THE FRENCH RADICAL PARTY

FROM HERRIOT TO MENDÈS-FRANCE

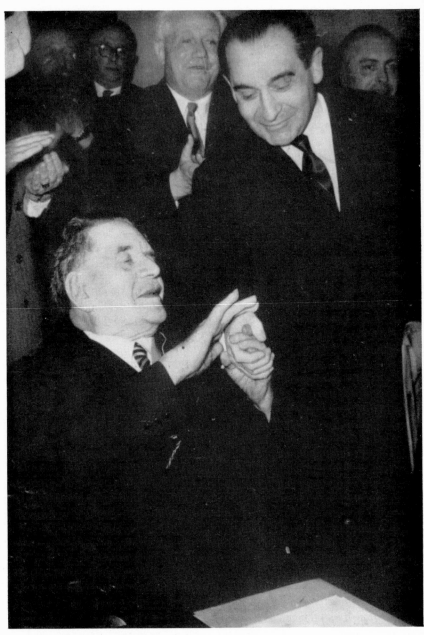

Edouard Herriot and Pierre Mendès-France at Radical
party's congress at Marseilles, October 1954

The French Radical Party

FROM HERRIOT TO MENDÈS-FRANCE

FRANCIS DE TARR

with a Foreword by
PIERRE MENDÈS-FRANCE

LONDON
OXFORD UNIVERSITY PRESS
NEW YORK   TORONTO
1961

Oxford University Press, Amen House, London E.C.4

GLASGOW NEW YORK TORONTO MELBOURNE WELLINGTON
BOMBAY CALCUTTA MADRAS KARACHI KUALA LUMPUR
CAPE TOWN IBADAN NAIROBI ACCRA

PRINTED IN GREAT BRITAIN

For Geraldine

CONTENTS

ILLUSTRATIONS

FOREWORD

France is living through a period of grave political crisis—the consequence of the hesitations, the divisions, and the equivocations of the past ten years. Situated at the centre of the political spectrum, the Radical party has suffered more than any other party from the effects of this crisis, and the author of this book assigned himself a difficult task in setting out to describe them.

The first of these effects is found in the party's internal divisions, which are reflections of the divisions which separate Frenchmen.

The author has analysed Radical 'tendencies'. He has carefully distinguished between the *radicaux classiques*, the *radicaux de gauche*, the *néo-radicaux*, the *radicaux gaullistes*, the *radicaux 'de gestion'*, and lastly those whom he calls—using a term which I do not like because of the ambiguities it creates or permits—the *mendésistes*. It is clear that Radicals have been divided on the most important contemporary problems, as have been, indeed, all Frenchmen. At the same time, however, on each of the great contemporary problems it has been possible to see side by side Radical leaders and party members who were opposed on other problems.

At bottom, it is not from the multiplicity of parties, as is sometimes said, that France has suffered and suffers still. It is because the parties, during recent years, have not been able to keep their doctrine in close touch with their action (this would have regrouped political formations, fortified their unity, and insured their efficiency). The reason for this is that the problems that face us during the second half of the twentieth century no longer correspond either to the traditional arguments or to the anachronistic vocabulary which we have never succeeded in discarding.

All this is true of the Radical party as of the others, and even more perhaps after the failure of the 1955–7 effort during which we tried to remedy both this weakness and this inadaptability.

This leads me to another observation. It is possible that the author did not use strong enough terms in describing the true state of the Radical party before 4 May 1955. The mass of the

party's members had remained sincerely and deeply attached to
an ideal of progress and of democracy of which radicalism, in
other times, had been the interpreter and the instrument. Afterwards, the workings of democracy had become corrupted in the
heart of the party itself. Certain men, business groups, had taken
control of the party's administrative machinery and were nulli-
fying the desires and decisions of the party's members. A veritable colonization had delivered up the party to those who were
using it both to promote the personal careers of a few and to
defend certain interests, notably in North Africa. On 4 May 1955
—the date of a violent and memorable Special Congress—it was
not, as some have said, a *coup d'état* which took place in the heart
of the party. It was a revolt of the rank and file of the party who
were tired of seeing themselves led by the coterie which had
been reigning arbitrarily for years. On that day, the opposition
was finally able to express with éclat the provincial federations'
profound desire for a change; their faithfulness to the true tradition of Gambetta, of Pelletan, of Herriot; and their wish for a
policy which would be reasonable but firm concerning private
interests and intransigent the moment the independence of the
State and the liberty of its citizens were at stake.

The events which followed showed us that we were not mistaken in basing hopes on a regeneration of radicalism. Many,
very many, were those who joined us in our combat. They were
not activated by the desire to win high positions or to protect
privileges, but rather by the hope of influencing the course of
events and of carrying out a policy of peace and reform by
means of the alliance which was proposed to other republicans,
notably to the Socialists.

It was not our fault that these hopes were not fulfilled. Unfortunately, whether from weakness or by design, France's
governments decided not to apply the programme submitted to
the voters and ratified by them in the elections of 2 January
1956. Then doubts, the choice of the path of least resistance,
and the lack of the energy and courage needed to resist attacks
and threats reappeared in the heart of the Radical party itself.
The party's members, old and new, became worried about the
persistent governmental weaknesses and their easily predictable
results. I made myself their spokesman among Radical cabinet
ministers in an attempt to get the latter to alter the policy which

was being followed. But while some deputies and ministers thought less and less about keeping their promises, the party's members, becoming discouraged, often gave up trying to exert on them the necessary pressure which is the mainspring of democracy. When it was clear that I was no longer able to make the will of the party respected, I drew the obvious conclusion and relinquished the leadership of the party.

If my friends and I had been only one internal division among others, it is likely that we would have been tolerated more easily. But our aim was not the victory of one group or faction, but was to transform fundamentally the action of radicalism. It was certainly this that others meant to prevent us from doing.

The events that followed, however, were to show that our opponents in the party were not capable of overcoming the dangers that we had tirelessly denounced. The Fourth Republic did not take long to die. One might dream about what might have happened if the republican politicians, if the ministers of the Left, Radicals and others, instead of giving way had had the strength of will to keep their promises, to resist pressures of all sorts, to serve only the public interest. . . .

In any case, the battle that we fought went beyond, far beyond, the limits of the Radical party, for on it depended perhaps one of the last chances of the Fourth Republic. It is for this reason that the readers of this work will be grateful to its author for the effort that he has made for them in gathering elements of information which were previously unknown or scattered and for having written a book of great interest. It is an important and scrupulous analytical study and also a clear and useful synthesis that the author is offering us and for which I wanted to be the first to thank him.

PIERRE MENDÈS-FRANCE

Paris, September 1958

AUTHOR'S INTRODUCTION

A biographer of Edouard Daladier has written that the Radical party, politically progressive but socially conservative, is as typically French as the tragedies of Racine, and just as unintelligible to foreigners.[1] The self-styled party of the 'average Frenchman', the Radical party has always prided itself on representing basic national characteristics. More than any other French party, it has traditionally managed to represent varied and often conflicting segments of French opinion. One objective of this book is to shed light on the state—or states—of mind that this party has come to represent.

France's oldest political party, the Radical party dominated French politics from its founding in 1901 to the collapse of France in 1940. From Combes and Clemenceau to Herriot and Daladier, Radicals always played prominent roles on the French political scene. At the time of the liberation, however, many observers concluded that the Radical party had seen its day. In the brave new world that was to be post-war France, the Radical Party was expected to join the Third Republic in oblivion.

After 1944, however, the Radical party confounded its critics by making a remarkable return to power. It never won more than 8 per cent. of the votes in any post-war general election, nor did it ever control more than 10 per cent. of the seats in the National Assembly, but as a strategically located centre party it soon became an indispensable part of any governmental coalition, and its many able leaders were soon again among the men who were leading France. Radicals headed ten of the twenty-one governments that were formed during the Fourth Republic; they participated in all of them. These are records that were unequalled by any other French political party.

During the years that followed the war, however, the Radical party, like the country that it prided itself on representing so well, was often deeply divided. This was a characteristic which the Radical party has shared with many other political parties, and was a characteristic that had never been absent in its own

---

[1] Yvon Lapaquellerie, *Edouard Daladier*, Paris, 1939, p. 121.

past history. In addition to sharing allegiance to a common core of 'radicalism', Radicals have always embraced and defended conflicting bodies of ideas. The main objectives of this book are, first, to identify the common core of radicalism and, second, to analyse the ideas and actions of Radicals and groups of Radicals who played representative, and often crucial, roles in the evolution of the Radical party during the fourteen years between the liberation of Paris in August 1944 and the fall of the Fourth Republic in May 1958.

*
* *

This book, therefore, is a study of a group of men, their ideas, and their role in French politics during a fourteen-year period. It is not a study of the Radical party's internal organization or social composition, though the importance of these two factors is undeniable.[2] The imprecision of the party's statutes and the traditional looseness of its discipline gave rise to a very flexible party structure, a flexibility skilfully utilized by the party's competing leaders. To many Radicals, indeed, the party has been more an electoral machine than a means to advance a political programme, and any study of the spectrum of radicalism must include a consideration of the tendency on the part of many Radicals to equate doctrine with tactics. The composition of the Radical party's membership has also inevitably affected the formation and evolution of the groups that have formed within the party. The role of these two factors—structure and social composition—will be noted, but they will not be subjects of primary emphasis.

Although the scope of this book is limited, the problems that it must deal with are vast. The many governments that held power in France during the years that followed the war grappled with a series of basic problems—economic, political, ideological, and international. Whether as individuals, as members of a party, or as members of a group within a party, Radicals played important roles in successive attempts to surmount the many problems that their country faced. The failure of Radicals to find and force through solutions to many of these problems was also the failure of the Fourth Republic and of the traditional

[2] For an outline of the Radical party's structure, see Appendix I.

methods of French parliamentary democracy. The Radical party
provides a unique vantage point for the study of this failure.

*

* *

With a few notable exceptions, it is undeniable that Radicals—
and Radical leaders in particular—have not been inclined to
arrange themselves in coherent groups convenient for analytical
study. It is often difficult, when viewing the Radical party, to
differentiate clearly between groups, cliques, and influential per-
sonages surrounded by an entourage. In a party with a plethora
of strong personalities, there has been an abundance of leaders,
but not always enough followers to go around. Many Radicals
have shared characteristics with more than one segment within
their party; many Radicals have also changed their allegiance
during the course of the evolving French political scene. In
choosing a limited number of categories, therefore, it has been
necessary to make somewhat arbitrary choices. At the same time,
no attempt has been made to assign each Radical to a specific
category.

As well as typifying varying aspects—and extremes—of radicalism, most of the groups that have been chosen will also be used
to represent a period in the post-war evolution of the Radical party.
One exception to this rule is the first category—the *radicaux
classiques*. These are the most traditionalist of all Radicals. Survivors from an earlier era, they may be said to represent the
past, a past that has remained alive in contemporary France.

During the immediate post-war period, the position of the
Radical party was virtually dependent upon the skill and tenacity
of one man, Edouard Herriot. Under his leadership, the Radical
party slowly recovered from its crushing defeat in France's first
post-war general election in 1945; fought against the constitutional projects advanced by France's two post-war constituent
assemblies in 1946; and after the inauguration of the Fourth
Republic in January 1947 went on to play an increasingly important role in the formation and leadership of France's successive governments. Herriot's immense popularity among the rank
and file of the party and his great oratorical skill gave him
a unique position above the conflicting groups and cliques.
For many of his compatriots, he was the personification of

radicalism. More than any other Radical, therefore, Herriot belongs in a category by himself.

Perhaps the most cohesive Radical group in post-war France was that formed by the _radicaux de gauche_ in 1944–6. Of marginal importance politically, they are of interest primarily because they represented the extreme left of the Radical spectrum of opinion. Staunchly defending themselves as the only true Radicals, they bitterly opposed their party's rightward evolution, and, increasingly isolated and ill at ease, they had all left the party by April 1946.

The departure of the _radicaux de gauche_ coincided with the rise of their bitterest enemies, the _néo-radicaux_. The prefix 'neo' is, of course, one that is subject to change. In the present context, the title '_néo-radicaux_' will be limited to a group of right-wing Radicals who played a prominent role in the party's evolution from 1945 to 1955. No Radical would willingly accept the title _radical de droite_, but opponents of the men who constituted this group provided them with even more pejorative names: _radicaux d'affaires_, _radicaux-libéraux_, _radicaux-capitalistes_, and, more extreme still, _radicalo-réactionnaires_. Led by Léon Martinaud-Déplat, who served as the party's administrative president until his ouster by the _radicaux mendésistes_ in 1955, the _néo-radicaux_ sought to 're-vitalize' the party and its doctrine along new lines. Unlike the _radicaux de gauche_, who were fond of citing the old Radical slogan, 'No enemies on the left!', the _néo-radicaux_ looked to the right for allies and supporters.

A fifth clearly discernible group was made up by those Radicals who supported de Gaulle during the years between 1947 and 1951. This was the period of the rise of the RPF; many, but not all, of the _radicaux gaullistes_ were attracted by opportunistic more than by ideological reasons. Like the _radicaux de gauche_, the _radicaux gaullistes_ were of marginal importance in the Radical party. They are, however, of interest in illustrating the consummate skill that Radicals have traditionally displayed in making and utilizing electoral alliances, the flexibility of their doctrine, and the ability of Radicals to have representatives in diverse political camps.

The next category of Radicals that will be discussed—the _radicaux de gestion_—belonged to a political tradition as old as politics itself. These were Radicals who, priding themselves on their *vocation gouvernementale*, placed a very high priority on keeping their governmental services at the service of the Republic. In their view, it was their party's duty to play an active role in governing France, even when sharing governmental responsibilities might mean supporting policies contrary to their party's official objectives. Compromisers, bargainers, conciliators, administrators, and caretakers, the *radicaux de gestion* were willing to adapt their policies to the needs and desires of the day. Many Radicals, in varying degrees and at different periods, have answered this description. During the post-war years, two Radicals provided particularly striking examples—Henri Queuille and Edgar Faure. After serving twenty times as a cabinet minister in the Third Republic, Queuille was to be in even greater demand in the Fourth Republic. He served as either a minister or as premier without a break from July 1948 to June 1954; the first of his three premierships made post-war history by lasting thirteen months, from September 1948 to November 1949. Faure was the only French politician to form more than one government during France's 1951–6 legislature; after a short period as premier in 1952, he returned to power after Mendès-France's fall in February 1955. Mendès-France's defeat had been attributed by many observers to the machinations of René Mayer, a fellow Radical who had served as premier for five months in 1953. His replacement by a fellow Radical helped to crystallize the growing opposition of many Radicals to the flexible approach to politics that was typified by the *radicaux de gestion*.

On 4 May 1955, almost three months to the day after Mendès-France's fall from power, his followers in the Radical party won control of the party's administrative machinery, and a new and tumultuous period in the party's history began. Unable to continue with his plans for renovating France, Mendès-France devoted much of his time during the next two years to the task of trying to renovate the Radical party. But by 1957 it was becoming evident that many Radicals were not willing to follow the new paths that the *radicaux mendésistes* were laying down for them. The premature general election of 2 January 1956—brought about by Faure's controversial dissolution of the National Assembly the previous month, an act for which he was expelled from the Radical party—had constituted a partial success for the *radicaux mendésistes*, but they were to become increasingly isolated during the last years of the Fourth Republic. At odds with the policy that was being carried out in Algeria, Mendès-France resigned from Guy Mollet's government in May 1956. A year later, unable to enforce discipline in the Radical party's parliamentary group, he resigned from his position as leader of the party. The following year was the last year of the Fourth Republic. Two young *radicaux de gestion*, Maurice Bourgès-Maunoury and Félix Gaillard, led the two governments that were formed during 1957; but by the end of the year, rent with quarrels and divided into competing political formations, the Radical party was almost as moribund as the latest Republic that it had come to represent so well.

*
* *

It will be noted that I have used the term 'Radical party'. This has been done to conform to the most prevalent current usage and to minimize confusion. The party's official title is *Le Parti républicain radical et radical-socialiste*, which may be translated as 'The Party of Radical and Socialistically Radical Republicans'. Selecting the most fitting abbreviation is, of necessity, an arbitrary task. Many writers, especially in the past, have used the expression 'Radical-Socialist party', with an explanatory note for the non-initiated that the party is 'neither radical nor socialist'. The French Radicals would be the first to agree that they are not Socialists. They have maintained, however, at least on the modern French political scene, a monopoly of the term 'Radical'.

The word 'Radical' was first used in France in the 1830's, during the reign of Louis-Philippe, when it was borrowed from England by Frenchmen who opposed the monarchy but who could not call themselves 'republican' without appearing disloyal to their country's régime. In 1847, Ledru-Rollin, who was to be one of the leaders of the Revolution of 1848, proclaimed that he and his followers were *ultra-radicaux*. Increasing numbers of Frenchmen, often holding conflicting opinions, were to use the term during the remaining decades of the nineteenth century, particularly during the latter part of the Second Empire and after the founding of the Third Republic. When *Le Parti républicain radical et radical-socialiste* was founded in 1901, the key importance of the word 'radical' in the new party's title was illustrated by a spirited debate among the party's founders. The more

conservative founders wanted to place a comma between the words
républicain and *radical*. The "socialistically radical" elements, however, although willing to ally themselves with 'radical republicans', flatly refused to join forces with less committed
'republicans', and the comma supporters lost.

Adopted with difficulty, the party's cumbersome title has not
been altered during subsequent history, but it is clear that the
term 'radical' has not remained unaffected by its cohabitation
with a political party. Writing in an official party newspaper in
1945, a Radical editorialist, for example, went so far as to proclaim that 'the France of yesterday is the France of today and
the France of tomorrow. A country like France cannot cut itself
off from its past. A nation is a long tradition.'[3] Such statements
clearly typify a state of mind at variance with the dictionary
definition of a radical, 'one who advocates radical and sweeping
changes in laws and methods of government with the least
delay'. They can serve, however, to illustrate the point that it
will be necessary to maintain not only an open mind concerning
the name of the party under consideration, but also a determined
willingness to accept the leaders and spokesmen of the Radical
party as the authoritative interpretators of radicalism, even if
some of their ideas may seem to upset preconceived notions
concerning people who call themselves radical. It is *their* 'radicalism', and theirs alone, that is the subject of this book.

*
* *

In the course of this study, the words and deeds of all those
who have spoken, written, or acted in the name of the Radical
party have been considered as legitimate sources of information.
For words, the most fertile sources were the verbatim records of
speeches and remarks made at the party's various meetings and
congresses. The most complete form of these verbatim records
is the unpublished stenographic record on file in the party's
headquarters in the Place de Valois, Paris. This record was of
particular importance for the early post-war period and for the
party's more private meetings during the entire period. The
party's official newspaper, *L'Information Radicale-Socialiste*, began
publication on 8 July 1946, and during the succeeding years

[3] *La Dépêche de Paris*, 5 July 1945.

provided verbatim records of many of the speeches and reports made at party congresses and executive committee meetings. Unless otherwise specified in footnotes, the sources for all statements made at party meetings held prior to July 1946 are the relevant stenographic records, and for the subsequent years are the relevant issues of *L'Information Radicale-Socialiste*. Another basic source of information was, of course, the *Journal Officiel*. Except when otherwise stated, the sources for parliamentary speeches and voting records are the relevant series and issues of this key publication.

This book could not have been written without the aid and co-operation of many people. I owe an especial debt of gratitude to those officials of the Radical party who, during the winter of 1955–6, gave me a warm welcome, provided me with working space and access to their records, arranged interviews, and made it possible for me to attend party functions and to participate freely in the life of the Radical party. I wish to thank in particular M. Paul Anxionnaz, then secretary-general of the Radical party; M. Georges Scali, then administrative secretary; and M. André Schmidt, editor of *L'Information Radicale-Socialiste*.

For material assistance that helped make it possible for this book to be written, I wish to thank Brigadier-General and Mrs. Charles A. Lindbergh, and also the William Garland Trust, Yale University. For invaluable assistance in gaining access to sources of information, I am greatly indebted to M. Michel Galas.

Many persons read the manuscript, both in the formative stages and after it was completed; to all of them I express my sincere appreciation. For helpful advice and comments during the early stages, I wish to thank, in particular, Mr. Frederick Watkins, Mr. William Scott, Mr. Henry Monroe, Mr. Joseph Nogee, and Mr. William Zartman. Among those who read the completed manuscript, I am particularly indebted to M. François Goguel, M. Jean Touchard, M. Claude Nicolet, and above all to Mr. Philip Williams for the invaluable nature of his comments and suggestions, and to M. Pierre Mendès-France for his great kindness in writing a Foreword.

FRANCIS DE TARR

Palagio de' Pesci
Fiesole, Italy
January 1960

ABBREVIATIONS

MRP	*Mouvement républicain populaire*
MURF	*Mouvement unifié de la résistance française*
PRL	*Parti républicain de la liberté*
RGR	*Rassemblement des gauches républicaines*
RPF	*Rassemblement du peuple français*
UDSR	*Union démocratique et socialiste de la résistance*

1

General Concepts of Radicalism

'Il y a tant de partis en France, et tant de divisions dans les partis, qu'il ne reste un seul mot de la politique qui soit parfaitement clair.'
JULES SIMON, *La Politique Radicale*, Paris, 1869, p. 1.

At a meeting of the Radical party's executive committee in February 1949, the party official in charge of propaganda rose to voice a strong complaint: that morning he had heard someone say that the party did not have a doctrine. Such a statement, he declared, was clearly inadmissible. Radicalism was not just a state of mind, as people so often said, but was a doctrine, 'a scientific and powerful doctrine'.

Other Radical spokesmen have been less exuberant in their claims. When Alain, who is often cited as the principal philosopher of radicalism, offered his book *Eléments d'une doctrine radicale* to Radical ministers in the government, one of the latter is said to have commented: 'If we had a doctrine we would be the first to know about it.' Thirty years later, while searching for a definition of 'Radical doctrine', the present writer was told, with a smile, by one party official: '*Eh bien*, it's the immortal principles of 1789 and all that.'

Although they may have differed—or been indifferent—concerning precise questions of terminology or content, all Radicals have been united in paying tribute to 'radicalism'. Radicals have shared, if in varying degrees, a common *état d'esprit* and a common body of symbols and concepts. And, despite their manifest differences of opinion on contemporary problems, virtually all of the party's spokesmen have taken pride in proclaiming their allegiance to a common heritage.

What more can be said concerning the common denominators of radicalism?

*
* *

In times of unity or division, in times of victory or defeat, but especially during electoral campaigns, Radical orators have never failed to pay allegiance to *les grandes principes*. The sacrosanct and universal character that these principles have come to possess may be seen by the fact that many of those who proclaim them do not feel the need to identify them further.

Fortunately, some Radical spokesmen have been more explicit. They have invoked the names of glorious precursors; they have exalted the 'immortal principles of 1789'; they have stressed their love of country and their respect for private property; they have defended Individualism, Democracy, and the Republic; they have rejected both Catholicism and Marxism which, they complain, place Church and State above the individual and demand conformity to a revealed body of doctrine; they have identified the Radical party with the Republic and with France.

In writing and speaking about their ideological heritage, Radicals have claimed an impressive and at times startling array of 'glorious ancestors'. One Radical historian has traced the precursors of radicalism as far back as Adam. 'The first man, in his hours of optimism, was a Radical.'[1] Another Radical authority, after noting that spokesmen of the French Communist party were claiming Plato, Thomas More, Campenella, Babeuf, Fourier, Saint-Simon, Cabet, Proudhon, and Robert Owen, countered by forcefully claiming for the Radicals Heraclitus ('whom the colossal Nietzsche ranked above all the ancient philosophers'), Montaigne, Rabelais, Erasmus, Etienne Dolet, Michael Servetus, Descartes, 'all the Encyclopedists, artisans of the French Revolution', Ledru-Rollin, Louis Blanc, Edgar Quinet, Michelet, Victor Hugo, Gambetta, Pelletan, Léon Bourgeois, Henri Brisson, René Goblet, and Herriot.[2]

Still another authority, after remarking that the history of the Radical party during the Third Republic *was* the history of the Third Republic, declared that this statement could be extended to cover the entire history of France, and went on to trace the Radical heritage to the story-tellers of the Middle Ages who showed 'a critical and satirical spirit toward social oppressions'.[3]

[1] Gaston Maurice, *Le Parti Radical* (*Préface de Jacques Kayser*), Paris, 1929, p. 15.

[2] Antonin Douzet, *L'Information Radicale-Socialiste* (hereafter cited as *I.R.S.*), 25 February 1949.

[3] Jammy-Schmidt, *Idées et Images radicales* (*Préface d'Edouard Herriot*), Paris, 1934.

In discussing later periods, he mentioned François Villon, 'irreverent toward the sacrosanct established powers', noted the laicism of Molière, La Fontaine, and Boileau, and added Emile Zola to his party's quota of glorious ancestors.

While emphasizing their ideological links with all periods of French history, Radicals have been most emphatic, however, in stressing their direct descent from the heroes of the French Revolution. It is from the Revolution that Radicals have drawn much of their inspiration, strength, and vocabulary. In forming their party in 1901, it was the Radicals' objective to 'group all the sons of the Revolution'. This preoccupation with the ideals of the Revolution has never dimmed. Radical orators, as well as Radical audiences, have always revelled in the vocabulary and symbols of the Revolution, often revealing a knowledge of Revolutionary chronology that would rival the knowledge of certain Americans concerning the battlefields of the American Civil War. An orator at the party's congress in 1946, for example, after declaring that the Revolution had been a victim of bad justice and bad money (two Radical themes in 1946), went on to regale his listeners. 'And you know what followed. It was Thermidor that ended the Epic and began the Adventure. It was Floréal that replied to Thermidor and, to conclude, it was Brumaire. But, it was the *coup de force* and the *assignat* that made possible Brumaire, and behind the pyramid of *assignats* there was Bonaparte.'[4] The speaker was given a long ovation by his enthusiastic and appreciative audience.

Although they have emphasized certain aspects of the Revolution, most notably its vocabulary and its defence of private property, Radicals have also stressed their willingness to accept the Revolution as a whole. On a theoretical level, they have claimed all the *philosophes*—as one Radical historian has written, they have refused to oppose, as 'modern critics in particular have done with some vigour, the *philosophes* against each other'.[5] Radicals have also proclaimed their solidarity even with the more extreme elements among the leaders of the French Revolution. In a speech at the party's congress in 1945, a right-wing Radical declared that it was not displeasing to be considered as the spiritual heirs of the Jacobins, and added that although the latter committed abominable acts 'they put their ardent love of country

[4] Gabriel Cudenet, president of the RGR, 1946-9.   [5] Maurice, *op. cit.,* p. 195.

and of liberty and their scorn of life at the service of this grandiose and monumental affair called the Convention, which opened new vistas to the modern world'.[6] During the post-war years, however, many Radicals did not extend this tolerance to include young Radicals who belonged to the *Club des Jacobins*, and who declared that they wanted to carry into the realm of action some of the ideas expressed by the original Jacobins.

The core of the *grands principes* to which Radical orators proclaim their allegiance may be said to be the famous *Déclaration des droits de l'Homme et du Citoyen*—the 'immortal principles of 1789'. The respect and reverence of Radicals for this enumeration of basic political liberties was never more evident than during the constitutional debates of 1945 and 1946. The political forces then dominant in France were determined to 'renovate' the 1789 Declaration by putting major emphasis on economic and social rights, and some called for a complete rewriting of a document that Radicals held as sacred. The importance that was attached to this issue may be seen by the fact that the Constitutional Committee of the First Constituent Assembly (November 1945 to April 1946) spent almost a fourth of its time discussing the Declaration of Rights that was to be included as a preamble to the proposed constitution.

Under the leadership of Herriot, Radicals eloquently argued and campaigned for a retention of the 1789 version, with its guarantee of private property and its emphasis on political rights. Unable to achieve this objective, they then tried to limit changes to the addition of several relatively mild articles concerning the guarantee of social and economic rights. Herriot, who agreed that it was necessary to establish economic democracy, argued that the builders of the new France could find no better motto than *Liberté, Egalité, Fraternité*, and that they could find no sounder foundation on which to base a republican régime than the *Déclaration des droits de l'Homme et du Citoyen*.[7]

Other Radical leaders joined Herriot in expressing dismay that fellow Frenchmen could want to alter the venerable charter of their liberties. After noting that some people were claiming that the Declaration had become old and no longer suited the modern world, Daladier observed that this was 'like saying that the

---

[6] M. Mauclair (Seine).

[7] *La Dépêche de Paris*, 17 July 1945.

statues in the Pantheon had become old'.[8] Although unable to carry the day, Radicals did not cease to proclaim their love for their beloved statement of political values or their disdain for the new version that was to be adopted. The 1789 Declaration was the charter not only of French democracy but of all democracy, Herriot told his fellow deputies.[9] It had conquered the world; 'How much time would be necessary for the principles of 1946 to have the same effect?'

*

* *

As befits intellectual descendants of the leaders of the eighteenth-century Enlightenment, Radicals have also rejoiced in representing the forces of Reason and Progress. Going further afield in identifying ideological relationships, Herriot once wrote that 'to be a Radical is to renew the ancient assertion that no one will enter the Garden of Thought if he is not first a geometrician', and noted that the Radicals, like the architects of ancient Greece, propagated the cult of the straight line.[10] After adding that 'to be a Radical is to revere Reason and to make it the measure of all things', Herriot further identified his fellow Radicals by stating that to be a Radical was 'to remain optimistic and to affirm that there is in the world, in spite of everything, much more sun than shadow, more knowledge than ignorance, more goodness than evil'. Radical party statute writers, probably exercising reason, never have attempted to equate the entrance requirements of the Radical party with those of the Garden of Thought; but Herriot's latter two characterizations of his fellow Radicals have never ceased to find an echo in Radical oratory.

It was undoubtedly Herriot himself, however, who provided the most concise statements of the Radical concept of Reason. At the party's congress in 1946, after acknowledging that there were not very many women in the party, he stated that he did not wish to attribute this state of affairs to the fact that the party represented Reason. Such an explanation, he remarked, would be discourteous to women. He offered, however, another explanation: there are two kinds of reason—*la raison froide* and *la raison passionée*. Radicals represent the former, and 'it is evident

---

[8] *Congrès extraordinaire*, April 1946.   [9] *Journal Officiel*, 8 March 1946, pp. 636–9.
[10] In preface to Jammy-Schmidt, *Idées et Images radicales*, p. 3.

that, up till now, women have chosen impassioned reason'. 'To be a Radical is to remain optimistic.' Radicals have always been agreed in considering Condorcet among their more important precursors. In paying tribute to Condorcet's celebrated *Outline or Historical Picture of the Progress of the Human Mind*, Herriot once called it 'a complete exposition of the central philosophy of the Revolution';[11] another Radical authority declared that it was from this book that 'radicalism and its most dazzling formulas emerged'.[12] At the same time, Radicals have also been careful to temper their optimism with realism. In an official declaration issued at the party's congress in 1951, it was stated that 'we are essentially, as in 1901, a party of evolution and of progress'; the declaration continued, however, on a more restrictive note by adding that 'no audacity shocks us in the degree that it is reasonable and possible'.[13] As a final warning, the author of the declaration added, in capital letters, that 'HUMAN PROGRESS IS INFINITE, ON CONDITION THAT IT BE CARRIED OUT IN STAGES'.

While paying tribute to the general principles of the Declaration of the Rights of Man, affirming their faith in Reason and Progress, and stressing the universality of their *grands principes*, Radical spokesmen have never failed to emphasize the French context and character of their fundamental concepts. Patriotism, a *culte de la patrie*, is a basic Radical principle, and the representativeness of the party and its close identification with traditional French values have never ceased to be regular themes and a general source of satisfaction for Radical orators. At the first congress that the Radicals held after the Liberation, Théodore Steeg, then the party's president, declared that 'our party sprang forth from the French soul, of which it has at certain times

---

[11] Edouard Herriot, *The Wellsprings of Liberty* (*Aux Sources de la liberté*), New York, 1939, p. 172.

[12] Jammy-Schmidt, *op. cit.*, p. 6.

[13] The declaration was written by Maurice Faure, deputy from Lot. In a public opinion study made in 1952, the *Institut Français d'Opinion Publique* reported that 11 per cent. of the Radical party's electorate gave the conviction that they were working for progress as their principal reason for belonging to the Radical party. *Sondages*, 1952, No. 3, p. 86.

expressed the rich diversity, as at other times the harmonious unity'. Mendès-France, at the first meeting of the executive committee held after the special congress of 4 May 1955 (at which he and his supporters had won control of the party's administrative machinery), declared that 'our party is nothing other than the mouthpiece of the general interest'. Spokesmen for any party, of course, may claim that their party represents their country as a whole, but Radicals have been especially insistent in claiming that their party 'represents more than any other the profound instinct of the Nation, its vital instinct',[14] and in stressing the 'certain identity of radicalism and French continuity'.[15]

Both France and the Republic are favoured subjects in Radical oratory, and during certain periods and in moments of emotion Radical speakers have attempted to monopolize both terms for their party. A campaign slogan frequently used by Radicals before the Second World War was, 'The Radical party is France itself!' An even more ambitious claim was made at a meeting of the party's executive committee in March 1951 by Léon Martinaud-Deplat, then administrative president of the party. Turning towards Herriot, the party's president, he proclaimed: 'This man is the Republic in person!' All present enthusiastically rose and gave their president a standing ovation.

While conceding to no one a more intense patriotism, Radicals, as befits free men, also attach a great importance to individualism. Their cult of country is matched only by their cult of the individual. They are devoted to France, but, while proud to equate France with their party, they are less inclined to equate France with the State. In the liberal tradition, they feel that society exists to further the development of the individual, and it is the role of the individual that they champion. They are traditionally suspicious of all that tends to circumscribe the activities of the individual or subordinate his welfare to the interests of the State.

The individualistic aspects of radicalism are best expressed in the writings of Alain, the 'philosopher of radicalism' who presents individualism as the foundation of radicalism.[16] Alain's writings still find favour among Radicals. The halls of Radical

---

[14] Paul Bastid, 1946 Congress.

[15] Edouard Ramonet, deputy from Indre, *Congrès extraordinaire*, 1946.

[16] Alain (Emile Chartier), *Politique,* Paris, 1952, p. 17.

congresses always include banners that quote some of his memorable slogans; a party official described him, in 1949, as 'the greatest of modern philosophers';[17] and new editions of his books are kept on display in party headquarters and at party meetings. His systematic distrust of power, however, and his eloquent entreaties to control and resist it, 'to construct every day a little barricade',[18] may be considered, in terms of contemporary Radical opinion, as an extreme view. Radicals have never ceased to pay tribute to individualism; but the individualism of Alain, and in particular his outlook on life, may be said to have been typified during the contemporary period more by the *radicaux classiques* than by Radicals in general.

The passage of time has had varying effects on another traditional keystone of radicalism: anti-clericalism. Radicals have not differed as to the basic principle of the separation of Church and State, but disputes concerning the implementation of this principle, especially with regard to the question of State aid to Church schools, have not been met with unanimity on the part of contemporary Radicals. Long considered by many Frenchmen as the core of radicalism, and indeed of republicanism itself, anti-clericalism is no longer considered by most Radicals to be the most crucial issue in French politics and the *raison d'être* of their party. This is not to say that it has not remained a vital issue to certain Radicals (especially the *radicaux classiques*) or that it has not been a subject of debate among all groups of Radicals. It is in these contexts, and not in a treatment of the more generally accepted concepts of contemporary radicalism, that the spectrum of Radical opinion concerning the precise implementation of the separation of Church and State will be investigated.

*

* *

Radicals have been able to profit from their possession of a flexible body of generally accepted ideas. Like Hinduism, radicalism has had the advantage of being able to assimilate diverse views. And, like Hindus, Radicals have prided themselves on

[17] Antonin Douzet, *Comité exécutif*, 9 February 1949. On another occasion, Douzet quoted André Maurois as having stated that 'People will speak of Alain in a hundred years as they spoke of Descartes a century after his death.' *I.R.S.*, June 1950.

[18] Alain, *Eléments d'une doctrine radicale*, Paris, 1925, p. 124.

their assimilative power. In a resounding speech in 1951, one Radical deputy proclaimed that the Radical party was the only party that offered its members an opportunity to be free and independent individuals, and went on to tell his Radical audience that there was 'room in these ranks for all religious and philosophical conceptions'.[19] On another occasion, an inspired Radical orator went so far as to present the assimilative approach to politics as a veritable political law. 'The main task of a great party is the same as that of a good stomach: not to reject, but to assimilate.'[20]

Some Radicals, however, have lamented the lack of virility of some of their party's cherished concepts, and have been emphatic in calling for a more precise and selective enumeration of their party's political objectives. 'It is always fine to reaffirm one's loyalty to the Rights of Man and one's attachment to the irreplaceable motto *Liberté, Egalité, Fraternité*, but perhaps there are more and better things to do than that.'[21] The basic ideas of radicalism were stated at the end of the eighteenth century— during the pre-industrial era. The nineteenth century did fairly well on these ideas, but there has been a steadily widening gap between political ideas and political reality. Radicals have long continued to put major emphasis on the 'immortal principles of 1789', but as the writer of a book highly regarded among *radicaux mendésistes* has observed: 'When an ideal becomes a principle, it is not a subject of enthusiasm: it is only a subject for a dissertation.'[22]

This evolution has affected many of the symbols much employed by Radicals. The word 'liberty', for example, which has been a potent rallying-cry in history, has lost much of its emotional appeal in contemporary France. Where liberty is already possessed, the word inevitably loses much of its power to arouse emotions. 'Brightest in dungeons, Liberty, thou art.' Most of the French electorate has not had experiences similar to those of the Prisoner of Chillon. In a poll taken in France during 1954 to see how the French conceived of happiness, only four persons in a thousand put liberty in first place![23]

[19] Jacques Genton, deputy from Cher, 1951 Congress.
[20] M. Mortier (Seine-et-Marne), *Assemblée générale*, January 1946.
[21] Vincent Badie, deputy from Herault, 1945 Congress.
[22] Maurice Laure, *Révolution, dernière chance de la France*, Paris, 1954, p. 147.
[23] Cited by Albert Camus in *L'Express*, 2 December 1954.

Not only have Radical symbols become devalued with time, but other political groups have become skilled in their usage. The revolutionary vocabulary used by Communists is not very different from that used by Radicals, and in their dealings with Communists the Radicals have had to contend with masters in the art of manipulating symbols. During the period after the liberation, even de Gaulle revealed himself as a skilled user of Jacobin vocabulary. The ability to speak *en radical-socialiste* is not limited, manifestly, to members of the Radical party, nor can the latter monopolize the teachings of their many precursors. In February 1956 the president of the newly constituted Poujadist group in the National Assembly informed a Radical deputy that Poujade and he never went to sleep at night without reading the 'magnificent speeches of Robespierre'.[24]

In some cases Radicals have even given up, at least temporarily, their most valued terms. In giving a report at the party's congress in 1944, a speaker stated that he wanted to use the word 'liberation' and not 'revolution' as groups to the right and left of the Radicals were doing.[25] To strengthen his argument, he noted that the Communists were not speaking of 'revolution', but of 'union'. A year later, a Radical editorialist echoed this unprecedented Radical distaste for the term 'revolution'. Noting that this word had been on the lips or in the writings of all those speaking or writing in the name of the other political parties, he went on to offer a stinging analogy: 'Indeed! Was it not the same under Pétain!'[26] It was clear that Radicals were not, as in 1901, setting out to 'group all the sons of the Revolution'. The symbol no longer was being applied to the same concept.

*

*   *

Located between the Socialists and the conservatives in the spectrum of French opinion, Radicals have often discussed their likenesses with, and differences from, the former. In regard to the latter, they have been brief and concise. If there is any one symbol that Radicals have insisted on disavowing, one symbol that they have been willing to cede to their opponents, it is that of 'conservatism'. Indeed, all French political groupings have

24 Paul Vahé, *L'Express*, 21 February 1956.   25 M. Isoré.
26 *La Dépêche de Paris*, 16 March 1945.

shared the Radical repugnance for this politically unpopular word. This was especially evident during the period immediately following the liberation. In refuting attacks against the party, Herriot declared at the party's congress in 1946 that the Radicals, who are devoted to Reason and to her sister, Science, had the right to protest when people call them conservatives, 'using in this manner a very petty, a very vulgar, a very mediocre insult, an insult found in all the political garbage cans'.

In regard to their Socialist neighbours on their left, Radicals have had to be less pejorative in discussing doctrinal and political positions, since they share their title in their party's official name and have often been allied with them for electoral purposes. In comparing radicalism and socialism, however, Radicals have made precise distinctions. 'There is', wrote one Radical historian, 'such a profound antipathy between certain principles, notably on the subject of property, that no confusion is possible.'[27] In addition to defending private property as one of the inviolable rights of man, Radicals have denied the reality of the class struggle and have claimed to be more realistic in method and less doctrinaire than the Socialists.

In addition, all Radicals have agreed on one point: Radicals are not Marxists. In a speech at the party's congress in 1946, Herriot admitted that he had an interest in, and admiration for, certain aspects of Marxism. He read Marx, considered him a powerful thinker, and thought that he represented 'a moment in intellectual evolution'; but Radicals, he went on to say, were not the slaves of any dogma. In Herriot's view, the theory of class consciousness was antiquated, and what Radicals wanted was 'fraternity among all the French' and the movement of the smallest, the *plus petit*, 'towards more comfort and security'.

When discussing the differences between radicalism and socialism, Radicals have not hesitated to take advantage of the French Socialists' own doctrinal contradictions. A speaker at a special congress in 1946 declared that Léon Blum, who had proposed the suppression in his party of the *Internationale* and the term 'class struggle', had shown himself in this way to be a partisan of a 'humanitarian and progressive socialism'.[28] 'That, Mesdames and Citizens,' he concluded, 'is, quite simply, radicalism!'

[27] Jammy-Schmidt, *op. cit.*, p. 33.   [28] M. Maniglier.

c

In contending with their Socialist opponents, however, Radicals have been as much inclined to reject with scorn as they have been to assimilate with discretion. Noting that Calvin had spoken of the predestination of societies, an orator at the party's congress in 1946 called Marxists 'social Calvinists', and stated that to the 'prophecies of Marxists' Calvinism, we oppose the magnificent laugh of Voltaire and the sceptical frown of Descartes'.[29]

*
* *

In summary, it may be said that there is an identifiable core of radicalism. Radicals share a common body of ideas and utilize a common body of symbols. Glorious ancestors and the Revolution; France and the Republic; Progress and Reason; individualism and patriotism; respect for private property; and separation of Church and State: these form the bedrock of radicalism.

It is clear, however, that Radicals have had to share their ideas and vocabulary with members of other political parties. This has been a source of advantages as well as of problems. It is to a party's honour to have had its ideas become public property. James K. Vardaman, who was elected governor of Mississippi in 1902 (the same year that Emile Combes, a leader of the newly founded Radical party, became premier of France), had what could be called an ideal campaign issue. 'His contribution to statesmanship was advocacy of the repeal of the Fifteenth Amendment, an utterly hopeless proposal and for that reason an ideal campaign issue. It could last for ever.'[30]

In contrast, the major issues that Radicals staunchly advocated during the same period were won and became part of history. In their subsequent evolution, therefore, Radicals were faced with an ever-growing need to revitalize their ideas and to define new objectives, and it was in undertaking this task that differences among Radicals became most evident. Allegiance to a common core of popularly accepted ideas has enabled Radicals to make

[29] Gabriel Cudenet.

[30] V. O. Key, *Southern Politics in State and Nation*, New York, 1949, p. 232. The Fifteenth Amendment, adopted in 1870, declares that the right of citizens of the United States to vote shall not be denied or abridged by the United States or any State on account of race, colour, or previous condition of servitude.

eloquent speeches, and has made it possible for them to claim that they represent traditional French values. This common core of radicalism has not proven sufficient, however, to unite contemporary Radicals, or to enable them to carry out a cohesive programme of action.

II

The Radicaux Classiques

'On m'a dit plus d'une fois: "Vous êtes le dernier radical, ou peu s'en faut.
Cette espèce disparaît comme a disparu l'aurochs!" J'en riais bien. Maintenant
j'en ris encore mieux.'

ALAIN, Eléments d'une doctrine radicale, Paris, 1925, p. 13.

A cartoon published in a December 1948 issue of a French
satirical weekly portrays two small boys looking at Santa Claus,
with one of the boys exclaiming: 'Look! A Radical!'[1] In the
minds of many of their compatriots, Radicals have been accredited
not only with a virtual monopoly of beards, but those Radicals
who wear beards have continued, at least during part of the
period under consideration and to certain observers (particularly those who draw cartoons), to be the true personification
of the Radical party. In a country of which it has become almost
a truism to state that the past has at least as much influence on
political life as the present, a group that is widely recognized as
being representative of the past is not without a special significance. This significance is heightened, of course, to the extent
that what may be considered as the 'past' to some areas and to
some people still is considered as the present, and possibly the
future, to others.

Aside from their reputed proclivity for growing impressive
beards, the *radicaux classiques* may be denoted by other readily
identifiable characteristics. Although they represent the traditional, easy-going radicalism of the past, in which local interests
and tactics are of more direct concern than dogmas and programmes, they are also highly susceptible to the charms of eloquence, and at the proper occasions excel in the enunciation of
a bold political philosophy. Progressive in spirit, conservative
in habits, they are always staunchly republican. Found primarily

[1] *Le Canard enchaîné*, 8 December 1948.

among the older generation that distinguished itself in the war of 1914–18, *la Grande Guerre*, they also may be identified geographically and occupationally. The most characteristic of them come from rural areas and small towns south of the Loire, and in particular from the south-west. Their ranks are made up of tradesmen, merchants, artisans, small property holders and, in general, of that part of the middle classes that emerged for the first time as a political force at the time of the Revolution.

*

* *

More than any other group of Radicals, the *radicaux classiques* have been steadfast in their allegiance to the basic tenets of radicalism. They have been more than loyal to them: they have been satisfied with them, and on occasion eloquently and even aggressively satisfied. In regions that are economically still in the nineteenth century, the ideological quarrels and problems of an earlier day are of greater concern than in more modernized areas. They are, indeed, in a local context, contemporary. This is particularly true regarding the traditional Radical attitudes towards the Church and the political Right. In many French villages there has continued to be competition, and sometimes bitter rivalry, between the local *curé* and the schoolmaster, or between the *curé* and the mayor. Those to the right of the Radicals have been grouped traditionally under the stinging epithet 'reactionaries'. One authoritative representative of traditional radicalism, a memorable employer of this term, has disdainfully and gleefully described Independents as *'des réactionnaires qui se cachent!'*, 'reactionaries in hiding'.[2] The old republican rallying-cry used at the turn of the century, *'Ni réaction ni révolution!'* (sons of a Revolution are not necessarily in favour of a new revolution), still finds enthusiastic users in Radical congresses. A delegate at a special congress in 1946, for example, declared that the slogan, 'Neither reaction nor revolution, progress in all its forms!', which was used by 'our fathers, who founded the Republic', still had conserved its force and nobility and was 'the doctrine that tomorrow can rally the cream of the French people for

[2] Philibert Lautissier, Mayor of Lignières (Cher), pop. 1623. Interview, 28 October 1955.

the triumph of the Republic and the salvation of the *Patrie*'.[3]

The *radicaux classiques* are skilled in proclaiming and presenting grandiose political programmes in which noble objectives
are eloquently expressed, but realistically hedged, and an able
orator can always find appreciative listeners at a Radical congress. The president of the Federation of Gironde, in welcoming
delegates to the party's congress at Bordeaux in 1952, provided
a spirited description of his fellow Radicals which was directed,
in particular, to those now under consideration. 'To be a Radical',
he said, 'is to safeguard the virtue of effort; it is to understand,
with the universal Goethe, that life is but a combat; it is to
correct the scriptural texts and to write with a firm hand.' Before concluding his speech, the orator did not forget to cite
Stendhal and Hugo on the wonders of Bordeaux or to list the
various wines of the region with slogans as to their respective
qualities, '*vin de Sauterne*: *du soleil en bouteille*', etc. For, as he
pointed out, without the products of the Bordeaux vineyards,
'there is no banquet . . . or congress'. This is a sentiment that
would meet with general Radical agreement, although, of course,
spokesmen for other regions favoured by nature would stress
the importance of the contributions to be made by their own
vineyards.

Banquets and congresses (the two go together) are the favourite
scenes of political activity to followers of the old Radical traditions. Reminiscing about the past, a delegate at the party's first
post-war congress said that 'in those days, one came to a congress as one went to a play, to hear the celebrities young and
old'.[4] He added that 'amidst the laudatory epithets, the old
tenors seemed to gain renewed force as in a fountain of youth,
and everyone returned to his province delighted with the per-
formance and rejuvenated by the luxurious hotels in which he
had stayed, the good meals he had eaten, and the distinguished
wines that had accompanied them'. Banquets and congresses have
not declined in popularity and often serve to stimulate eloquent
restatements of traditional Radical ideals. Radical orators have
remained true to old traditions by continuing to merit praise
such as that given by a provincial paper which, reporting a local
Radical celebration in 1949, described the local senator as speaking in 'this splendid language with the magnificent flights that

[3] M. Le Bail (Finistère).   [4] M. Langlois (Deux-Sèvres).

the *Berrichons* know'.[5] The orator's concluding remarks were described as 'a magnificent rhetorical passage in which he affirmed the high value of liberty'.

The *radicaux classiques* represent many of the traditional attitudes held by those who inhabit the French countryside. Their way of life, the quiet rhythm of their days, and their views of the outside world have been a traditional source of inspiration to many who have described French life. The novels of Balzac, Flaubert, and Emile Zola in earlier periods, Gabriel Chevallier's more contemporary stories of the Radical municipality of *Clochemerle*, these and a multitude of other literary works portray the scenes and the atmosphere in which Radicals and their competitors carry on their political activities. Helpful documentation is provided by all mediums that use France and the French as subjects. Jacques Tati's popular film *Jour de Fête*, issued in 1949, was made in the little commune of Saint-Sévère in the Indre *département* of central France. The local municipal government, controlled by Radicals, provided all possible assistance—the local *curé*, incidentally, was not enthusiastic.

To study the *radicaux classiques*, then, is to study a fundamental and characteristic side of French life, a way of life that has found a plenitude of able portrayers. This way of life is often considered, by the portrayers as well as by those portrayed, as representative of the life of the 'average Frenchman'. *Le français moyen*—the phrase has been attributed to Herriot—is taken as the antithesis of the Parisian, *'le beau Monsieur de Paris'*. The superiority of country over the town, of the provincial town over the great city, is a common theme of the spokesmen of classical radicalism. Alain approvingly cited Balzac's *Les Paysans* for showing how the *Messieurs* that come from Paris must adapt and conform to country ways, if they wish to remain; in another passage he pointed out that Montesquieu and Montaigne lived in the country.[6] It is Alain himself, however, who has provided some of the most vivid characterizations of this as well as of other basic attitudes and ideas of the classical Radicals. His defence and idealization of the country as compared to Paris, the small as compared to the large, the individual as compared to the State; his opposition to a strong government and centralized

---

[5] *Le Berry républicain*, 5 December 1949. Marcel Plaisant, senator from Cher.
[6] *Politique*, Paris, 1952, p. 271 and p. 244.

power: all these themes familiar to Alain are reflected in the ideas and attitudes of the old-school Radicals.

To Alain, political life consisted of an unending battle between the Citizen and the Powers-that-be. The State is a dangerous machine that must be diligently controlled. 'Power corrupts all those who participate in it.'[7] The people elect deputies in an attempt to control power; 'It elects not so much chiefs as *controleurs*.'[8] Alain argued that it was not desirable to have important people, great bankers, shipbuilders, lawyers, etc., as deputies, for they might think too much of their fortunes or naturally incline to exercise tyrannical power. 'I would often prefer an honest man who had not succeeded too well.'[9] Or, as one author once observed: 'The ideal of the controlled official is evidently Lebrun, Foreign Minister of the Convention, who went to his office between two policemen and was finally guillotined.'[10]

In Alain's opinion the true role of the Radical party and its members was to limit and control, not to lead. 'This art of cracking the whip defines, according to me, the party of the future, the true Radical party, which I would call "the party of governmental opposition"!'[11] Alain's name for those who think they are born to lead, for the 'permanent conspiracy of the rich and ambitious, the great chiefs, parasites and flatterers',[12] for those who think that they are indispensable, is the *Importants*. When a deputy becomes a minister, he changes his skin and becomes an *Important*. 'He was a deputy always ready to resist and threaten the powers-that-be; he takes power and sees all questions from a different angle.'[13] Once caught up in the machinery of power, it is impossible to escape. Very few men, unfortunately, know how to disdain or to resist the lure of power.

Alain's distrust of power has not prevented *radicaux classiques* from desiring to participate in its exercise. Few members of a political party would care to follow faithfully all Alain's entreaties. Radicals have been willing to oppose and control those in power, but they have been even more willing to replace them.

Radicals, and especially *radicaux classiques*, have been more at ease in joining Alain in his denunciation of non-governmental forms of power—social, military, ecclesiastical, and economic

---

[7] *Eléments d'une doctrine radicale*, p. 27.   [8] *Ibid.*, p. 14.   [9] *Ibid.*, p. 93.
[10] Albert Thibaudet, *La République des professeurs*, Paris, 1927, p. 243.
[11] *Eléments*, p. 92.   [12] *Ibid.*, p. 54.   [13] *Ibid.*, p. 80.

power. The old-school Radicals have shared Alain's distrust of Paris as the centre of power and even more as the centre of French social life. Radical militants still share Alain's fear that their deputies will be seduced by the flattery and social poison of Paris. 'There is a court there', Alain warned, 'today as in the past, and courtesans, even without a king. There is rich and ornate life; the man who permits himself to enter it loses for ever his independence of judgement.'[14] In another passage Alain declared that 'there is not one example of a *salon* whose devotees accept the sovereignty of the people'.[15] A delegate from Normandy, where Alain first won fame, echoed this fear when he asked at the party's congress in 1945 whether 'certain Radical leaders had not gone astray in the sweet-smelling paths of the boudoirs of the extreme right'.[16] He then asked his listeners whether they remembered 'the old, the healthy doctrine of Alain, the doctrine of the people', and whether they wanted, 'yes or no, to be controlled by the elector, or absorbed by the *salons* of Paris'.

These are charges that Radical ministers and deputies have always been eager to disprove. Most Radical politicians have been masters in the art of maintaining close relations with their constituents, and they lose respect for those of their colleagues who have been less successful. Daladier has been quoted as calling Reynaud a '*Parisien*' in an attempt, while in a fit of rage during a ministerial crisis, to express 'his contempt of the man who had lost his earthy roots'.[17] Reynaud had been defeated in his home constituency in Basses-Alpes and was representing the electoral district of the Paris Stock Exchange—a sharp demotion in Daladier's eyes. In a speech at the party's congress in 1955, Mendès-France stressed the need to aid provincial universities where, he declared, there was a better atmosphere than at Paris. It is unlikely, however, that any Radical leader would want to see the implementation of Alain's wish to have the government moved 'to Tours, to Orleans or to Chateauroux', where 'politics would be more clear, less Parisien, more national', or to conduct

[14] *Ibid.*, p. 59.   [15] *Ibid.*, p. 47.

[16] M. Soyer (Seine-Maritime).

[17] Pertinax (André Geraud), *The Gravediggers of France: Gamelin, Daladier, Reynaud Pétain, and Laval*, New York, 1944, p. 184. Pertinax cites Georges Mandel as his source.

the affairs of state wearing 'a farm labourer's frock and wooden shoes'.[18]

Alain's irreverence towards the powerful—'An *Important* ruined and humiliated provides the best possible spectacle for my taste'.[19] —is particularly attractive to those who have become reconciled to remaining small and unimportant. In many cases, however, 'reconciled' is too weak a word. The *radicaux classiques* have come to typify those who participate in a cult of the *petit*. They represent those who not only are reconciled to being *petit*, but revel in that state. Writing at a time when the *radicaux classiques* were the dominant element in the party, Albert Thibaudet stated that the economic programme of radicalism consisted in the use of the mystical prestige of this one epithet, *petit*—'the little farmer, the little tradesman, the little property, the little savings, the little shareholders'.[20] It is clear that these conditions carry prestige among many French voters. 'To acquire a little property,' André Siegfried once wrote, 'a little house, a little business, a little income from investments, is the dream of millions of French people.'[21] These may seem limited objectives, but they have continued to be kept in mind in planning French electoral campaigns. A French business newspaper, distributed in the Radical party's headquarters before the 1956 general elections, began an appeal to voters with the title 'Little employer or future little employer, little property owner or future little property owner ...'[22] Openly to ask for higher support or to encourage more expansive ambitions would not have been in keeping with sound electoral policy.

Perhaps the most abiding attitude and ideological keystone of the *radicaux classiques* has been their anti-clericalism. The most important ideological and political issue at the turn of the century, when the party was founded, was that of the relations between the Church and State, and this has remained a living issue in the hearts of virtually all old-school Radicals. The evolution of the Radical attitude towards the Church question has been

---

[18] *Eléments*, pp. 77–8. For a study of the mutual attitudes of Parisians and provincials, see *Sondages*, No. 2, 1951, pp. 17–19.

[19] *Eléments*, p. 17.   [20] *La République des professeurs*, pp. 259–60.

[21] André Siegfried, *France. A Study in Nationality*, New Haven, Conn., 1930, p. 12. See also p. 78.

[22] *La Volonté du Commerce et de l'Industrie*, December 1955.

reflected in radicalism's relationship with French Masonry. Masonry was an important aspect of radicalism; many Radicals have received their intellectual formation and political apprenticeship in provincial Masonic lodges. The Masonic way of life, the Masonic comradeship, has been a lasting feature of the Radical way of life. The influence and position of Masonry has lessened since the Second World War, but it continues as a force, varying and difficult to assess, among Radicals, and in particular among the old-school Radicals. In the spectrum of Radical opinion concerning the proper degree of *laïcisation* of the State, the *radicaux classiques*, as would be expected, belong among those with the most extreme opinions.

*

* *

Congresses, banquets, and eloquent appeals to defend the Republic can be counted on to arouse the interest of older Radicals, and moves to counter the machinations of the reactionaries and of the *curés* continue to have their support. Perhaps the most important ingredient in the make-up of the *radical classique*, however, is his abiding concern with tactics and personality. Both of these factors are of primary importance on the local level, and the local level, as we have noted, is the most characteristic habitat of the followers of traditional radicalism. There are 37,983 communes in France, each with its *conseil municipal* and mayor: the opportunities for local rivalries are endless. Questions of doctrine and of ideas often give way in importance to conflicts between personalities. 'A Radical in origin, and perhaps still a Radical at heart, Larondelle attacked radicalism ferociously, since for him radicalism meant simply Piéchut, the man he hated most in the world.'[23]

In a clash between vague doctrines and the inexorable logic of local situations, the latter may be expected to take precedence, although ideally these two factors should complement each other, with the former confined to the realm of speech-making. No personal ambition should be allowed to preclude the announcement, in vague but grandiose terms, of a future of Peace and Prosperity or the stern advocacy of Justice and Progress. These, of course, are not characteristics that are limited to the Radical

[23] Gabriel Chevallier, *Clochemerle Babylone*, Paris, 1954, p. 245.

party, or even to its most traditionalistic wing, but it must be noted that some of the *radicaux classiques* have placed at least as high a priority on electoral campaigns and disputes as on the other aspects of traditional radicalism. Unlike some of their less traditional colleagues, however, they have continued to accompany their concern to win elections with an interest in the traditional tenets of radicalism. Certain Radicals may be said to have specialized in having no doctrine except a desire to win office. By most *radicaux classiques*, however, this desire has been accompanied by at least an appeal to traditional Radical values.

A primary requisite of a *radical classique* who aspires to office is that he be an *homme du pays*, a local man. It usually is required that he also be a strong personality, a *notable*, and have a personal following in his constituency. Such a candidate, of course, is a strong opponent of proportional representation. 'A son of the people,' Alain once wrote, 'always blushes a little when he betrays the Republic, but one fine morning you will discover that he is anti-Semitic, or else *proportionaliste*.'[24] Deputies elected by an electoral system with single-member constituencies and two ballots—the Radical ideal and the method in favour during most of the Third Republic—usually began their careers as *conseiller municipal*, then became mayor of their commune or town, next adding to their experience by becoming *conseiller général* of their *département*. Radical candidates at all levels nearly always are well known in the regions in which they run for office and count on the support of their local *comités*. Working in a local context, they are very careful to take local conditions into consideration. It is in this task that the *radicaux classiques* traditionally excel, and it is on the local level that doctrine has been equated most often with tactics and personality. Despite their decline on the national scene after the Second World War, Radicals were able to maintain their strong local positions in many areas, and much of this success may be ascribed to the tenacious role played by the *radicaux classiques*. As the official Radical newspaper commented in 1955 concerning local and cantonal elections: 'The man counts as much as, if not more than, the political ideas that he represents.'[25]

Examples of this phenomenon are legion. The mayor of a

[24] *Eléments*, p. 65.

[25] 'Physionomie des élections cantonales', *I.R.S.*, 28 April 1955.

small commune in central France with a population of 557 inhabitants has been mayor for over thirty-five years; he was mayor before the war, he was mayor under Vichy, and except for a period after the Liberation, has been mayor since the war.[26] He also serves as a *conseiller général* of his *département*. Radicals have controlled his *mairie* since the party was organized; he succeeded his father-in-law in office, and his wife was *secrétaire* of the *mairie* during the First World War while her father was in the trenches. Although strongly attacked after the Liberation, he won the municipal election by a comfortable majority: 250 people voted for him. Of particular significance is the fact that he is the only registered Radical in the commune. It is his personality, not his party membership, that has made his position. During his first thirty-five years as mayor he had never heard of Alain. Even the Communist party, which long attacked him as 'Le caïd à l'éternel sourire', eventually supported him in cantonal elections. This durable personage was also careful to remain on good terms with the schoolmaster and the *curé*—the town being run by the schoolmaster, the *curé*, the mayor, and the mayor's wife.

The mayor of a larger town in the same *département* has described himself as one of the three Radical party members in a Radical electorate of 600.[27] The *département*'s only successful postwar Radical candidate for the National Assembly received 12,552 votes in the general elections of June 1951; in March 1951, the *département*'s Radical Federation had paid for 230 membership cards.[28] A comparatively young man, this deputy could not be considered a *radical classique*, but his success illustrates the importance of a personal clientele as a basis for party activity. In his opinion, the local Radicals follow men and not ideas. They were voting for him, and not for his programme or party label.

The weakening of the ideas of traditional radicalism among

[26] M. Dubreuil, Mayor of Maisonnais (Cher), pop. 557, and *conseiller général du Cher*. Interview, 28 October 1955.

[27] Philibert Lautissier, Mayor of Lignières (Cher), pop. 1,623. Interview, 28 October 1955. According to his estimates the electorate also included 350 Communists, 150 Socialists, and 150 'réactionnaires'.

[28] Radical party archives. The successful candidate later declared that the federation's leaders could have purchased 1,000 cards but did not wish to entail the extra expense. Interview with Jacques Genton, deputy from Cher, Paris, 3 November 1955.

the *radicaux classiques* themselves has contributed to this situation. With a decline of party activity in many areas, deputies naturally came to depend primarily on local Radical mayors, *conseillers généraux*, and personal friends to aid in advancing their cause. As a vice-president of the party declared at the party's congress in 1951 (held after the general elections of that year), 'certain gloomy spirits' could consider that the party's electoral publicity had consisted, 'in truth, of personal publicity made by our candidates who were aided by a certain number of militants'.[29] This tendency has led, during the period under consideration, to a greater emphasis by many *radicaux classiques* on the tactical and personality aspects of traditional radicalism, with a relative decline in the importance attached to certain of its ideological postulates. The deputy described above, a toiler in a former stronghold of traditional radicalism, has said, with sadness, that only two issues still matter: conscription and taxes. Others would supplement this list with, at least, the question of Church schools and the electoral law issue.

The degree of susceptibility to restatements of the basic tenets of radicalism and the degree of faith in their inherent value remain, along with ability to act effectively on the local political scene, as reliable measuring rods of the true *radical classique*. It has been necessary, though, to take cognizance of the fact that there has been a shifting of emphasis among these factors and to note a tendency on the part of certain of the traditionalists to neglect ideological questions, while concentrating a preponderant interest on tactics.

*

* *

We have seen that a characteristic attitude of traditional radicalism has been a mistrust of power. This mistrust of the central power, however, has a close corollary: the desire to participate in the fruits of power. The distrust of *power* is more than matched by the desire for *patronage*. Participation in the government has come to mean a way of gaining protection against the State. The deputy is seen as the delegate of his constituents and is expected to advance their material welfare and to gain favours from the administration. Such an attitude is not limited, of course, to the

[29] Raymond Grimal, 'La Propagande', *I.R.S.*, October–November 1951.

radicaux classiques, but the latter are particularly insistent in placing a strong emphasis on this part of a deputy's life, and the lot of the Radical deputy who conscientiously tries to maintain a close relationship with his constituents can be a particularly onerous one. One Radical deputy, for example, once received from one of his female constituents a letter that began: 'I was told that your wife accompanied you this week on your trip to Paris. As I know that her figure is about the same as mine, I would be very happy if she would buy a girdle for me . . .'[30]

Constituents expect their deputies to provide personal services and to protect their interests, but they are less exigent about the problems of the outside world. On this level they are more willing to follow the lead of the deputy or, perhaps more often, to remain indifferent. Many deputies take this attitude for granted. This approach to political life is present, in varying degrees, in virtually all political parties, but it must be said that the Radicals —in keeping with the state of mind best represented by the *radicaux classiques*—have provided some particularly striking examples of this attitude. In an official report on foreign policy at the party's congress at Marseilles in 1954, a speaker noted that 'we are living probably the most decisive weeks of the last ten post-war years'—Mendès-France had been in office four months —and concluded by declaring that 'it is the hour when the parliamentarian, who holds by his vote such a heavy responsibility, a veritable portion of the national sovereignty, must act in complete independence and only obey the commands of conscience'.[31]

The president of the Radical Group in the National Assembly —a deputy from the same south-western *département*, Dordogne —on retiring from his post the previous month to move to the Senate, stressed the problems inherent in the position that he was leaving. It was, he said, 'a difficult role in a party like ours, and one which is less that of a chief than that of a referee. The parliamentary group wants a conciliator and not a dictator.'[32]

The 'elders' of the party—those who have made their careers amidst the traditions of radicalism, who have spent decades learning how to manipulate assemblies and congresses and in

[30] François Muselier, *Regards neufs sur le Parlement*, Paris, 1956, pp. 142–3.
[31] Henry Laforest, deputy from Dordogne.
[32] Yvon Delbos, *I.R.S.*, 21 September 1955.

participating in the give-and-take, mutual concessions, compromises, and favours of life in the Chamber of Deputies, Senate, and the National Assembly—are recognized masters in the art of conciliation and temporizing. In order to exercise this art, moreover, it has been necessary to aspire to and win high positions in government. A presidency is a coveted post in the eyes of all old-school Radicals—in party congresses the title *Monsieur le Président* is heard at least as often as *Citoyen*. On one memorable occasion during the party's congress in 1952, the astute Edgar Faure addressed his listeners collectively as *Messieurs les Présidents*. If, despite the claims of radicalism, there is a paradise on Earth, there is no doubt that in the dreams of any ambitious *radical classique* it would consist in being elected to the presidency of the French Republic.

*

* *

What conclusions may be drawn as to the ideas and the role of the *radicaux classiques*?

It is clear that they represent a declining but still tenacious element both on the French national scene and in the life of the Radical party. They have been the most steadfast guardians of many of the most traditional Radical symbols. At the same time they have also typified the Radical tradition that puts a premium on flexible doctrines. In Alain's words, 'the Radical is by nature a philosopher; he knows that every doctrine is provisional, and that no doctrine is adequate for the events to follow'.[33] Bold political ideas are useful ingredients for a speech, but in the words of one local practitioner, it is better to lose one's head over a woman than over a doctrine. Except on special occasions or when confronted by certain special issues, the old-school Radical is a congenial and amenable person.

The *radicaux classiques* have been careful not to reject the good things from the past merely because they are from the past. Supporting the ideal of progress, they have been careful not to confuse change with progress. They have been most durable in those parts of France that have been the least dynamic economically. They have always been more interested in old ideological quarrels and in political tactics than in social and economic

[33] *Eléments*, p. 24.

reforms. In this respect, they reflect the fear that a strengthened and modernized state would benefit primarily the powerful leaders of business and finance, who, contrary to the interests of equality, are already too powerful. The *radicaux classiques* may be said to be the representatives of *status quo* France—the France which one critic has described by saying that its clocks keep a different time, a time based on its sleepy small towns.[34]

But this is also the France where one can live so well, 'like God in France' in the words of a German proverb that, like the *radicaux classiques*, comes from an earlier day but still survives. The old ways have their advantages and defenders. Speed is not an unmitigated blessing. Alain, who often stressed his dislike for machines and wrote fondly of the 'happy carpenter' and the 'happy wood-worker', has argued, in one of his *propos*, that trains should not go too quickly.[35] At the same time, the *radicaux classiques* manifestly do not represent many of the more dynamic aspects of France. Alain made his comment on trains in the early part of the century; by mid-century, France had the fastest trains in the world.

In the context of much that typifies modern-day France, it may be argued that the *radicaux classiques* and the ideas that they represent are anachronistic. In an earlier day they and their predecessors, putting the emphasis on political objectives, won great victories. Once political liberties and rights were ensured, however, they became satisfied and tended to leave the task of pushing for economic and social reforms to the Socialists and Communists. This is a problem that has not been solved with the passage of time. Social classes that did not profit as fully from the Revolution of 1789 as did the ancestors of the *radicaux classiques* are still awaiting their turn. Despite the old Radical slogan of 'No enemies on the left', the state of mind that the old-school Radicals have represented has not proven convincing to the rising working class, nor does it provide answers to their problems.

In a period when increasing numbers of their compatriots were demanding reforms, it was no longer possible, or tactically wise,

[34] Herbert Lüthy, *The State of France*, London, 1955. First published as *Frankreichs Uhren gehen anders*, Zurich, 1954.

[35] *Propos d'un Normand*, 1906–14 (Paris, Vol. I: 1952; Vol. II: 1955), vol. 2, pp. 212–13.

D

for Radicals to join Alain in defining 'the true power of the voters' as being exercised 'rather by the resistance to the powers-that-be than by reformative action'.[36] In a novel written at the turn of the century, Anatole France has one of his characters say that although the Republic governs badly, he can excuse this as it governs little. In September 1949, at the opening of a cabinet meeting, all the ministers in the government congratulated the Radical premier, Henri Queuille, for the successful completion of a year in office. As a testimonial of their esteem they presented him with the collected works of Anatole France.[37] He had presided over the first post-war government to have lasted a year, a notable achievement, but his was a government accused of *immobilisme*, of governing little, and it fell the following month in face of demands for greater economic and social reforms. Governing little was no longer enough.

Old habits of living, especially in the provinces, work in favour of the traditional brand of radicalism. Despite the upheavals of war, industrialism, and the *mystique* of the resistance, old traditions have persisted. The *radicaux classiques* represent a way of life that may appear outmoded to many observers, but it can be argued that it is a way of life that does provide a subtle understanding of the true dynamics of existence. More concerned with the art of *savoir-vivre* than with being up-to-date, the *radicaux classiques* represent an attitude that is undoubtedly more conducive to the preservation of psychological roots than to the development of intercontinental missiles.

But the world has continued to change, if not to progress, and the position of the *radicaux classiques* has become more difficult. Not only the world, but France, and indeed the Radical party itself, has changed. At the party's congress in 1946, one delegate, declaring that the liberty of the world was menaced, warned that the day would perhaps come when Frenchmen who want to play *boules*—a leisurely game popular in southern France —would be forced by collectivism to play football. Ten years later, in July 1956, a young, newly elected deputy proposed a law that would make rugby, 'considered by the sporting elite as the king of sports', obligatory in all French schools.[38] This

---

[36] *Eléments*, p. 123.   [37] *Journal Officiel*, 27 October 1949, p. 5931.

[38] *Le Monde*, 31 July 1956. Paul Ferrand, deputy from Creuse. Elected on a *union des gauches* list in 1956, as a '*radical de gauche*', Ferrand was later inscribed as a *progressiste*.

proposition was not greeted with enthusiasm by the representatives of any party, but by this time there was no doubt that some of the most unexpected affronts to the *radicaux classiques* could originate among those who claimed allegiance to the same party label.

During the post-war years the Radicals themselves were to provide some of the most searching criticisms of their traditional ways of doing things and of the tendency of some of their members to think in terms of the past. In an official report at the party's congress in 1954, one of the party's rising young leaders expressed this concern when he declared that the Radical party 'does not mean to be the conservatory of a great past, but the architect of the national future'.[39] Such a role is not compatible with the ideas, objectives, and attitudes of the *radicaux classiques*. Yet, in the opinion of this orator, if the party 'were content to scrape along on positions won in the past and on the sentimental loyalty of its traditional cadres, it would slip little by little into oblivion and mediocrity'.

[39] Félix Gaillard. Elected deputy in June 1946, at the age of twenty-six, Gaillard began a spectacular ministerial career the following year, and became premier in October 1957, on his thirty-eighth birthday, the youngest man to preside over France's destinies since Napoleon became First Consul in 1799. Gaillard was elected president of the Radical Party in September 1958.

III

The 'Symbol of Radicalism':
Edouard Herriot

'*Le radicalisme semble être quelquefois moins la doctrine d'un parti que la popularité d'un homme.*'

JACQUES FAUVET, *Le Monde*, 7 April 1946

'*Cet homme c'est la République en personne!*'
(*Les délégués, debout, ovationnent longuement le président Herriot*)

LÉON MARTINAUD-DÉPLAT, Administrative President of the Radical party, at a meeting of the Executive Committee, 18 March 1951

One antidote for splits and divergencies within a political party is for that party to have a chief who can foster harmony and promote a synthesis. In the Radical party, where this has always been a task of heroic proportions, one man has been outstanding in playing the role of peacemaker: Edouard Herriot. From his return from German captivity in 1945 to his death in 1957, no other Radical served as president of the party. Herriot, however, was more than a beloved leader and a respected peacemaker. If any one man may be said to have been the personification of the Radical party and of radicalism, it was the party's venerable president. At the party's congress in 1945, Théodore Steeg, who had served as president before Herriot's return, called him 'the symbol, the incarnation of our party'; at the party's congress in 1956, Mendès-France, *premier vice-président*, 'certain of expressing, at least for a few moments, the unanimous feeling of the party', asked Herriot to remain at the helm, 'not only as the symbol of radicalism, but as the most certain guarantee of its force and of its profound unity'.

In 1956, as in previous years, Radicals were still clinging to their aging leader and pleading with him not to resign. His resignations, or threats of resignation, were a source of anxious concern to Radicals during the years that followed his return from Germany. As one political writer declared in 1947: 'Everyone knows that the Radical party is above all a man: its president; and nobody knows what would happen to the party if it were to lose its chief.'[1] At a meeting of the party's executive committee in March 1951, Léon Martinaud-Déplat, the party's administrative president, bluntly warned his listeners of the dire effects that would ensue if they lost their president: 'You would be emptied of your substance.' Declaring that it was 'not possible to find in his life, vis-à-vis Radical doctrine, a single error that has been committed', he added that 'the republicans of the country know this, and it is with him that we must go forward to "tomorrows that sing" '.

Thus Herriot was not only considered indispensable, but in the minds of many Radicals was credited with an almost papal infallibility. In his later years, indeed, certain party members and outside observers called him 'the Pope'—not always with unmitigated respect. At the same time, however, other Radicals attributed to him an even greater infallibility than the doctrinal infallibility attributed by Roman Catholics to their spiritual leader. In the words of the president of the Radical Federation of Calvados, in a speech of welcome at the party's congress at Deauville in 1953, Herriot was 'the great Frenchman who has never made a mistake and whom one can follow without fear'. Leaving aside the question as to whether or not—or to what extent—Herriot may be considered as infallible, there is no doubt that he was a unique figure in the Radical party and is of central importance in any study of radicalism and the Radical party.

*

*   *

Herriot had a long and active life. In an effort to shed as much light as possible on the party and the body of ideas that he came to symbolize (Herriot, the 'symbol of radicalism', may also be said to represent, more than any other man, the spectrum of radicalism), certain of the more representative and significant aspects of his life and career will be selected for special analysis. This analysis will include a consideration of his background and intellectual formation, his entry into political life, his choice of

[1] Jacques Fauvet, *Le Monde*, 20 September 1947.

the Radical party, and his political career. What factors went into the making of a Radical symbol? How did Herriot use his great authority?

A compromise will have to be made between providing a case study of the development and evolution of this 'symbol of radicalism'—whose life has formed a unified whole—and studying a specific period in the life of the Radical party. Perhaps the most revealing and representative part of Herriot's life was the soul-searching period of the German invasion and the subsequent Vichy government: his activities during the war years can serve to symbolize the immediate heritage and position of the party and its ideas during the early post-war years. Herriot's role as a leader of the opposition and as rebuilder of the Radical party was undoubtedly one of the high points of his long career, and one in which he had ample occasions to describe and defend the ideas for which he had always stood. His brief experience as honorary president of a Communist-front, post-war resistance organization; his more than a half-century as mayor of Lyons; his long periods as president of the National Assembly and as president of the Radical party: these facets of Herriot's life are also among those that must be studied in order to gain an insight into the remarkable position that Herriot was able to attain.

*

* *

Radicals have identified Herriot with their party's history and doctrine; Herriot never rejected this identification. Radicals have identified Herriot with the Republic and with France; Herriot once referred to himself as 'an old Frenchman who does not have a drop of blood that is not French'.[2] Born in 1872, he was a few weeks under seventy-three on his return to France in May 1945. His father, whose family came from the Vosges region of eastern France, was an infantry officer who had fought against the Austrians in the Italian campaign of 1859 and against the Germans in 1870; he died while on active service in Algeria in 1889.[3] His mother was from Vendée in western France. Herriot's official biographical sketch in the *Annuaire de l'Assemblée Nationale*

[2] 1946 Congress.

[3] Edouard Herriot, *Jadis*, vol. 1, *Avant la première guerre mondiale*, vol. 2, *D'une guerre à l'autre*, 1914-1936, Paris, 1948, 1952; vol. 1, chapter I.

stated that his grandfather was the son of a labourer, who retired as a corporal, and had married a seamstress.

After making a brilliant record in the *lycée* at La-Roche-sur-Yon, a small town in Vendée where his father was stationed, Herriot was awarded a scholarship to the famed *Collège Sainte-Barbe* in Paris. At nineteen he entered the *Ecole Normale Supérieure*. After completing his year of military service in 1895, he was appointed professor at the *lycée* at Nantes. He was transferred to the *Lycée Ampère* at Lyons the following year. Lyons was henceforth to be his home and a central factor in his life.

Despite his active political life Herriot carried on with conspicuous success the distinguished literary career that he began during this period. While doing his year of military service, he wrote a biography of Philo, the great Hebrew philosopher and a contemporary of Jesus Christ. Possibly his greatest literary work was his magistral doctoral dissertation—first published in 1904—on Madame Récamier, the beautiful *lyonnaise* who had a famous *salon* in Paris during the early years of the nineteenth century.[4] Among the score of other books that Herriot wrote were erudite historical, political and literary studies, books based on his travels, and memoirs. His subjects included Beethoven, Diderot, Zola, Mistral, Rodin, Madame de Staël, Lamartine, Chateaubriand, and many others. His studies led him to all parts of French history. 'One is no more a Bonapartist for admiring Napoleon,' he once wrote, 'than one is a Royalist because one cherishes Joan of Arc.'[5] They also brought him many honours and much respect. In awarding Herriot an honorary doctorate in 1939, Dr. Nicholas Murray Butler, President of Columbia University, described him as 'one of the best-balanced and wisest minds in the public life of these grievously troubled times; a statesman who has happily retained his love of letters and the fine arts'.[6] In December 1946, he was elected to the French Academy in recognition of his many literary and political attainments.

Herriot's early surroundings marked him profoundly in his political life. He often expressed pride in his modest origins—

[4] *Madame Récamier et ses Amis*, Paris, 1904.

[5] 'Remerciement à l'Académie, le 26 juin 1947.' Reprinted in Edouard Herriot, *Etudes françaises*, Geneva, 1950, p. 263.

[6] Cited in frontispiece of Edouard Herriot, *The Wellsprings of Liberty* (*Aux Sources de la Liberté*), New York, 1939.

stressing their modesty—and had a profound and eloquent love for France, French history, and the French countryside. In a speech at the party's congress at Deauville in 1950, Herriot spoke of his emotion on his return to France after his captivity: '. . . this delightful country of France, at the same time so strong and so fragile, so quick to take offence but so rapid in recovery; this country of France where the countryside itself seems to think; this countryside where there is not one little stream that does not sing a song for us, in which we do not find the echo of some local dialect or some childhood memory; this country which is not a country of plutocrats or of millionaires; this country where so many little thatched or tile-roofed houses grouped in the bottom of a valley, built on the summit or nestling on the sides of hills testify to the modesty and simplicity of the inhabitants; this country that we all love'. The sincerity of such descriptions was matched only by the warmth of the receptions that they received by his Radical listeners.

Herriot often expressed his admiration for his father. In his memoirs he wrote that his father had been inspired with a love of ancient literature during his military experiences in Italy, and had communicated this love to his son. 'I owe to him,' Herriot proudly acknowledged, 'the beginning of my Latin education.'[7] His father had fought with distinction against the Germans in 1870 and had a sister living in conquered territory; even more than most of his generation, therefore, he was grief-stricken over the loss of Alsace and Lorraine. All of Herriot's childhood was pervaded with the recital of the woes of Alsace. Other early influences were also to affect Herriot's intellectual formation. As a boy, he spent his summers with a great-uncle, who was a country priest, and he occasionally served as an altar boy. One of his aunts was a governess at the house of Maurice Barrès, the renowned Catholic writer. Barrès became one of Herriot's early friends and helped him while he was a poor student in Paris; on one occasion he gave Herriot an overcoat—the young student's first one.[8] Although a staunch advocate of laicism in his later political career, Herriot was always tolerant of the opinions of others and never carried his secular opinions to the extremes attained by many of his Radical contemporaries.

[7] *Jadis*, vol. 1, p. 10.
[8] 'Rencontre avec Edouard Herriot', *I.R.S.*, January 1957

In Herriot's intellectual and political development, a crucial role was played by the Dreyfus Affair, which as he later recalled, was 'to alter my life and impose new duties on me'.[9] At first he had been incredulous. 'For an officer's son such as I was, no slightest doubt was permissible.' The rising tide of evidence, however, soon convinced him of Dreyfus's innocence. When the *Ligue des Droits de l'Homme*—founded to fight for a revision of the case—opened a section at Lyons, Herriot was among the first to join.

Until aroused by the Dreyfus Affair, Herriot had not played an active role in politics. 'I had confined myself,' he later remarked, 'to joining, on my arrival in Lyons, the Radical *comité* of the sixth *arrondissement*.'[10] After this step, however, he was to remain 'constantly faithful' to the Radical party. 'I have never separated myself from it,' he wrote many years later.[11] 'Certainly, an *homme public* may change his doctrine; but if he has made a mistake, that is to say, if he has deceived the public, the best thing for him to do is to seclude himself in retirement and be silent.' Throughout his long political career, Herriot always stressed with pride his close links with his party's history. At a banquet held in February 1952, to celebrate the fiftieth anniversary of the formal organization of the party, Herriot declared that he had 'lived all the life of the Radical party' and noted that he had been one of the first *rapporteurs* in its congresses.[12]

After his decision to play an active role in politics, Herriot was soon on his way to a brilliant political career. During his long political life, he was never officially a candidate for any post. It was always sufficient for him to have been, in the words of the traditional French expression, 'at the disposal of his friends and in the service of the Republic'. He was elected *conseiller municipal* at Lyons in 1904. In 1905, the year he won his doctorate at the Sorbonne, he was elected mayor of Lyons. Then thirty-three years old, he was the youngest mayor in France. Except during the three years of enforced absence after his dismissal by the Vichy government, he continued to serve as mayor of Lyons until his death; his fiftieth anniversary as mayor was celebrated in 1955. In his memoirs, Herriot stated that 'in my long public life the problem that has occupied me most continually has been

[9] *Jadis*, vol. 1, p. 130.   [10] *Ibid.*, p. 139.
[11] *Ibid.*, vol. 2, pp. 646–7.   [12] *I.R.S.*, February 1952.

that of the administration of the town of Lyons'.[13] 'I have loved the town of Lyons,' he concluded, 'as one loves a human being.' France, the Republic, the Radical party, Lyons: these were the central themes of Herriot's life. They were linked with each other (a popular saying maintains that 'Paris is the capital of France, but Lyons is the capital of the Republic'), and Herriot with all four.

Herriot was always particularly proud of being mayor of Lyons, but he won many other titles during his long political career. In 1910, he was elected *conseiller général* of the Rhône *département*. In 1912, at the age of forty, he was elected senator; he was the youngest senator in France. He was a cabinet minister for the first time in 1916 and was elected deputy as well as president of the Radical party in 1919. He held the latter post until 1924, when he became premier; he was again president of the party from 1931 to 1935, and was the party's only president from his return from Germany in May 1945 until his death in March 1957. He was premier for ten months in 1924–5 and won international fame for his advocacy of collective security, arbitration and disarmament, for his proposal of the Geneva protocol, and for his re-establishment of relations between France and Russia. After his government was overthrown by the Senate for its financial policies, he was elected, for the first time, President of the Chamber of Deputies. He was again premier for three days in 1926 and for four and a half months in 1932; the latter government fell when Herriot insisted that the current instalment on the American war debt be paid.

The one high office that Herriot did not attain was the presidency of the Republic. He was a prominent presidential possibility during most of the 1930's—and two decades later was again mentioned as a possible candidate. In an article published before the presidential elections that were held in December 1953, *Le Progrès de Lyon* declared that Herriot would not officially be a candidate, 'but if on the fateful day 474 ballots bearing his name are put in the ballot-box, he will not refuse to enter the *Elysée* on 16 January'.[14] Herriot, however, in a letter read to the National Assembly on 1 December 1953, declared that his age and health obliged him to ask that his term as president of the National Assembly not be renewed, and that for the same reasons

[13] *Jadis*, vol. 2, p. 664.   [14] Cited by *Le Monde*, 26 November 1953.

he would not be a candidate for the presidency of the Republic. 'It would not be honest on my part,' he wrote, 'to solicit or accept a mandate that I could not fill.' After ten fruitless ballots in the most lengthy presidential election in French history, his name was one of those suggested as a compromise candidate, but on the thirteenth ballot the voters had recourse to a less known figure—René Coty. The following month, in January 1954, at eighty-one years of age, Herriot was unanimously elected honorary president of the National Assembly. A few months earlier, at the Radical party's congress in 1953, he had been elected president of his party 'for the duration of his life'. From *conseiller municipal* to virtually all the presidencies but one, Herriot's career provided inspiration and leadership that won the respect, and often the adulation, of his fellow Radicals.

*

* *

How did Herriot, the 'symbol of radicalism', use his great authority?

His first major post-war task was to resuscitate his party and to defend its ideas and interests amidst the avalanche of new political forces that swept over liberated France. In order to be an effective leader of the opposition, however, he had to re-establish his own personal authority and prestige. The 'symbol of radicalism', like radicalism itself, had not survived the war with reputation unscathed—his record during the Vichy period was to be an occasional subject of partisan debate, especially during the political campaigns of 1945 and 1946. An analysis of the comportment of the revered leader of the Radicals during the tragic years of defeat and occupation can serve to typify the attitude of many of his colleagues and compatriots and to provide a background for, and possibly an illumination of, some of the problems faced by the party after the Liberation. It was in the light of this record that Herriot had to operate in the impassioned political life of post-war France, and it was with this record as an immediate background that Herriot became known as the symbol of radicalism.

In June 1940, Herriot was hostile to an armistice with the German invaders and favoured moving the government to North Africa. On 18 June, he and Jules Jeanneney, the President of the Senate and a fellow Radical, wrote a letter to Albert Lebrun, President of the Republic, to express their formal opposition to making a separate peace.[15] On 17 June, however, Pétain had replaced Reynaud as premier, and on 22 June an armistice was signed with Germany. Full powers were voted to Pétain on 10 July in a special joint session of the two houses of Parliament. Herriot presided over a meeting of the Chamber of Deputies on 9 July; as president he did not vote in either of the two crucial roll calls of these two days, but part of the speech that he delivered in opening the 9 July session was to be used against him after the liberation. After speaking of the great misfortune that had afflicted France and after paying tribute to deputies who had fallen in battle, he had asked his listeners to rally around Pétain: 'Around Marshal Pétain, with the veneration that his name inspires, our nation has grouped itself in its distress. Let us take care not to upset the unity which, under his authority, is now established.' His speech was followed with 'loud and prolonged applause from all the benches', and the Chamber voted 593 to 3 for a revision of the constitution. On the following day Pétain's constitutional project was adopted by a margin of 569 to 80.

In this period of confusion and dismay, Pétain was at the height of his popularity, and Herriot, like the bulk of his compatriots, was thinking more of reorganization than of resistance. When questioned at Pétain's trial in 1945 concerning his remarks four years earlier, Herriot replied: 'I was rather waiting for this question. I had no prejudice against the Marshal. Our relationship had always been courteous. He had his legend. I wanted to believe it. I did everything possible to believe it. I had to give up believing it.'[16] In his speech at Vichy, Herriot did not make a call to resistance, as some of his later critics have pointed out, but there was nothing in his speech that was against the honour of France or that was, in the context of the period, unrepresentative of the general attitude of most of his compatriots.

Herriot expressed another aspect of this attitude at the 10 July session by defending those deputies who had gone to Morocco

[15] Edouard Herriot, *Episodes, 1940–1944*, Paris, 1950, pp. 81–83.

[16] *Le Monde*, 1 August 1945. See also Geo. London, *Le Procès Pétain*, Lyons, 1945, pp. 151–3.

on the *Massilia*. In Auriol's words, he did it 'with simplicity and courage. A few screams from the mercenaries interrupted him. But he was listened to.'[17] 'What a shame,' Auriol went on to note, 'that he did not, from the first day, call for the rallying of those Frenchmen who were clearsighted. Only he was able to do it.'

Herriot later wrote that his confidence in Pétain ended the following day when the latter proclaimed himself *Chef de l'Etat* and assumed 'all governmental and legislative power'.[18] Henceforth Herriot did not cease to manifest his opposition. He was dismissed as mayor of Lyons on 20 September 1941. On 30 August 1942, he sent his Legion of Honour award to Pétain when the same distinction was given to Frenchmen who had fought with the Germans against the Russians.[19] On 25 August 1942, a decree was published in the *Journal Officiel* ordering the dissolution of the two parliamentary chambers on 31 August. On the latter date, Herriot and Jeanneney addressed a sharp letter to Pétain in which they formally accused him of dereliction to the engagements he had made before the National Assembly.[20] 'If,' they wrote, 'in spite of your engagements, you intend to deprive the nation of the right to decide for herself her definitive régime, or if without the authorization of the Parliament, you try to drag France into a war against her former allies, while you yourself have declared that honour forbade this, we, by this letter, protest in advance in the name of the national sovereignty. . . . Liberty cannot die in the country that gave it birth and from whence it spread throughout the world.' Soon afterwards, after refusing to promise not to leave France, Herriot was arrested and spent the remainder of the war in captivity. When the southern zone was invaded by the Germans in November 1942, Herriot became their prisoner, and in August 1944 he was deported to Germany.

A persistent theme pervaded Herriot's war period and had repercussions in the political situation in France after the war: should he have left France and put his great authority more directly on the side of those who were still fighting Germany? Could he, and those who followed his lead, have played a more active role in the resistance? After the war he was to point out,

[17] Vincent Auriol, *Hier . . . Demain*, Paris, 1945, vol. 1, p. 130.
[18] *Episodes*, p. 148.   [19] *Ibid.*, pp. 165–6.   [20] *Ibid.*, pp. 159–65.

concerning himself and certain other leaders, that if, 'as it appears is regretted, we did not give political directives to the whole of the resistance movement, it was for a little reason that I mention to you in passing: we were ourselves in prison, and our communications with our friends and the country got through with difficulty or not at all'.[21]

There is no doubt that persistent efforts were made to get Herriot to leave France, and it is probable that if he had wished to do so, Herriot could have left. In early 1941 Churchill sent a letter of invitation to Herriot by a secret agent, and arrangements were made to fly Herriot to Switzerland, but he declined this offer.[22] After entry of the United States in the war, efforts were redoubled. On 23 December 1941, General Donovan, head of the Office of Strategic Services, wrote a letter to President Roosevelt suggesting the desirability of taking up with the British Prime Minister 'the deplorable condition of the whole Free French movement in this country and inquire into the advisability or possibility of getting out of France some leader, perhaps like Herriot'.[23] In a conversation with Lord Halifax on 27 December 1941, Sumner Welles, the United States Under Secretary of State, took an unfavourable view of the Gaullist movement, and Herriot was proposed again as an alternative. 'I said,' Welles reported, 'that I felt that if some man like Herriot would get out of France and lead the movement, the situation would undoubtedly be very different.'[24] Admiral Leahy had been visited by Herriot on his arrival in Vichy in January 1941, as American Ambassador, and again in April 1942, before his return to the United States. 'Herriot,' he later wrote, 'was hopeful of going to the United States to discuss with President Roosevelt future relations between France and America, but since he and the president of the French Senate were the only two effective leaders still anxious to preserve representative government in

---

[21] 1945 Congress.

[22] Interview with André Enfière, Paris, 15 January 1956. Enfière was in close contact with Herriot during the war years; his activities are described in Robert Aron, *Histoire de Vichy 1940–1944*, Paris, 1954, pp. 635–6; Adrien Dansette, *Histoire de la Libération de Paris*, Paris, 1946, pp. 101–9; and Jean Tracou, *Le Maréchal aux liens. Le temps du sacrifice*, Paris, 1948, p. 366, pp. 371–5, and p. 385.

[23] William L. Langer, *Our Vichy Gamble*, New York, 1947, p. 212. (OSS Files: Donovan to the President, 23 December 1941.)

[24] *Ibid.*, p. 223. (Memorandum of conversation, 27 December 1941.)

France, he did not feel he should leave at that time.'[25]

Like Weygand and finally Giraud, Herriot was the subject of much solicitation on the part of Allied leaders. The proposals to Herriot continued after his arrest. At one stage Laval told a secret agent that he would let Herriot leave if the agent could promise that he, Laval, would not be condemned to death; the agent was only able to promise that he would not be assassinated.[26] In very poor physical condition, Herriot preferred not to try to escape. In a speech after the war, following a reference to his friendship with President Roosevelt, Herriot declared that 'several times, during the last war, he called to me to come to him, in the most flattering and touching terms. But France was so unhappy, the persecutions were so numerous, that I did not wish to leave her.'[27] 'Let others judge,' he added, 'whether I was mistaken or correct.'

The question of Herriot's departure is especially significant for what might have resulted: his party certainly would have been in a stronger position after the Liberation. Of more direct concern to Herriot after the war were charges resulting from his role in Laval's desperate attempt in August 1944, just before the liberation of Paris, to convoke the 1936 Parliament. As one historian has written: 'This last desperate measure has never received the attention it deserves. Its implications are fantastic.'[28] Laval's objective was to re-establish a constitutional authority which would put a mantle of legality over the whole Vichy régime and which could welcome the Allies and de Gaulle. Laval visited Herriot in his room on 12 August, told him he was free, and had him brought to Paris—under German escort—where he explained his plan and declared that it was 'according to the

[25] William D. Leahy, *I Was There. The Personal Story*, New York, 1950, p. 36. Regarding the latter visit, Leahy added: 'He declared he would not undertake work of any kind for the Laval government. Herriot and his followers did not believe that de Gaulle or his movement had committed any offence against France but, on the contrary, were fighting for French survival and for French ideals. The veteran leader of the Radical-Socialist Party impressed me as a very able and courageous French patriot—a type not often met in Vichy. He advised me that America must not have confidence in anything that Laval promised or said. Herriot spoke convincingly, but when speaking, did not look at his hearer.'

[26] André Enfière, Interview, Paris, 15 January 1956.

[27] *Jadis*, vol. 2, p. 647.

[28] David Thomson, *Two Frenchmen: Pierre Laval and Charles de Gaulle*, London, 1951, p. 106.

wishes of the Americans'.[29] In later years, Herriot remained convinced that this project had the backing of the United States authorities. 'I was to learn later,' he recalled in 1950, 'that for some time, the United States had been advising Laval to abandon the government and pass it on to me. I never have had, incidentally, official confirmation of this thesis; I cite it because it appears likely to me.'[30] Herriot, who was lodged in the Prefecture of the Seine, had several conversations with Laval and refused to co-operate. 'The conditions were such that I refused with indignation.' Events were moving quickly, and on 16 August he was arrested again and soon was deported to Germany. This episode aroused concern among resistance leaders—varied reports circulated as to the tenor of the conversations—and the confusion created by his forced presence in Paris nearly cost him his life.[31] After being interned at Potsdam, Herriot was liberated by the Soviet Army in April 1945, and was repatriated via Moscow, Teheran, Damascus, and Cairo.

*

* *

After his return to France, Herriot found not only his personal position questioned but also most of the ideas and institutions that he had spent his life defending. His attackers associated him with the past that they were trying to reject. 'Herriot is the Radical party,' proclaimed a Gaullist Minister of Education, 'he is the Third Republic in decay, he is the régime of the inter-war years, he is the weak system that was incapable of organizing the victory. It is a finished past that France wants no longer.'[32] Herriot, who did not hesitate to cite these words, accepted the challenge to fight on a wide front.

Though seventy-three and seventy-four years of age, Herriot took a vigorous part in the electoral campaigns and constitutional debates of 1945 and 1946. Refusing to accept his old apartment

[29] *Episodes*, pp. 198–9.   [30] *Ibid.*, p. 199.

[31] 'His execution was planned for 13 August, as is seen in "note 22" of Lebacq, Chief of Staff of the *Secteur Nord*, and it was the refusal of a man named Louis that prevented a bloody error.' Lucien Galimand, *Vive Pétain, vive de Gaulle*, Paris, 1948, p. 214. See also Dansette, pp. 107–8.

[32] Cited by Herriot in *La Dépêche de Paris*, 9 October 1945, from an article by René Capitant in the *Journal d'Alsace*.

in the Palais-Bourbon, he dedicated himself to the task of fighting a government that refused to allow the automatic return of the Third Republic, that had promulgated an electoral law which he felt was directed against his party, and that was expropriating many of his party's newspapers. His arguments won respect if not always agreement. He was re-elected a deputy in the October 1945 general elections—one of the small group of twenty-three Radical deputies that was to be even further diminished by the resignation of the *radicaux de gauche* a few months later. At this low point in the party's history, even some of his fellow Radicals lost faith in him. Nine years later, in the happier setting of the party's congress at Marseilles in 1954, he recalled a remark made to him at the party's headquarters one gloomy evening following the party's defeat. 'You are too old,' he had been told, 'do not participate in politics any more, occupy yourself with making collections, in writing if you wish, but don't participate in politics.' Herriot did not follow this advice, and by the end of the First Constituent Assembly he had regained much of his prestige.

Herriot had returned to France in May 1945; the First Constituent Assembly was elected in October. This was a tumultuous period. To Herriot and his fellow Radicals, France presented an unprecedented and confused spectacle. From September 1944 to November 1945 de Gaulle held almost unlimited control. The Third Republic was discredited in the eyes of most Frenchmen, who associated it with past humiliations; and the Radical party was considered, not without reason, as typifying the Third Republic. The desire for change was dominant. A new régime, new leaders and new ideas were the order of the day. Some Frenchmen were even surprised when de Gaulle included the retention of the Third Republic as an alternative in the constitutional referendum of October 1945; at least one factor in de Gaulle's decision was the strong case that Herriot presented after his return from Germany.

Before analysing Herriot's defence of the Third Republic, it is necessary to take cognizance of his role in the brief post-liberation flirtation between the Radicals and the Communists. This *rapprochement*, although it may appear remarkable in retrospect, was solidly based on both ideological and tactical reasons. One link between the two parties was a common hostility to de Gaulle: Radicals were suspicious of his tendency to exercise power personally; Communists saw de Gaulle as a major obstacle to their ambition to assume power. Many Radicals were still nostalgic for their old slogan of 'No enemies on the left'; the *radicaux de gauche*, who were later to leave the party and some of whom were to become *progressistes* and Communists, were still in the party and holding positions of influence. Both Communists and Radicals were calling for a return to the pre-war status of Church–State relations. At the height of their power and basking in their resistance-won prestige, the Communists were useful allies to Radicals who were under attack for their lack of activity during the war years. Weakened by the war, the Radicals were, in the eyes of the Communists, eligible to serve both as tactical allies and as candidates for complete destruction or assimilation. By using them, for example, against de Gaulle (then at the height of his popularity), they could compromise them in the eyes of the public. With expert tacticians on both sides, however, the brief *rapprochement* did not outlive its mutual usefulness.

During the early part of 1945, Radicals did not hesitate to participate in Communist manifestations. On 3 February 1945, for example, a Communist *comité d'organisation* sent a letter to the Radicals inviting them to participate in a parade to be held 11 February 1945, 'to commemorate the anti-fascist manifestations of 11 February 1934'; the letter listed titles of banners that were to be carried, cries to be chanted (e.g. *Les traîtres au poteau!*), and songs to be sung (e.g. the *Internationale* and the revolutionary *La Jeune Garde*).[33] The Radical party's *bureau* designated four members as delegates; these included Dr. Bernard Lafay, who was later to be a prominent leader of the right-wing *néo-radicaux*.[34]

In July 1945, Radicals and Communists—joined by deputies on the extreme right—voted together in the Consultative Assembly to defeat a compromise plan advanced by Auriol concerning the proposed elections and referendum. There were also agreements between Radicals and Communists in the cantonal elections held in September 1945. On 1 September, the Communist

---

[33] Radical party archives. Letter, with enclosures, from '*Parti Communiste Français Région Paris-Ville*, 120 *rue Lafayette*' to '*Comité Directeur* (sic) *du Parti Radical et du parti radical socialiste*', 3 February 1945.

[34] Radical party archives. Carbon copy of letter from Pierre Mazé, *secrétaire général*, to Lafay, 9 February 1945. Letters of designation were also sent to Messrs Bauzin, Grosclaude, and Kayser.

Party's *comité central* passed a resolution calling for the unity of all 'democratic groups and parties'.[35] These included the *Confédération Générale de Travail*, the *Ligue des Droits de l'Homme*, the Socialists, the Radicals, and of course the Communists. Joint electoral lists were formed by Communists and Radicals in several areas. The Radical Federation of the Seine joined the Communists in forming a group entitled *Renaissance française*; in most cases, however, only one or two Radicals had places on the joint lists that were formed. In discussing these alliances, a writer in *Le Monde* observed that the party of the extreme left was repaying, in 1945, the favour that the Radicals had granted in 1886 in accepting workers' candidates on *their* lists.[36] He added that, 'at that epoch such an affinity on the same ballot aroused as bitter criticism as at present'.

Such alliances were of considerable assistance to the Radicals in the municipal elections of 29 April and 13 May 1945, and helped the Radicals in the cantonal elections of 23 September of the same year in which the Radicals ranked third in popular vote after the Socialists and the Communists. Radicals and Communists differed in their attitudes to the first question of the referendum of 31 October 1945 (whether the Assembly should be a constituent one), but were united in opposing the second question concerning the establishment of a non-sovereign assembly. Faced with these two questions, Radicals replied with a forceful *non-non*. Although Radicals and Communists observed a tacit truce during the electoral campaign of October 1945, joint Radical–Communist tickets were established in only one small district. It was after their disastrous defeat in this election that the Radicals began to move towards the right.

In this period of flirtation between Radicals and the Communists, Herriot's role was highlighted by his perhaps most unusual presidency. In June 1945, a few weeks after his return from Germany, he became president of the *Mouvement unifié de la résistance française*, an ephemeral organization formed from the pro-Communist wing of the *Mouvement de libération nationale*, a federation of resistance organizations that had split in January

---

[35] Radical party archives. '*Résolution du Comité Central du Parti Communiste Français: Pour assurer aux prochaines élections le triomphe du programme du Conseil National de la Résistance et d'une majorité démocratique decidée à l'appliquer*' (1 September 1945).

[36] *Le Monde*, 23 September 1945.

1945. He was also named honorary president of the *Union de la Jeunesse républicaine de France*—the new name for what had previously been called the Communist youth organization. These two presidencies, and especially that of MURF, were to cause more than raised eyebrows among certain of his fellow Radicals, especially during the subsequent evolution of the party; but it can be argued that, as usual, Herriot's actions were in keeping with the dominant—if only temporarily dominant—feeling within the party.

Herriot came under heavy fire from many of his colleagues and followers at the party's congress in August 1945. It was not long, however, before he had completely extricated himself from what were becoming increasingly embarrassing presidencies. During the course of the congress, several delegates asked him to clarify his position concerning his presidency of MURF. On the last day of the congress a delegate from Vaucluse was particularly insistent in asking for an explanation. 'Having accounts to render in our federations,' he said, 'we ask you to clearly explain your position on this point. As we must board our train in an hour and a half, we would be happy to know your position as soon as possible.'

Herriot's reply was characteristic of his skill in oratory, his control over his party, and his ability to land on his feet in an awkward situation. He started by minimizing the gravity of his acts. 'Thus,' he said, 'I am guilty of having given my name to one of these algebraic formations of which I spoke yesterday and which I do not understand very well. Formerly, one took the train to go to Paris to attend a meeting. Now, one takes the SNCF to go to a meeting of the MRP, in passing a stage that is called the RIN or the RIEN . . . or something of this sort!' (Smiles.) He then provided a frank explanation: 'Here are the facts, *Messieurs les juges*!' He had been visited by a young person, 'very friendly and full of authority', who had asked him to join 'this hieroglyphic party'—'You will note in passing that it was formerly a step forward to abandon writing by hieroglyphics, but that now we are going back to it.' On asking what the movement was, he was told that it was 'a unified movement, an attempt to unite the French Resistance'. He replied that he agreed with this principle and that he was in favour, keeping apart the question of opinions or parties, of a union of the French. 'Indeed,' he observed, 'above the parties there is France, which must remain united.' After consulting an assistant, who saw no reason why he should not join, he had asked the person to write him a letter and had then replied favourably. He then told his listeners that the fact that the organization included Communists and was not approved by the Socialists did not bother him. People knew well enough, he argued, that he was a staunch Radical. When he had favoured a *rapprochement* with the Soviet Union in 1924, people had said: 'Indeed! Here is Herriot who has become a Communist! Communist or Anarchist!' He was, however, no less a good Radical. After a final evocation of his wartime arrest, 'on direct orders from Hitler', Herriot concluded his explanations by proclaiming: 'Let people leave me in peace! (applause); whether it pleases them or not I intend to defend my party!'

When the question arose again at a party meeting in January 1946, Herriot pointed out that he was not president of the party when he joined MURF. By the time of the party's congress in September 1946, he was able to confine his references to MURF largely to puns based on the similarity of the movement's title and the French word for wall—*mur*. In explaining a slight accident that had befallen him, he declared: 'It is nothing. I missed a step on the stairs and fell against a *mur*. Still the MUR! (laughter and applause). In picking myself up, with a certain amount of difficulty, I told myself: "After all, it is better to make a bad step physically than a bad step in politics" (laughter).'

*
* *

By the spring of 1946, there was no doubt that Herriot was back on his feet politically. His leadership of the hopeless struggle to maintain the political framework of the Third Republic—this alternative had been opposed by over 96 per cent of the voters in the constitutional referendum of 21 October 1945—had won attention and respect, if not support, and his brilliant leadership of the small group of Radical deputies in the First Constituent Assembly added greatly to his prestige. Again and again he reiterated his basic themes: defence of the institutions that had made France great; opposition to the plans and methods of the dominant political forces of the day.

Herriot was particularly forceful in arguing for the need not to break the thread of continuity with the past—the dictionary definition of the term 'radical' was, even more than usual, inapplicable to Radical opinion during this period. In a speech at the party's congress in 1945, he noted that he had been struck by a detail in the Roman ruins at Vaison, 'in a region that you know well, Daladier. One sees there decapitated statues; the clothes and insignia remained permanently; they only changed the heads when there was a fluctuation in opinion, a municipal or a general revolution.' Herriot saw in this custom 'the proof of the great political wisdom of the Roman Republic'. 'It was thus,' he explained, 'that the Roman Republic reconciled the necessary change of men with fidelity to institutions and ideas.' Declaring that 'human material wears out as does other', and that it was 'not heretical to say that one wants to replace it from time to time,' Herriot concluded: 'Let people lay the blame on men, against the heads, as long as they leave in place the togas, costumes, insignia, and rules of the Republic!' Once again, the ranks of Radical precursors could have been opened to Edmund Burke, or Joseph de Maistre. In this same speech, Herriot approvingly cited the British for having been able to make profound political transformations in their régime without changing their institutions. Herriot was willing that the Republic be reformed. 'But,' he said, 'I do not want it to be killed.'

In a speech at a rally in Paris's *Salle Wagram* two days before the referendum vote, he made a last appeal to his compatriots to vote *non-non*.[37] He agreed that his party was probably 'going against the current' of prevailing opinions, but added that he was asking his party, 'once more, to look for duty much more than for success'. He warned of the dangers of abolishing the second chamber, one of his basic themes: the Radicals' defence of the Third Republic included, of course, the Senate in which they had long wielded great power. At the party's congress in 1945 he had argued that the issue of a second chamber was a problem of mechanics. 'There is,' he said, 'no motor that can function without a brake, and I defy the most resolute partisan of the single chamber to go on a road in a car without a brake, above all if his car is rapid.' In an editorial, he cited an authority

[37] Speech at *Salle Wagram*, Paris, 19 October 1945. Reprinted in *L'Action du Groupe Parlementaire Radical et Radical Socialiste a l'Assemblée Nationale Constituante* (*Novembre* 1945–*Avril* 1946), Paris, 1946, pp. 8–12.

dear to many of those who opposed him on this issue. 'Stalin,' he wrote, 'as a true statesman, understood this well in insisting on having two chambers in Soviet Russia.'[38] At the *Salle Wagram* he referred his listeners to de Tocqueville's *Souvenirs*, in which de Tocqueville described the agitation in 1848 in favour of a single chamber. The success of this agitation, he pointed out, enabled the *Prince-Président* to arbitrate his conflicts with the chamber and led to the *coup d'état* of 2 December 1851. In the same speech, Herriot cited other examples of the nefarious results of single chambers. The Revolutionary *Convention*, although admirable, did not provide for a safety outlet and resulted in the arbitration of the guillotine; and the Weimar Republic, with a single chamber elected by proportional representation, resulted in Hitler.

Herriot was able to declare at the party's congress in 1946 that the Radicals had been at least partially successful in their campaign to have two chambers; 'We have at least a chamber and a half (smiles).' In their struggle against proportional representation, however, Radicals could not claim an even partial success. In April 1946, at the First Constituent Assembly, Herriot sponsored a *contre-projet* against the principle of proportional representation, which he had described in a speech at the party's congress in 1945 as 'absurd in all countries, but especially absurd in France, in this country of common sense, where it will never be possible to make the voter understand that, although he is part of the sovereign people, he does not have the right to choose his candidates without interposition'. In an eloquent speech in the Constituent Assembly on 2 April 1946, Herriot provided a résumé of his arguments against proportional representation. It violated the principle of popular sovereignty; the voter was not free to make his own choice; by establishing rigid lists, the parties became all-powerful, and the formation of new parties was hindered; by favouring large monolithic parties, proportional representation violated the principle of parties and fostered equivocal unions between smaller parties that differ 'not in degree but in nature'. France, a country of nuances and not of violent contrasts, Herriot argued, could have its general interest best expressed by allowing 'each part, each division, by means of one or several representatives, to make known its ideas,

[38] *La Dépêche de Paris*, 14 October 1945.

interests, and needs'. Herriot's argumentation was of no avail, however, and his proposals were defeated by a vote of 452 to 109. Radicals later were to gain concessions in the application of the various electoral laws that followed, but during the Fourth Republic they never succeeded in bringing about a return to the electoral system under which they flourished during the Third Republic.[39]

During the constitutional debates of 1945 and 1946, therefore, Herriot was unable to defeat the supporters of proportional representation, nor could he wield enough power to have a constitution written that he and his followers could support. After the defeat of the first constitutional project on 5 May 1946, however, Radicals could claim that their influence was growing. The Declaration of Rights that Herriot and his colleagues had opposed so eloquently in the First Constituent Assembly was replaced in the Second Constituent Assembly by a more general preamble that was entitled 'Declaration of Principles'—the discussion of principles aroused fewer conflicts than that of rights. The result of a series of compromises, the new preamble opened with a reaffirmation of the contents of the 1789 Declaration of Rights and included the newer social and economic principles that had been generally accepted. During the preliminary negotiations, the Radicals and the anti-clerical parties on their left had prevented a manœuvre by the MRP to have the 1848 Declaration of Rights included as well: they correctly recognized a scheme to introduce a guarantee of freedom of instruction through the back door.[40] In Radical eyes, the 'Declaration of Principles' was not comparable to their immortal Declaration of Rights; it was on a different plane and was not an affront.

*

* *

A consideration of Herriot's role during the period of constitution-making must include mention of an eloquent speech on colonial problems that Herriot made in the Second

[39] Such a return was brought about in 1958 by the leaders of the new Fifth Republic with results that surprised many Radicals. After the general elections of November 1958, it was calculated that if the system of proportional representation had been maintained, the Radical party, which had won only 13 seats, would have won 23. See *Le Monde*, 6 December 1958.

[40] Gordon Wright, *The Reshaping of French Democracy*, London, 1950, p. 200.

Constituent Assembly on 27 August 1946. 'By his speech on the rostrum of the Constituent Assembly,' one of his fellow Radicals later declared, '*le Président* Herriot saved the French Empire.'[41] In his speech, Herriot attacked the very liberal French Union chapter in the proposed constitution and led many of his fellow deputies to reconsider their attitudes concerning the new proposals. Herriot and his fellow Radicals were not the only opponents of this chapter. Led by Bidault, the MRP provided much of the influence and voting strength that forced a revision. But, at least in the eyes of Radicals, it was Herriot who supplied the inspiration which led to a drastic revision of the proposed chapter. At a meeting of the Radical party's executive committee in February 1952, Vincent de Moro-Giafferri, a veteran Radical deputy and member of the two constituent assemblies, recalled the dramatic scene. He declared that if Herriot ('who I recall was very tired that day'), responding 'to the entreaties of René Mayer and myself but above all to his sense of duty, had not gone up to the rostrum to repulse a certain Chapter VIII that my colleagues remember well, we would have found ourselves in an unbelievable situation which would have made France the colony of the territories that not long ago, for their welfare and not for our profit, she could call her colonies'. He then said that the government—Bidault was president of France's *Gouvernement provisoire* —'was agreed to have us vote this Chapter VIII'. 'The president of the commission and the *rapporteur général* had approved it,' he continued, but 'when Herriot stepped down from the rostrum, the government and the commission withdrew their project.' Moro-Giafferri, who had been arguing that the Radical party was guiltless—'virgin'—of all responsibility in 'this adventure', i.e. the new French Constitution, concluded that 'on that day (we must remember it, my dear colleagues, it is an honour we must keep before the eyes of the public), on that day the words of Herriot saved the work of Jules Ferry and of Paul Bert'.

In his speech, Herriot strongly opposed a sentence in the chapter's preamble that condemned colonial systems based on oppression. Such a statement, he argued, which he approved in principle, was not applicable to the French pioneers, who with 'almost insignificant means', had travelled along the shores of the great rivers of America and founded such cities as Montreal

[41] Gabriel Cudenet, 1946 Congress.

(where the mayor once told him that he administered more Frenchmen than Herriot did at Lyons) and Detroit (whose mayor had once drawn his attention to a picture at the City Hall which portrayed Louis XIV giving a charter for the founding of Detroit). Adding that the sentence in question was even less applicable to the colonial achievements of the Third Republic, Herriot asked whether there were any nation that could equal France's record in the struggle against racial and colour prejudice.

Herriot also advanced more specific objections. He warned that the chapter would lead to secessions, as each colony was to be allowed to choose whether it should be an *Etat libre* connected to France by an international treaty, or politically autonomous, or completely integrated within the Republic. Noting a 'terrible contradiction' in having overseas territories connected to France by an international treaty in the framework of the French Union, he asked how a free or autonomous *Etat libre* could be prevented from having international treaties with other countries. He then remarked that an article that granted French citizenship, with all its rights and duties, to all who lived in the French Union would mean that France would become the 'colony of its colonies'— in a vast French Union, metropolitan Frenchmen would be in a minority. By having the right of secession, overseas citizens would have, indeed, more rights than French citizens. Noting that there was nothing in the proposed chapter concerning defence ('Do you believe that if we abandoned Dakar there would be no one to take our place?'), he concluded by pleading for a complete revision of the chapter.

Less than three months later, in the electoral campaign of November 1946, Radical propagandists proclaimed that this chapter, 'examined in a commission presided over by M. Philip, Socialist, and reported by M. Coste-Floret, MRP', would have made France the colony of its colonies and that it was Herriot's speech that had 'aroused the conscience of the Chamber and led the government to intervene'.[42] In later years, Radical spokesmen continued to argue that by his speech on 27 August 1946, Herriot had saved the French Union. Speaking for a cause close to his heart, Herriot had acquired yet another claim to fame.

[42] Radical party archives. *Service de documentation* for November 1946 general elections (mimeographed).

In general, however, the interventions of Herriot and his fellow Radicals in the political issues of this period usually did not result in specific measures being taken or programmes revised. Herriot, the defender of the Third Republic, spent much of his time expressing his eloquent but forlorn opposition to the new rulers of France and to the way that they were governing his country. A writer in *Le Monde* on 4 April 1946 compared the activities of the small Radical group to guerrilla warfare. 'Crowded around their chief,' he wrote, 'the last unit of their parliamentarians have given themselves the mission of harassing the Government of the day and its majority with unexpected thrusts, proposing little, criticizing all.'

In his speeches and articles Herriot proclaimed the need to return to the traditional liberties of the past: liberty of commerce, opinion, expression, press; 'the liberty to say what one has to say without having to clear with a series of *comités de contrôle*'.[43] 'We are no longer human beings,' he complained, 'but are numbers. We carry the number of our food ration card, and it is by this that we are known and recognized.' In November 1946 he published articles entitled 'For a Second Liberation' and 'Climate of Dictatorship' in which he vigorously attacked the governmental scandals of the period.[44] 'One no longer dares,' he wrote, 'to open a newspaper for fear of learning that a high official has speculated on trouser buttons or shoe laces. Here is the work of the trust of trusts, the trust of the State, with its hierarchy of incompetence and irresponsibility.'[45] At a meeting of the Radical party in January 1946, he spoke of the 'Republic of the Black Market'. At the party's congress at Nice in 1947, pointing out that the Black Market was a result of the government's mismanagement of the economy, he compared the situation in France to that in England. Churchill, he recalled, had told him that the King had waited six months to have a new suit, as he had wanted to wait his turn. On a recent trip to England, Herriot added, he was given banquets without bread, with only soup, one course and a dessert—and felt very honoured.

The 'modern' and 'scientific' methods of their adversaries did not impress Herriot and his fellow Radicals. At a meeting of

[43] *La Dépêche de Paris*, 20 October 1945.
[44] *Ibid.*, 1 November 1946 and 5 November 1946.
[45] *Ibid.*, 26 October 1945.

the Radical parliamentary group in August 1946, Herriot declared that there were three sorts of falsehoods: 'ordinary lies, perjury, and statistics'.[46] That summer Yves Farge, the Minister of Food, had arranged to have three women—each belonging to one of the three major parties—fly in an aeroplane over the regions of Normandy and Charolais in order to take pictures of cattle and in this way confirm statistics on the quantity of post-war cattle as compared to pre-war cattle. Such methods were greeted with considerable scepticism by Radicals.

The nationalization projects and general economic policies carried out during the early post-war period were a subject of special concern to Herriot and his fellow Radicals and provided Herriot with ample occasion to discuss the question of the proper role of the State. In a speech in October 1945, after noting that many false ideas had been expressed as to the party's attitude on nationalization, Herriot declared that the party was in favour of a 'return to the collectivity of the economic sectors in which competition had disappeared', and proposed 'their management by co-operative administration in each instance where private management menaces the general interest or the independence of the State'.[47] At the party's congress the following year, Herriot was considerably less favourable. 'Now,' he said, 'we voted for these nationalizations, and this perhaps is not the best thing we have ever done (laughter and applause). We voted for them because, one fine Sunday, as is said in the song (smiles), they brought to us in the morning, with the obligation to finish it by evening, a project that, unlike the English one, resolved in a few lines, almost in a few moments, a problem of the most serious gravity, that of the nationalization of the banks. . . .' The nationalizations, in Herriot's view, were poorly conceived and poorly managed. The State, he argued, was 'a *mauvais commerçant*' and it was 'not proper that it should act in commercial matters'.[48] Herriot argued that the *esprit d'épargne*, the spirit of saving, that had represented the force of France and had made France a creditor throughout the world, had been cruelly hurt by the nationalizations. Herriot also led the Radicals in their

[46] Cited by Jean Masson, deputy from Haute-Marne, 1946 Congress.

[47] *La Dépêche de Paris*, 20 October 1945.

[48] Speech at Agen (Lot-et-Garonne), 31 October 1946. *La Dépêche de Paris*, 1 November 1946.

Party poster, 1946: *Nous la libererons!*

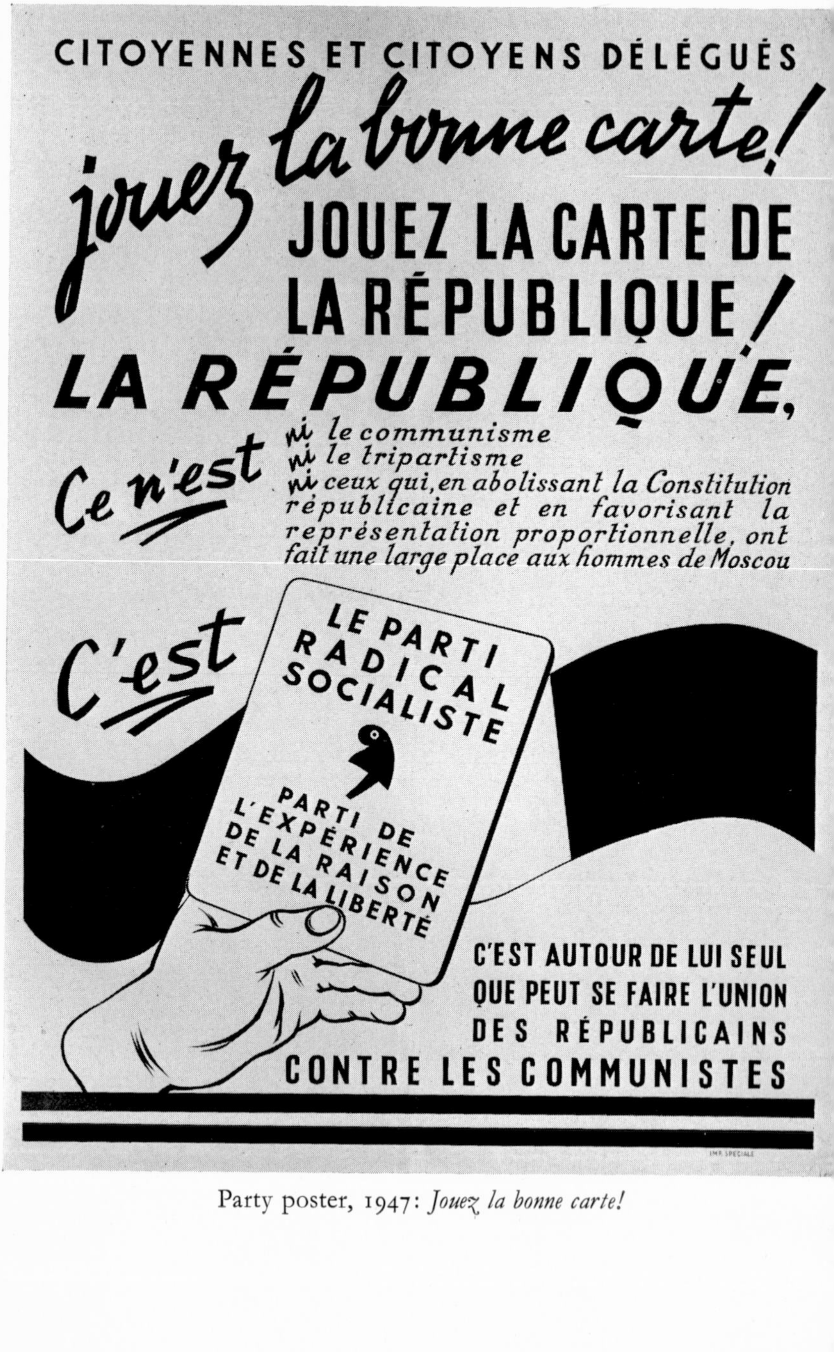

Party poster, 1947: *Jouez la bonne carte!*

attacks against *dirigisme*, government management of the economy ('a word that has not yet been formally introduced and which grates on my ears a bit'),[49] and at the party's congress at Nice in 1947 said that France was under the control of a purely bureaucratic *dirigisme*. Under the old régime a king had said: *L'état, c'est moi!* Now a huge group of officials was saying: *L'état, c'est nous!* For Herriot, the State was the French people, and its proper role was one of arbitration. 'For us,' he declared, 'the State is not a master, the State is an arbitrator! The State is not a power that has the right to absorb all the resources of the nation in order to then distribute them according to its whims and fancies! The State is an arbitrator whose arbitration must be represented by the law!'

Herriot and his fellow Radicals were particularly bitter concerning the State's intervention in matters pertaining to the press. Herriot led the battle against the drastic press law of 11 May 1946, which, making no distinction between those newspapers that had collaborated and those that had not, arbitrarily transferred to the State the property of all those newspapers that had continued to appear during the occupation.[50] Much of the strength of the pre-war Radical party had been based on its provincial newspapers. In the early post-war period this strength was nearly destroyed; lack of newspapers was a basic reason that Radicals cited in explaining their losses in the elections of 1945 and 1946. 'We were fighting,' said Herriot, in a reference to the October 1945 elections, 'with wooden sabres against machine-gun nests.'[51]

In an eloquent speech in the Constituent Assembly shortly before the press law was passed, Herriot, paraphrasing Proudhon, concluded that such an expropriation was theft.[52] Citing numerous examples, including that of the famed Radical newspaper, *La Dépêche de Toulouse*, whose owner Maurice Sarraut had been assassinated by the Vichy militia, Herriot defended the role played by Radical newspapers—and others—that had continued publication during the war. Many had worked closely with resistance

[49] *I.R.S.*, 16 October 1947.

[50] For information on the post-war French press laws, see Jean Mottin, *Histoire politique de la presse 1944-1949*, Paris, 1949, and Raymond Millet, 'Devant la presse de la IV République', *Le Monde*, 27 March–11 April 1947.

[51] *Journal Officiel*, 13 March 1946, pp. 711–15.   [52] *Ibid.*

groups. Editors and writers had been imprisoned and deported, and some had returned from concentration camps to find their newspaper plants occupied by others. Herriot said that to correct the so-called errors of the Third Republic it was a serious mistake to want to return to the Second Empire, and added that to condemn a whole enterprise because one member had been guilty was, indeed, a 'return to the Middle Ages'. He read to his colleagues a passage from a pamphlet that Mirabeau, whom he described as 'father of the freedom of the press', had addressed to the members of the *Etats Généraux* in 1788. After a Communist deputy had interrupted him to declare that this was 'no reference', Herriot proceeded to refer 'to another text, to the immortal principles of 1946 that we are engaged in writing', and cited a clause that forbade expropriation for private use. Herriot's efforts to prevent passage of the press law failed, but a subsequent Radical campaign to wreck the effectiveness of the law by impeding its application proved to be very successful, and the law expired in December 1948.

The success of the Radicals in their campaign against the May 1946 press law was due to the rise of their influence in the government. When Ramadier invited them to participate in his government in January 1947, they had asked for the ministries of Justice and Information and had obtained the former for themselves and the latter for their ally, the UDSR. Herriot's political situation rose with that of his party: he was now no longer the leader of a small but vigorous opposition group. Radical deputies, though still relatively few in number (after numbering seventeen in April 1946, they were thirty in June and forty-three after the elections of November 1946), soon began to accede to positions of authority. Their rise was facilitated by the eviction of the Communists from the government in May 1947; by the increasing difference of opinion between the MRP and the Socialist party; and, above all, by the experience of the older Radicals in negotiation, compromise and manœuvre— these skills were particularly evident in 1947 when they managed to support and oppose the same Government, that of Ramadier.

On 21 January 1947, Herriot was elected by 429 of 558 votes to succeed Auriol as President of the National Assembly after the latter was elected President of the Republic. Herriot was now back in the same position that he had held until the end of the Third Republic. His return to popularity had been fittingly consecrated, and his record vindicated.

A majestic and respected President of the Assembly, he presided over the often tempestuous debates with great authority. His task was not always simple. 'There is, indeed,' he said in 1950, 'no reason why politics should be divorced from politeness. How times have changed, at any rate!'[53] In carrying out his duties, he was careful to honour the ways of the past. He characteristically followed the traditional ritual of walking from his hôtel de présidence to the salle des séances to open each meeting of the Assembly. 'Accompanied by two officers with their sabres unsheathed, he advances slowly between two ranks of Gardes républicaines who present arms while drums beat.'[54] Describing this scene in 1949, the writer of these lines concluded by saying that 'those who have seen Herriot perform this ritual walk know how well he succeeds in giving a true solemnity to this slightly outmoded ceremony'.

Herriot's leadership of the National Assembly could be as skilful as it was impressive. On one occasion he was able to save the government of his fellow Radical, Henri Queuille. At a difficult stage in the painful elaboration of the controversial 1951 electoral law, Queuille had failed by three votes to get the absolute majority necessary to override the Conseil de la République's rejection of a bill that the government had proposed. When the results of the vote were announced, Queuille, concluding that his government had been defeated, rose and walked towards the exit, thus announcing his intention to resign. But, 'at that moment the voice of President Herriot rang out: "One moment, Monsieur le président du conseil!"'[55] In the words of Le Monde,

[53] Speech at Bar-le-Duc, 25 July 1950. Reprinted in Etudes Françaises, p. 224. An anecdote published concerning Herriot's resignation in November 1956 from 'France-URSS' illustrates this facet, and others, of Herriot's character. On being told by one of his entourage that he should have written a harsher letter with a more direct reference to the Hungarian drama, Herriot replied, 'Il faut être poli', and asked for the name of the president of the organization so that he could address the letter. The aide returned in a few minutes and reported: 'Mais c'est vous Monsieur le Président.' 'Vous voyez bien. J'avais raison de vous dire d'être poli,' replied Herriot. . . . Demain, 22–28 November 1956.

[54] Jean Le Pavec, Le Monde, 4 October 1949.

[55] Citations concerning this incident are from Le Monde, 29–30 April 1951, Journal Officiel, 27 April 1951, p. 4123, and L'Année politique, 1951, p. 98.

Queuille 'stopped and amidst laughter returned to his bench'.
'I have a communication to transmit to the Assembly,' Herriot
continued, 'to explain to it what the jurisprudence is in such
a case.' Declaring that the refusal to adopt the bill at the second
reading meant that it should be sent back to committee, he went
on to cite two precedents. The Communists protested violently;
the Assembly 'seemed stricken with stupor'. There were 'loud
interruptions on the extreme left and on various benches to the
left and to the right'. Herriot carried the day, however, and an
acceptable compromise was eventually found. By his technical
dexterity and his forceful personality, Herriot had redressed the
balance.

From being the leader of an opposition group, therefore,
Herriot had become an important member of the group of men
who were governing France. This evolution was not one that
met with universal approval or agreement among his fellow
Radicals. Having been united in opposition, they were by no
means unanimous in supporting governmental participation. In
the roll call vote that had nearly brought about Queuille's downfall—by a margin of three votes—only twenty-one of the forty-
one members of the Radical group had voted with him. Thirteen
Radical deputies had voted against the bill, and the others were
absent or had abstained. Queuille had been saved by the one
Radical who, because of his position, did not participate in
parliamentary voting.

Herriot often found it necessary to defend the policy of
governmental participation, especially at the party's congresses
where his old rival Daladier—who was playing an increasingly
active role and was vigorously challenging Herriot's leadership
—was particularly outspoken in condemning the party's change
in position. In a speech at a special congress before the general
elections of June 1951, Herriot defended those Radicals who—
unlike Daladier—were enjoying the fruits and responsibilities of
power. He argued that the party that had opposed the Constitution had the right, 'as certain people have asked us', to remain
on its positions and 'watch as observers the difficulties against
which France was struggling, the poor France that had been
treated so unfortunately by circumstances and which after the
sufferings of the war was experiencing in such a harsh fashion
the ordeals of the peace'. But the Radicals, he stressed, had

chosen the most difficult path and had rushed 'with all our force, no matter how limited, to the aid of this France'.

Until his death in March 1957, Herriot continued to play an active role on the French political scene. Other characteristic and representative stands that he took will be considered in later chapters. He was a leader of the forces that opposed de Gaulle, both on the national scene and within his own party. He was an eloquent spokesman on the side of those who opposed German rearmament and, in particular, the European Defence Community. His position on both of these questions was solidly based on his ideological background and past experience. Also typical and predictable were his political stands in his constituency of Lyons, where in order to protect his personal position (a primary task and preoccupation of all true Radicals), he found himself involved, more than once, in bitter political controversies. One of these, as will be seen, led to his temporary resignation of the presidency of the party and the final exclusion of the *radicaux gaullistes*.

*
* *

A master in the difficult art of political manœuvre, Herriot was of great value to his party as a peacemaker. As the recognized symbol and respected 'Pope' of radicalism, he was always in great demand by all factions within the party. His support, or at least blessing, was a primary goal of any ambitious Radical leader or group. A significant step in Mendès-France's rise to power in the party was Herriot's closing statement at the party's congress at Marseilles in 1954. After observing that the congress had been animated, directed, and inspired by 'our very dear friend *le Président* Mendès-France', the aging leader declared: 'I gladly bow before him my person and my past.'

Herriot played a crucial role in the calling of the special congress of 4 May 1955, at which the *radicaux mendésistes* won control of the party's administrative machinery. During the last months of his life, however, he became increasingly reticent, both as a supporter of the party's *premier vice-président* and as the much sought-after symbol of the party's unity. After resigning as president in May 1955 and then again accepting the presidency of the party at the party's congress in December of that year, he declined

F

to continue as president after the party's congress at Lyons in October 1956. The man who had said ten years earlier that 'overwork is the hygiene of healthy people'[56] was weary both in mind and body. Heartbroken in face of his party's painful disunity, he refused to give in to demands that he continue to serve as president. 'It is rather clever,' he told the *congressistes*, 'to choose *le père* Herriot. Everybody will jump on him no matter what he does. *Eh bien*, I do not want to be president any longer, I am too old, too ill, and then I am deaf. I hardly understood a fourth of what you have said on this rostrum.'

Despite his age—he was eighty-four in 1956—and his concern as to the future, Herriot never ceased to affirm his faith in France, the Republic and radicalism. 'I have lived,' he once said, 'in the Radical faith, and in this faith I wish to live and die.'[57] He often stressed his pride in having remained faithful to his early ideals. 'I am a Radical of the old vintage! I have the right to say it! One of those who does not become "white" in growing old!'[58] A man who took pride in what he liked to consider as his humble origins, he always preferred simple but stable ideas and ideals. 'Oh, I am not a very complicated man . . . for me an honest *homme public* is one who conducts himself in public life as an honest man does in private life.'[59] He once wrote that his decision to join the Radical party rather than the Socialist party was based in part on his shock at seeing how people who pretended to be revolutionaries led easy and comfortable lives.[60] They reminded him of a sign that he had seen in the old quarter of Nice, 'Workers' restaurant. *Cuisine bourgeoise.*'

Although not noted for spartan eating habits (this would be heretical on the part of a symbol of radicalism), Herriot never deviated either from his unostentatious way of life or his unostentatious approach to politics. His simplicity was matched by his evident kindliness and sincerity. Basing his ideology on a firm bedrock of generally accepted and respected ideas and

---

[56] 1946 Congress.

[57] *I.R.S.*, December 1948. After Herriot's death on 26 March 1957, a long and inconclusive controversy ensued as to whether Herriot, in a conversation shortly before his death with the Archbishop of Lyons, Cardinal Gerlier, renounced his agnosticism and asked for a religious burial. See *Le Monde*, 15–16 November 1959 and 17 November 1959.

[58] *I.R.S.*, 16 October 1947.   [59] *I.R.S.*, December 1949.

[60] *Jadis*, vol. 2, p. 146.

putting his undeniably great abilities at the service of these ideas, Herriot had an honourable and honoured career. He played a unique role in the life of the Radical party and in the enunciation of radicalism, but during his last years he could no longer be counted as the arbitrator of the party's steadily increasing internal divergencies. The venerable symbol of radicalism could be accredited by his followers with the gift of infallibility, but it was not within their power to endow him with immortality.

IV

The Radicaux de Gauche, 1944-6

'*Le vrai radicalisme est rose foncé.*'

M. SIMON, *conseiller municipal* of Charenton (Cher), October 1955

Never failing to stress their faithfulness to the principles of 'authentic radicalism', the *radicaux de gauche* of the early post-war period found it impossible to remain in a party that they felt was no longer a *parti de gauche*. Priding themselves on representing a coherent body of ideas ('our doctrine—because we have one!'[1]), they had to agree that most of these ideas were at variance with the body of opinion that was becoming more and more predominant within the Radical party. Their departure from the party, however, did not go unnoticed. They were eloquent to the bitter end in defending their positions and in maintaining that it was they, and not their adversaries, who were 'the real Radicals'

The *radicaux de gauche* are—at least when compared to most Radicals who have formed groups within the party—readily identifiable both as to membership and as to ideas. But, as was to become particularly evident in their post-Radical party political evolution, the extreme 'left' side of the spectrum of radicalism contained its own spectrum of opinion.

Pierre Cot, for example, who was elected as a Radical in October 1945 and who left the party in April 1946, moved to the MURF bench in the First Constituent Assembly, and in August 1946, during the Second Constituent Assembly, moved to the front row of Communist benches, on Jacques Duclos' right hand. Commenting on this evolution, one journalist speculated that if Cot's leftward migration were to continue in the following legislature it might be necessary to install a jump seat for him outside the regular semicircle.[2] Cot was to become

---

[1] Serge Krikowski and Raoul Reynier, *Les radicaux de gauche au service de République*, Marseilles, 1946, p. 6.

[2] Cited by Gordon Wright, *The Reshaping of French Democracy*, London, 195 p. 208.

however, the best known of the *progressistes*, sharing a tenuous position slightly to the right of the Communists. In the general elections of November 1946, he ran as head of a Union list with the Communists in Savoie and in 1951 and 1956 was given second place on a Communist list in Rhône.

Another example of the more extreme left-wing *radicaux de gauche* was Pierre Meunier, who had served as *directeur de cabinet* for Cot when the latter was Air Minister in 1938 and who was secretary-general of the *Conseil National de la Résistance* during the war. He ran in the October 1945 elections on a Radical list and was defeated. The following month, still a member of the Radical party, he was chosen *directeur de cabinet* by the newly appointed Vice-Premier, Maurice Thorez. His subsequent political evolution was to parallel that of Cot. Like Cot he was elected in conjunction with the Communists in the legislative elections of 1946, 1951, and 1956, and like Cot he faithfully patterned his behaviour in the National Assembly on that of his Communist colleagues. Other *radicaux de gauche* who were subsequently elected as deputies on *Progressiste-Communiste* lists include Pierre Dreyfus-Schmidt, mayor of Belfort, who was a successful candidate for the National Assembly in 1946 and 1956, and Robert Chambeiron, elected in 1946. Both Chambeiron and Dreyfus-Schmidt had been elected to the First Constituent Assembly as Radicals.

Many of those who were active as *radicaux de gauche*, however, did not have the desire or opportunity to carry on political careers at the national level. These included Madeleine Jean Zay, widow of the former Radical Minister of Education who had been assassinated by the Vichy militia; Albert Bayet, president of the *Fédération Nationale de la Presse* and the author of pre-war books on radicalism;[3] Pierre Le Brun, secretary-general of the *Confédération Générale de Travail*; and two pre-war Radical ministers: Justin Godart, who served briefly as mayor of Lyons at the time of the Liberation, and Jammy-Schmidt, a prominent Mason and author of two books on radicalism.[4]

---

[3] *Notre morale (Préface de Ferdinand Buisson)*, Paris, 1926; *Le Radicalisme*, Paris, 1932.

[4] *Les Grandes thèses radicales. De Condorcet à Edouard Herriot. Préface d'Edouard Herriot*, Paris, 1931; *Idées et Images radicales*, Paris, 1934. Born in 1872, Jammy-Schmidt was active in pre-war politics. At the 1945 Congress he remarked that he was the only parliamentarian present who had also been at the party's first congress in 1901. He died in 1949.

A prominent member of what may be termed as the least *progressiste* part of the *radicaux de gauche* spectrum was Jacques Kayser. An active member of the Radical party from 1921 to 1946, Kayser was vice-president of the party in 1932–4, 1936, and 1937; he was serving as secretary-general of the party shortly before his exclusion on 2 May 1946. After his exclusion he withdrew from political activities and carried on his career as a writer and as a professor at the *Institut d'Etudes Politiques*.[5] In December 1955—after the victory of the *radicaux mendésistes* had been confirmed at the party's congress held the previous month—he successfully applied for readmission into the party's ranks.

Although they varied in the intensity of their feelings and have differed in their later political evolution, the *radicaux de gauche* of the 1944–6 period shared many of the same ideas and had a similar outlook and background. Three primary influences will be emphasized as having fostered their formation as a political grouping within the Radical party: certain of the old traditions of the party, and in particular the old slogan of 'No enemies on the left'; their personal experiences and activities within the party during the pre-war period; and the new hopes and spirit engendered in France by the resistance movement.

*

*　*

The *radicaux de gauche* were able to find a solid basis for many of their positions in the historical past of radicalism: it was by making a selective and judicious choice from the ideological background of their party that they were able to claim that they were 'the real Radicals'. They joined other Radicals in eulogizing 'the most glorious of our traditions, that of the French Revolution', but in listing their Revolutionary precursors, they were apt to include the leaders of the Paris Commune. 'We want to continue,' they declared, 'the work of the men of '89, '48, and '71.'[6] Their members and followers included men who had written basic texts on radicalism and Radical precursors. But, although they shared many of their heroes with their fellow Radicals, they were particularly bitter in proclaiming their

[5] M. Kayser is at present engaged in writing a book on the origins of the Radical party.

[6] Krikowski, p. 11.

disillusionment with the way that the objectives of these heroes had been and were being implemented. 'We desire that their ideas be neither betrayed, denied, nor even, in the obscurity of words, disfigured.'[7] Other Radicals have shared this disillusionment, but no group of Radicals has ever been as persistent or insistent as the *radicaux de gauche* in directing their indictments at fellow Radicals. In their eyes, many of the most flagrant betrayers were to be found in the ranks of their own party.

Although the *radicaux de gauche* were fond of evoking the Revolution and liked to recall the old Radical veterans of the nineteenth century who were often just 'one step ahead of the *gendarmes*', they were even more prone to draw their illustrations and comparisons from the early days of the Third Republic. It was then, they argued, that the party had an atmosphere of *élan*, of enthusiasm, and of faith. It was then, above all, that the party lived up to its old slogan of 'No enemies on the left'. For this was the crux and touchstone of existence in the minds and hearts of the *radicaux de gauche*: Radicals, even in a country in which a large segment of the '*gauche*' was now Communist, should not separate themselves from *any* of the parties on their left. The slogan that was operative in the days of Pelletan and Jaurès was revived again and again in a period when much of the *gauche* was under the control of Maurice Thorez and Jacques Duclos. The problems inherent in the advancement and implementation of such a programme were to typify the dilemma of the *radicaux de gauche* and their increasingly paradoxical position in a party in which most of the members saw at least as many dangers on the left as on the right.

The *radicaux de gauche*, however, did not limit their historical references to the distant revolutionary past and to the early days of the Republic; they were able to utilize arguments and programmes that they themselves had helped to enunciate and advance. The *cartel des gauches* that was formed for the elections of 1924—and *after* the 1920 *scission de Tours* that saw the birth of an organized French Communist party—was cited approvingly as a precedent worthy of emulation. But of more immediate interest were the political formations of the 1930's, and in particular the Popular Front.

[7] *Ibid.*

A pre-war political grouping within the Radical party itself may also be cited as especially relevant. Fighting for a rejuvenation of their party and for a reorganization of France, the *radicaux de gauche* were advancing arguments similar to those that had been advanced by the *Jeunes Turcs* of the 1930's.[8] The analogy is, indeed, closer: they were, in certain cases, the same people. The individual destinies of those who were called *Jeunes Turcs* have been very different. Gaston Bergery served as an ambassador of Vichy to the Soviet Union and to Turkey; Jean Zay was killed by the Vichy militia. Mendès-France, another prominent *Jeune Turc*, was almost the only one who remained in the party during the Fourth Republic. But the *radicaux de gauche* —who included in their ranks the ex-*Jeunes Turcs* Pierre Cot, Jacques Mitterand, and Jacques Kayser—were to argue after the war that it was they who were being the most faithful to the ideals of their earlier days. They were still revolting against the same leaders and the same ideas.

The intensity of this revolt during the post-war period ranged from the lack of recrimination shown by Kayser, who did not want to revive old quarrels, to the more violent attitude of Albert Bayet. The latter, who was particularly virulent in attacking Daladier (he submitted his resignation while Daladier was speaking at the rostrum at the Lyons congress in April 1946), summed up his attitude towards the party's pre-war record at the first post-war congress in December 1944. 'The policies of our party,' he proclaimed, 'during the five or six years that preceded the war were, in my opinion, policies of weakness and abandon and, to sum up, detestable!' Radicals were in power when Mussolini attacked Abyssinia and when Germany decided to occupy Austria; they abandoned Spain and signed the Munich pact. The only bright spot during this period was the formation of the Popular Front, but the hopes based on this alliance were betrayed by the party's leaders—and in particular, by Daladier.

The authors of a pamphlet issued by several of the *radicaux de gauche* after their eviction from the party in 1946 noted that the *Jeunes Turcs* 'outlined the path of our movement', but they

---

[8] For information on the role of the *Jeunes Turcs* in the Radical party, see Alexander Werth, 'Le mouvement "Jeunes Turcs" un phénomène radical d'entre les deux guerres', *Les Cahiers de la République*, vol. 1, no. 2, 1956.

traced the immediate origins of the group to the party's congress held at Marseilles in October 1938, when a group of Radicals— including Cot, Léon Perrier and François de Tessan—addressed a strong letter to Herriot denouncing the 'Rightist attitude of Daladier and all its evil consequences for Democracy'.[9] The letter declared that the party, 'proud of its traditions, its organization and its deep roots', saw its destiny—'like the destiny of the country itself'—dependent more than ever 'on the closest possible alliance of the middle classes and the working classes', and added that even a partial rupture—or even a weakening— of this alliance 'constitutes the only chance and the *jeu*, henceforth classic, of *césarisme* and fascism'. The writers concluded that the party must follow the policy of 'No enemies on the left', and must 'maintain the confidence of both the middle and working classes'.

These goals had been obstructed by 'the anti-social acts of Daladier' and 'the drama of Munich', but the spirit of the resistance movement was to provide the *radicaux de gauche*—along with those Frenchmen of all parties who participated in the liberation of their country—with much cause for hope and optimism. The Communists had played a large role in the resistance; they had, more than ever, the backing of the bulk of the working class. Radicals, the *radicaux de gauche* argued, could not refuse to co-operate with the Communists if a new and better France were to be built. 'Do you think,' Cot asked at the party's congress in 1944, 'that we will reconstruct the foundations of French democracy if we allow ourselves to be cut off from the other democratic parties?' Many *radicaux de gauche* had been active in the resistance and had had occasion to work with Communists; they had come to take such co-operation for granted. Such war experiences, however, had alienated them further than ever from many of their less active Radical colleagues.

Recognizing the strong desire in France for regeneration, the *radicaux de gauche* proposed to ally the 'republicanism of old' with the 'new spirit of the Resistance'.[10] At the same time they stressed the need to be realistic and to realize that France's position in the world had been altered since 1939. In a report at the party's congress in 1945, Kayser pointedly remarked that 'we are the same men who were discussing all these problems in

[9] Krikowski, p. 3.   [10] *Ibid.*

1939, we are the same country, but we are no longer acting in the same world' and emphasized the need to 'carry on a constant effort of imagination and reason in order to discuss the issues of 1945 on the basis of conditions in 1945, and no longer on the basis of information that was valid from 1919 to 1939'. After making a reference to the national parks of Canada and the United States ('protected areas that many people visit with astonishment; one sees in them rare animals that have not gone through the usual evolutionary process and which are forbidden to hunters; one also sees flowers and plants that cannot find elsewhere conditions propitious to their blossoming and which it is forbidden to pick'), he declared: 'Citizens, we can become the foremost national park in the world!'

Kayser went on to explain that people would 'look at us with curiosity as the anachronistic representatives of an evolved epoch' and as 'men who were incapable of adapting themselves to the rigour of new times'. Foreign statesmen would spend their vacations on the *Côte d'Azur*; delegations would come to see 'the beauties of Paris or the splendour of our cathedrals and museums'; people would 'celebrate the happy virtues of France and observe our *duels d'idées* as at a show that had become harmless'. France had been gravely hurt by the catastrophe of 1940; the Vichy government 'was a terrible blow to our prestige in the world'; France was 'no longer in the first rank of the great powers', but Radicals must never reconcile themselves to seeing their country become a national park, even the foremost one in the world.

It became increasingly clear that the *radicaux de gauche*, unlike many of their colleagues, were welcoming the new political atmosphere that had pervaded the France of the resistance and the Liberation. Far from wanting to return to the ways of the Third Republic, they were in the vanguard of those calling for change and reform. They did not feel that they were in a hostile and alien world, but rather that they were riding the wave of the future. It was their party, unfortunately, that was dragging its feet.

Their dissatisfaction with their colleagues was evident at the party's first congress after the Liberation—the *petit congrès* of December 1944. Several speakers expressed their disappointment in the order of the day presented by the *Commission de politique générale.* Complaining that the Commission's report lacked 'tributes to the Resistance, to Bir-Hakim, and to the national insurrection', Bayet declared that more dynamism was needed. After observing that a certain number of Radical militants had hoped that the debates would have given rise to a report that was 'shorter, more vigorous, more filled with realities and hopes', Kayser noted that there was nothing in it about 'the soldiers who were fighting in Alsace, in the Alps, and on the Atlantic front, often without shoes, warm clothes, and modern weapons'. Declaring that the congress's applause for Louis Saillant—the labour leader who had succeeded Georges Bidault as president of the *Conseil National de la Résistance*—had 'sealed our collaboration with all the forces of the resistance around clear and simple ideas for the resurrection of the *patrie* and of democracy', Kayser stated that he would have preferred it if the final order of the day had been 'limited to recording these clear and simple ideas in a few ardent and vigorous lines'. 'I regret,' he said, 'that the declaration that has been presented to you is so similar to our usual motions (applause), that it is heavy with balanced and conditional formulas.'

Cot was also insistent in stating his belief that the party's official statements should express the country's 'need for renovation and rejuvenation', and in arguing that the party must learn to 'adapt to the new conditions of political life'. He was particularly adamant on the need for change, but his arguments did not meet with universal agreement. 'Are we going to orient ourselves,' he asked, 'towards the left or the right? This is the problem that we must settle here! (A voice: "Let us simply remain ourselves!").'

Proclaiming the need for clarity, for change, and for vigorous reform, the *radicaux de gauche* were not reticent in advancing a programme of action. Cot left no doubt in his hearers' minds that his question was purely rhetorical. What was the clear and realistic programme that was offered by this articulate group? How did it differ from that of their Radical colleagues, and which were the issues that were mainly responsible for the split? An additional question may also be posed concerning this programme: how did it differ from that of the Communists?

*
* *

A theme common to most of the *radicaux de gauche* was the need for an energetic purge of all those who had co-operated with the Vichy government; they regretted the relative laxity of the purge that was undertaken in their own party. They called for drastic changes in the economic and social structure of France. Speaking in the name of their colleagues, the authors of *Les radicaux de gauche au service de la République* provided a detailed list of the reforms that they desired.[11] Advocating a complete implementation of the nationalization programme outlined by the *Conseil National de la Résistance*, they stressed the need to carry on the 'struggle against the trusts'. They asked for a simplification and reform of the tax system—'It is particularly inadmissible that over half of the direct taxes are made up by the tax on wages'—and emphasized the need for increased productivity. Besides advancing such general objectives as 'the nationalization of the great forces of production', they called for a more democratic recruitment—and a reduction in number —of government officials and stressed the need to encourage the intellectual elite, to improve laboratories, and to provide more funds in the budget for scientific research and for the popularisation of the results of this research. Women should be in a position of equality with men in regard to civic and professional rights and should receive equal salaries. 'Only a few retrograde souls can deny these truths, or become alarmed by them.' They declared that the army should be democratic—no longer an *armée de caste*—and one even more optimistic objective was cited— 'The proper utilization of skills will be practised: no more barbers in the kitchen or tailors in the infirmary.'

The social and economic measures advocated by the *radicaux de gauche* were particularly striking for the enthusiasm for which they were advanced. The Radical party as a whole, for example, had officially accepted the CNR's nationalization programme, but as was noted earlier, this acceptance was accompanied by manifest misgivings and increasing reservations. Many *radicaux de gauche* were equally enthusiastic in what they termed their '*défense permanente de la laïcité*'; this was an enthusiasm more in keeping with the ideas of many of their fellow Radicals—and, in particular, the *radicaux classiques*. The proponents of the old ways and the disciples of the new were often able to join hands over the

11 Krikowski, pp. 6–10.

venerable problem of Church and State relations. Albert Bayet, president of the anti-clerical *Ligue française de l'Enseignment*, continued to press his arguments in favour of an *école unique*. 'At the same age all the children of France enter elementary school; they are given the same lessons, sit on the same benches, under the same teacher. No distinction between the son of a rich man and the son of a poor man. Equality.'[12] This extreme version of the laic ideal was actively supported by most *radicaux de gauche*; a few, including Kayser, concentrated their efforts on other issues. Cot expressed a generally accepted attitude at the party's congress in December 1944. 'For us the principle of laicism is a principle that we do not intend giving up, for it is the basis of liberty of conscience and is probably the most solid foundation of the Republic.' There is no doubt that the *radicaux de gauche*, as a group, must be included among the most faithful defenders of the old republican ideal of laicism.

In their statements on foreign policy, the *radicaux de gauche* supported positions that were generally accepted by most of their compatriots—both in and out of the Radical party—during the early post-Liberation period; but as was the case with the prevailing economic and social attitudes, the *radicaux de gauche* were more enthusiastic in their support than most of their Radical colleagues. This was particularly true in their bitter repudiation of France's pre-war record in foreign policy. Bayet's violent attitude towards Daladier and the party's record in the 1930's has already been mentioned. In an article published a week before the crucial October 1945 elections, he noted that Daladier had behaved courageously at the Riom trials but added that he was wrong to make his *rentrée politique* in defending the 'disastrous policies that had been suggested and imposed by Georges Bonnet'.[13] Bayet wanted the past to provide a catalyst for the present. 'It is on the frank and universal repudiation of Munich,' he declared, 'that the *union des gauches* must be made today, as the union of the resistance was made yesterday.'

Although sharing Bayet's disapproval of France's pre-war foreign policies, other *radicaux de gauche* put primary emphasis

[12] Quoted in Krikowski, p. 6.

[13] *La Voix de Paris*, 18 October 1945. Bayet expounded his views on France's pre-war foreign policy in a resounding speech in the First Constituent Assembly, 21 November 1944.

on more contemporary problems. Their attitude towards Germany coincided with the general French opinion of the period: 'We demand a prolonged occupation of Germany, its complete disarmament, the internationalization of the Ruhr, and the full payment of all the reparations that are due us.'[14] They strongly approved the Franco-Soviet pact concluded by de Gaulle in December 1944 and backed close co-operation with the Soviet Union. In a speech at the party's congress in 1945, Kayser also called for close co-operation with the United States, the United Nations, and eulogizing Churchill, favoured a particularly close relationship with England. All the *radicaux de gauche* shared the general distaste for Franco Spain. 'Frenchmen will not feel free as long as Spaniards are enslaved by Franco.'[15] And, in problems relating to the proposed French Union, the *radicaux de gauche* were on the side of those who advocated liberal solutions. 'Do not forget that we are the sons of 1789—of those who proclaimed to the world their determination to free their brothers, and not to enslave or exploit them.'[16]

Although most Radicals were willing to support—or at least to applaud—many of these objectives that were outlined by the *radicaux de gauche*, there were other issues that made a rupture inevitable. These issues arose when action had to be taken in regard to specific questions: what stand should the party take concerning the constitutional referendum of October 1945 and, later, the proposed constitution of 5 May 1946; and what political orientation should the party follow in the face of its sinking position on the electoral scene? Differences over the 5 May 1946 constitution were to be the immediate reason for the exclusion of several *radicaux de gauche*; the new orientation chosen by the party was the fundamental cause.

*
* *

The attitude of many of the *radicaux de gauche* concerning the constitutional referendum and general elections of 21 October 1945, was vividly illustrated in *La Voix de Paris*, a new daily newspaper that had appeared on 30 June 1945, with the bene-

[14] Krikowski, p. 10.   [15] Albert Bayet, *petit congrès*, December 1944.
[16] Krikowski, p. 9.

diction of Herriot.[17] On 22 October *La Voix*'s headline proclaimed: 'France voted yesterday for the *union des gauches*.' On
the following day their headline explained: '*Daladier-le-Munichois*
drags the Radical party into defeat.' Declaring that the party
was now relegated to a position among France's splinter parties
and noting that silence reigned at the party's headquarters in the
Place de Valois, the writer of one article stated that in the opinion of
its militants the party had not done enough to rejuvenate its *cadres*,
had carried out too weak a purge, and was still too much the party
of the grey-beards. An editorialist remarked that he could not
help thinking of the British Liberal party which 'experienced a
similar defeat and whose nearly complete disappearance from the
political scene is now a *fait accompli*'. There was no doubt that
those who wrote for *La Voix de Paris* were skilled in concealing any
grief they may have felt after the most crushing defeat the Radical
party had ever sustained. Their hopes for the future, it was
explained, were in what they termed the '*union des gauches*'.

Certain of the *radicaux de gauche*—including Kayser, Madeleine
Jean Zay, and Pierre Guillon, the mayor of Poitiers—had submitted to the party's decision to campaign for a double '*non*' in
the referendum, but not without expressing their misgivings.
These three played active roles in the party's organization; many
of those among the rank and file were more outspoken. In a
study—published in *La Voix de Paris*, 7 July 1945—concerning
the relative advantages of having one or two houses in Parliament, only two of those whose opinions were cited favoured two
houses, while seven favoured a single chamber. In explaining his
position, one of the latter, Etienne Nouveau (who described
himself as a Radical and a member of the resistance group *Vengeance*)
declared that he favoured a single chamber because 'the old
grey-beards threaten to curb dangerously the achievements of a
democratic Assembly', and more moderately added that he did
not 'consider as traitors to the Republic those of my colleagues
who remain partisans of the co-operation of the Senate'.

During the same period, however, a new element of Radicals
with a programme diametrically opposed to that of the *radicaux*

---

[17] *La Voix de Paris* published 312 issues before expiring 1 July 1946. A letter
from Herriot was published on the front page of the first issue: '*Je ne puis que vous
apporter mes encouragements*.' Several editorials written by Herriot were published
during the first few weeks.

de gauche was gaining strength within the party. This group and their projects will be studied in detail in the following chapter; in the present context it must be noted that the formation of the *Rassemblement des gauches républicaines*, strongly supported by those whom Kayser described as *'ces nouveaux messieurs'*, was to coincide with the exclusion of the last survivors of the *radicaux de gauche*. The latter, who had found much to criticize in the radicalism of the latter part of the Third Republic and the radicalism of the war years and Liberation, found even more to criticize in the new vistas that were being displayed to the party in 1946.

In the eyes of the *radicaux de gauche*, Pelletan's old slogan was being changed to 'No enemies on the *right*!' The arguments that led to the formation of the RGR were launched at the unprecedented *Assemblée générale* that the party held on 12 January 1946, to study the reasons for their defeat in the October 1945 elections. Certain *radicaux de gauche* had drawn other conclusions from their party's recent record. Dreyfus-Schmidt declared that the report on the party's financial and economic policies that had been written by 'our colleague Laffargue' was 'certainly the most reactionary document proposed to the electors during all the electoral campaign' and went on to conclude that he could only say that 'our disagreement is irreducible and that our continued presence in the same party is no longer possible'. With Cot and the other *radicaux de gauche*, he was bitterly hostile to enlarging the party towards the right. They could not agree to participating in a coalition that would include many of their traditional opponents; they were even less disposed to having that coalition become the heart of the new political movement that some of its proponents envisaged.

After several stormy sessions, the formation of the RGR was approved by a special congress held in Lyons, 4–7 April 1946. At the same congress the status of Cot, who had abstained in the Constituent Assembly from voting on several Radical propositions and who had accepted the task of being *rapporteur* for a 'disgraceful constitution', was a subject of violent debate. One speaker did not want him expelled, but rather thrown out the door.[18]

---

[18] *Le Monde*, 6 April 1946. As *rapporteur*, Cot had played a very active role in trying to win acceptance for the constitution of 5 May 1956. In recognition of his role, this abortive constitution has often been called the 'Pierre Cot constitution'. See, for example, Wright, p. 182.

Cot, however, had already resigned from the Radicals' parliamentary group, and it was announced, amidst loud applause, that he was no longer a member of the party. On the same Sunday morning, at the final meeting of the congress, it was also announced that Bayet's letter of resignation had been refused and that he had been 'expelled from our party (loud applause)'.[19]

The remaining *radicaux de gauche* were expelled from the party at a meeting of the executive committee, 2 May 1946; the final criterion of a *radical de gauche* was the position he took concerning the coming constitutional referendum of 5 May. Eight of those who were still officially in the party and who had taken a position against the decisions of the Lyons Congress to oppose the proposed constitution made up this final cluster. Among them were Kayser, Guillon, Chambeiron, Le Brun, and Meunier.

Many of the *radicaux de gauche* were willing to leave the Radical party with a flourish; some had already found more congenial political companions. Others, however, were insistent in expressing their regret. Three of those who had belonged to the party's *Commission exécutive*—Kayser, Guillon, and Madeleine Jean Zay—issued a letter after their exclusion in order to explain why they had not given in to the majority.[20] Three sources for their motivations were emphasized: the history of the party, the usual methods employed in the party, and the general orientation of the party. They pointed out that in October 1945 they had submitted to a party decision, and although favouring a '*oui-non*' vote in the referendum (i.e. the establishment of a Constituent Assembly that would have sovereign power), had campaigned for '*non-non*'. They had been surprised, however, to see some official party candidates campaign for '*oui-oui*' or '*oui-non*' without any sanctions being taken. Concerning the party's methods, they cited the party's usual lack of clear decisions. At the *Assemblée générale* in January, two proposed texts were in opposition, but instead of choosing between them by voting, the delegates had put them together. They argued that there was no clear vote

[19] A letter of resignation sent by Bayet to Herriot was summarized in *La Voix de Paris* (of which Bayet was editor), 7 April 1946.

[20] Mimeographed letter sent by Jacques Kayser, Madeleine Jean Zay, and Pierre Guillon, Paris, May 1946, to those whom they had represented in the Radical party's *Commission exécutive*. I am indebted to M. Jacques Kayser for showing me a copy of this letter.

at Lyons, or they would have made their decision at that time: they were never given this choice.

The three writers explained that the essential reason for their decision, however, was their dislike for the new orientation of the party, which was 'no longer anything like that which we were pleased to find in it in bygone times'. For then it had been a *parti de gauche*, 'a party whose objective was to hold power in accord with all the left or to participate in governmental or parliamentary majorities, in *union des gauches* formations'. The new *rassemblement* was a 'resurrection of the old formulas of "*concentration*", against which, in our own party, we victoriously fought so many times between 1921 and 1939'. Those who had been expelled were being faithful to their political beliefs—beliefs which were those of 'the great majority of the party from its foundation until these past few months'—by fighting a *rassemblement*, which, 'despite the precautions taken by *le président* Herriot, had succeeded in imposing its law and its methods on our party'.

*

* *

There was, therefore, a considerable body of differences between the *radicaux de gauche* and those who were formulating the party's official policies, but an attempt to analyse their position must include an additional point of reference: how did the ideas and the programme of the *radicaux de gauche* differ from the ones advanced by those who would constitute the extreme left side of the much desired *union des gauches*?

The authors of *Les radicaux de gauche au service de la République* referred to their relationship with the Communists as the 'burning issue'. 'How many times have people said: Come, come! Don't tell us stories. You are Communists!' The writers termed this a 'naïve error', and asked why, if such were the case, they would continue to call themselves Radicals. Their *avant-garde* conceptions, they said, were sufficiently 'red' to make them immune against an additional 'reddening'. They argued that they had only accepted in Marxism—as in 'positivism and in other systems of thought'—that which is 'true and of use'. But they did agree that, 'aside from this point of doctrine', there was a 'programme of immediate action that we both share'.

This was a generally accepted theme among the *radicaux de*

gauche. Asserting their allegiance to the basic tenets of radicalism, they saw no reason why these tenets should preclude working in close co-operation with all the forces of the *gauche*. 'That which identifies us, in short, with the Communists in the civic combat', the authors concluded, 'is the same attachment to laic, democratic, and social principles'.

This facility for co-operating with the Communists was illustrated, as has been noted, by several prominent *radicaux de gauche* in their subsequent political evolution. Cot, Chambeiron, Dreyfus-Schmidt, and Meunier were members of the *Groupe d'union républicaine résistante*—later called the *Groupe de l'union des républicains progressistes*—in the National Assembly, a group that was officially affiliated with the Communist group.

Radicaux de gauche were also to participate in other organizations. A group of those who had resigned or been expelled from the party met in Paris on 8 May 1946, and formed the *Regroupement des radicaux et résistants de gauche*. They issued a manifesto the following day affirming their belief in the historic mission of the Radical party 'to unite in republican action the middle classes and working classes' and denounced those who were promoting *'le radicalisme munichois'* and *'le radicalisme d'affaires'*.[21] This group participated in a *Comité d'Entente* with a splinter group of Socialists and with the *Chrétiens progressistes* that was organized in April 1848 and subsequently joined the *Union progressiste* when the latter was formed in December 1950.

Not all the former *radicaux de gauche*, however, participated in these successive mutations in which the predominant themes were neutralism abroad and co-operation with the Communists at home. The subsequent evolution of French political life was to provide new causes for disillusionment. While some of the *radicaux de gauche* had become inextricably linked with the Communists, and some—less prominent—participated in *La Nouvelle Gauche* (yet another group devoted to promoting the elusive *union des gauches*), others gave up the struggle and retired to less onerous fields of activity.

The *élan* of the Mendès-France 'experience' was to arouse the

[21] *Le Monde*, 11 May 1946. I am indebted to M. Marc Jacquier, who was a prominent member of the *Radicaux et Résistants de gauche*, *secrétaire général* of the *Comité d'Entente des Mouvements Progressistes*, and *secrétaire* of the *Union Progressiste*, for showing me a copy of this manifesto and for providing me with information and documentation concerning the ideas and activities of these groups.

hopes of several—hopes that have been termed the 'temptation of Mendès-France' by one of those affected.[22] The latter, however, was able to resist the 'temptation'. Although he liked 'the Indo-China side of Mendès-France', approved his social and economic policies, and could tolerate his position on the laic question and his policies toward the United States and the Soviet Union, he could never forgive him for having supported the Paris Agreements that would allow the Germans to rearm.

The goals that were enunciated by the *radicaux de gauche* have yet to be attained; they are, indeed, further from attainment—particularly in regard to the formation of a *union des gauches*—in the post-Budapest world than in the period of optimism that followed the Liberation. Indeed, despite the tenacious optimism of some of those who have supported the ideal of a united and reformative *gauche*, the end of '*tripartisme*' and the eviction of the Communists from the Ramadier government in 1947 may be said to have marked the end of an epoch.

But none of the *radicaux de gauche* has ever expressed regrets for the programme that was advocated during the 1944–6 period. As Jacques Kayser, the only one who subsequently returned to the ranks of the Radical party, has said: 'It was only logical to have tried to work with the Communists. After all, de Gaulle tried.'

[22] Gaston Maurice. Interview, Paris, 19 December 1955. Maurice, who was a friend of Mendès-France during their student days, wrote a thesis on the Radical party for a law doctorate, *Le Parti radical (Préface de Jacques Kayser)*, Paris, 1929. He was twenty-two years old when he wrote the thesis. During the post-war period, he was a member of the *Comité National* of the *Radicaux et Résistants de gauche*, and served on the *Commission Exécutive de l'Union Progressiste*. He has written of his views on subsequent developments in the Radical party in the *Bulletin Mensuel des Radicaux et Résistants de gauche*, April 1948, and in *Le Jacobin*, June 1953 and 26 February 1954.

V

The Néo-Radicaux, 1945-55

'M. Paul Reynaud n'avait pas tort de constater dans un récent article de
l'Agence Economique une identité de vue à peu près totale sur la doctrine
entre ses indépendants et nos radicaux.'

LÉON MARTINAUD-DÉPLAT, Administrative President of the Radical party,
in an editorial in L'Information radicale-socialiste, 2 June 1949.

'Les indépendants? Ce sont des réactionnaires qui se cachent!'

PHILIBERT LAUTISSIER, Mayor of Lignières (Cher), October 1955.

In 1939 an anonymous but astute political observer declared that
in the Radical party there were no workers from the great industries, no representatives of the old landed aristocracy, and no
members of the *grande bourgeoisie d'affaires*, but noted that the
latter had links with the party without joining it.[1] The situation
concerning the third category was to be drastically changed after
the war. Members of the *grande bourgeoisie d'affaires* not only joined
the party, but also actively participated in its administration and
in the formulation of its policies.

The presence of right-wing elements within the Radical party
is not, of course, a phenomenon limited to the years after the
Second World War. Since the earliest periods in the party's history,
there have been Radical candidates who were elected with the support of the Right. During the Third Republic there were always
Radicals who could be counted on to support conservative policies in the Chamber of Deputies and—a more striking example
—in the Senate. From the days of *le petit père* Combes (whose
cabinet included the shrewd financier Maurice Rouvier as a
guarantee to the Right that income tax proposals would remain
shelved) to those of Daladier (*his* Minister of Finance was the
conservative Paul Reynaud), Radical governments did not always
distinguish themselves for carrying out social and economic policies that were distasteful to the dominant business groups. But

[1] *Esprit*, May 1939, p. 171.

the presence of right-wing opinion was never so preponderant within the party as it was to be during the years between 1946 and 1955, when conservative policies were to be followed not only as a matter of tactics and expediency, but were to be advanced as the *raison d'être* of the party. The supporters of conservative political and economic interests not only had links with the party: they joined it, led it, and tried to transform it into their own image.

*

*   *

During the period that followed the Liberation, it soon became clear that an influx of new members with new ideas had undertaken to revitalize the Radical party. 'Revitalize' is the term that the representatives of this group liked to use. In referring to this period in their party's evolution, the *radicaux mendésistes* were to prefer the word 'colonize'.

Not all of those, however, who supported the form of 'neoradicalism' that was to gain control of the party's machinery during the post-war years were new to the Radical party. What was 'new' was the frankness and fervour with which they promoted their ideas and the extent to which their efforts were successful.

Léon Martinaud-Déplat, for example, who was administrative president of the party from September 1948 (when he replaced Queuille in this position when the latter was elected premier) to the night of 4 May 1955 (when he was submerged under the forces of the *radicaux mendésistes*), had served as secretary-general of the party in 1930 and 1931. In the late 1920's and in the 1930's he had been a friend and protégé of Daladier; after the war he had new friends and new ambitions.

Other prominent spokesmen for the new and 'revitalized' form of radicalism advanced by the *néo-radicaux* could also cite long Radical pasts. Speaking at the party's *Assemblée générale* in January 1946, Georges Laffargue noted that his effort to become a deputy in the recent elections had been his first attempt to attain public office, but added that he had been a member of the Radical party for twenty-five years. In other of his statements, however, he made it clear that he had little in common with the *radicaux classiques* and the old traditions of radicalism. 'Our political vocabulary,' he told his listeners, 'has a strong resemblance to those old novels that people no longer read; it is no longer suitable for modern times and the realities of the present; we use words that are old, vague and out-of-date.' It was Laffargue's wish that the party should consider itself as a 'large industrial or commercial concern', and should seek 'new financial assistance'. At the party's congress four months later he noted that there were many women and young people who were participating in elections for the first time and warned his listeners that the old ideas and methods of radicalism could not induce these new voters to vote for the Radical party. 'I am afraid,' he said, 'that despite all your optimism and all your feelings of sailing before the wind, and all that you are able to imagine, you will not attract them to pure radicalism.' As a leader of the party's *Fédération de la Seine*, as a prominent senator (he was elected to the *Conseil de la République* in 1946), and as a vice-president of the Radical party, Laffargue was to distinguish himself during the post-war years as one of the most articulate supporters of a new and less 'pure' form of radicalism.

In general, however, the *néo-radicaux* were identifiable not only by the newness of the radicalism that they were advancing. Most of them were also new to the party, and virtually all of them represented regions that had not previously been considered Radical strongholds. And, as a third distinguishing characteristic, all *néo-radicaux* shared a common interest in the formation and activities of the new political group in which the Radical party played a central role from 1946 to 1955, the *Rassemblement des Gauches républicaines*.

These three aspects of neo-radicalism may be said to have been personified by Dr. Bernard Lafay, who joined the party after the war, served as its administrative secretary-general from 1946 to 1948, as senator from the Seine from 1946 to 1951, and as deputy after 1951. Born in 1905, Lafay won many decorations for his activities in the Battle of France and in the resistance and was the subject of a eulogistic citation signed by de Gaulle in April 1945.[2] After having played an important role in helping

---

[2] *Journal Officiel, Ordonnances et Décrets*, 26 April 1945, p. 2376. Lafay was described as '*le premier médecin résistant de France*'. Citing Lafay's record in a speech at the party's 1945 Congress, Pierre Mazé, the party's secretary-general, concluded: '*Encore un radical naphtaliné, probablement! (rires).*'

French workers avoid being sent to Germany during the war, Lafay was among the first to enter Paris's *Hôtel de Ville* during the Paris insurrection of August 1944 and distinguished himself by being the first to raise the French flag above the building.

Lafay provided a particularly striking example of the methods and ideas of the *néo-radicaux* in his successful campaign to become a deputy in 1951. In November 1946 he had made an unsuccessful attempt in Tarn, in south-western France, a region with long Radical traditions. In 1951, he was the head of the RGR list in the right-bank second sector of Paris, an area not noted for a Radical background. While the Radical candidate in the first sector lost 19,000 votes as compared to the 1946 results, and the one in the third sector lost 7,000, Lafay's list won 27,500 more votes than had been won in the previous election. In a sector that did not send any Radicals to the Chamber in 1936, Lafay's list had won 21 per cent. of the votes, and both he and Pierre de Léotard, the second candidate on his list, had been elected. De Léotard was the right-wing president of *Réconciliation Française*, a small party that was the spiritual and doctrinal heir of the *Croix de feu* and the *Parti Social Français*, pre-war groups led by Colonel de La Rocque. It was clear that a new form of 'radicalism', with new supporters and new allies, had won success among voters who had been hostile to the Radical slogans and programmes of other days and places.

Other areas with non-Radical backgrounds also participated in this political evolution. Jean-Paul David, the dynamic secretary-general of the RGR and the secretary-general of the anti-Communist organization *Paix-et-Liberté*, has served as deputy from Seine-et-Oise since 1946. Like Lafay, he has been a very active organizer and publicist, and, again like Lafay, he has represented voters who traditionally have supported moderate candidates. Other Radicals who have accomplished similar feats include Léon Martinaud-Déplat in Bouches-du-Rhône (who went down to defeat, however, in January 1956), André Morice at Nantes, Edouard Ramonet in Indre, and Emile Hugues in Alpes-Maritimes.

It was non-metropolitan France, however, that was to provide the most unique field of activity for the *néo-radicaux*, who were to find that they had much in common with the powerful *colons* of North Africa. The latter, whether joining the party or supporting it from the outside, saw in it a useful medium for advancing their interests. The *néo-radicaux* not only were pleased to have the electoral support of new allies but welcomed the powerful financial assistance that they brought.

The financial aspects of this relationship were aptly described by Gustave Maniglier, who served as delegate from the Ivory Coast at the party's *Assemblée générale* in January 1946. Agreeing with arguments advanced by Laffargue at the same meeting, Maniglier stressed the need not to be too squeamish in seeking financial assistance. 'We must not hang back on the choice of financial resources, one does not make propaganda with only words and men, money is necessary! What difference does it make if we associate ourselves with capitalistic organizations—that call themselves republican—which will advance the money necessary to make propaganda!' To illustrate the wisdom of his statements, Maniglier referred to a personal experience. He had succeeded in founding a newspaper—'but not with my hands and my pay' —in the area for which he was a delegate, and 'now you have a Radical deputy from the Ivory Coast'.

Whatever the means used, the neo-radicalism of the post-war years was to prosper under the African sun. Radicals were numerous in the *Conseil du Gouvernement* at Rabat, in the *Assemblée Algérienne*, and in the *Haut Conseil* of Tunisia. The 'North African Lobby', as its opponents called it, was able to extend its influence into the party's machinery and found—or provided—many able spokesmen among the party's leaders, both in the National Assembly and in the Senate.

One of the most powerful of these spokesmen was Henri Borgeaud, who was elected to the *Conseil de la République* in 1946 and who long served as president of the *Groupe Sénatorial de la Gauche Démocratique et du RGR*, the group that Radical senators join. Borgeaud, who was often described as the unofficial Governor-General of Algeria, long has played an important role in North Africa both financially and politically; his interests include newspapers, large vineyards, agricultural concerns, and cigarette, cement and construction companies. Borgeaud extended his influence from Africa to Paris, and for several years this influence was exercised in a considerable measure through the Radical party.[3]

---

[3] Borgeaud was the object of a spectacular but thwarted assassination attempt in Paris by Algerian terrorists on 31 October 1957.

Another North African *néo-radical*, Antoine Colonna, played a similar role in Tunisia. Like Borgeaud, Colonna was elected to the *Conseil de la République* in 1946; he long bore the title *Sénateur des Français de Tunisie*. Such men were to be among the bitterest opponents of Mendès-France and the warmest supporters of the methods and objectives of the party's *néo-radical* administrative president, Martinaud-Déplat. They succeeded in equating many of their interests and objectives with those of the Radical party.

Any discussion of important Radical politicians who have represented North African constituencies must include mention of René Mayer. Mayer, however, does not fit easily into any limited classification. Although recognized as a strong supporter of the interests of the French *colons* of the Constantine constituency that he represented for nearly ten years in the National Assembly, he is better known for his long record of political activity on the national scene and for his high position in the world of *les très grandes affaires* that centre around Paris. Born in 1895, Mayer is the grandson of a Grand Rabbi of Paris on his father's side and on his mother's side is related to the French branch of the Rothschild family. After a very creditable record in the First World War, he made a brilliant career in business. In 1925 he was appointed administrator of the autonomous port of Strasbourg, and the following year was given an important post as a railroad administrator. He became vice-president of a prominent railroad company in 1932, played a key role in the formation of the French National Railways System, and was a founder of *Air France*. He has never ceased to distinguish himself for the great number of financial, industrial, and economic organizations, both French and foreign, for which he has acted as an advisor or administrator.

Mayer's first governmental post was that of *chef adjoint de cabinet* for Pierre Laval when the latter was Minister of Public Works in 1925. When war broke out in 1939, he was in London as head of a mission sent by the French Ministry of Armaments. During the war he accomplished the unusual feat of serving under both Giraud and de Gaulle. Minister of Public Works in de Gaulle's provisional government in 1944 and 1945, he was the only minister who was defeated in the October 1945 elections. In the June 1946 elections he successfully transferred his electoral ambitions from south-western Charente-Maritime to the *premier collège* of the new Algerian *département* of Constantine, the constituency that he represented until the end of the 1951–6 legislature.

Mayer's political career during the Fourth Republic was advanced under the banner of the Radical party. He usually was with the *néo-radicaux*, if not precisely of them; he was, in any case, at ease in a party in which their ideas were in a dominating position. At the same time Mayer distinguished himself for his personal authority and for his undeniable courage and ability. He cannot be considered as a 'party man', and indeed it was probably this latter characteristic that made the Radical party attractive to him.

Mayer won fame—and notoriety—when as Minister of Finance in the Schuman government of November 1947 to July 1948 he launched the Mayer Plan which was designed to stabilize the economy by vigorous measures.[4] After holding the portfolios of National Defence, Justice, and Finance in several subsequent governments and after unsuccessful attempts to be invested as premier in 1949 and 1951, Mayer served as premier from January to June 1953.

The early part of his premiership was marked by *l'affaire* Boutemy. Mayer's Minister of Public Health, André Boutemy, had to resign from the cabinet after violent objections were raised concerning his activities as a Vichy prefect and as distributor of electoral subsidies for the *Conseil National du Patronat français*, a French employers' organization. In discussing the latter charge, a Communist spokesman alleged in a speech in the National Assembly that in the 1951 elections the Radicals had been given 500,000 francs for each deputy's campaign and 1,000,000 francs for that of each ex-minister—'even if this ex-minister, I state this precisely, was standing in the *département* of Constantine'.[5] Mayer defended his appointee's war record,

---

[4] Along with re-establishing a free market for gold and currency and providing an amnesty for those who had hoarded them, Mayer caused much controversy by withdrawing all 5,000-franc notes in order to combat the Black Market. The government was forced to adopt the latter measure in order to maintain the support of the Socialists, but it greatly reduced public confidence in the currency and hurt Mayer's reputation, particularly in rural areas.

[5] *Journal Officiel*, 17 February 1953, pp. 1065–8. See also, *Journal Officiel*, 22 January 1953, pp. 128–34. The Communist spokesman was Jean Pronteau, deputy from Charente. It has been said that the grants were doubled for the 1956 general elections. See Jacques Fauvet, *La France déchirée*, Paris, 1957, p. 135.

but no contradictions were offered as to the exactness of the statements concerning his party's financial resources.

Eventually overthrown on the well-worn issue of governing by decree-laws, Mayer did not participate in any of the succeeding governments. A bitter opponent of Mendès-France, particularly on North African questions, he played an instrumental role in the latter's defeat in February 1955. In November of the same year, after the *radicaux mendésistes* had consolidated their control of the party, Mayer was expelled from its ranks. In the meantime he had transferred his abilities to the international scene by becoming president of the European Coal and Steel Community.

It can be argued that Mayer's career, both within and outside the Radical party, should be considered as *sui generis*. Bitterly attacked by the Communists as the *rapporteur* of the Atlantic Pact and as the *homme de Rothschild*, respected but feared, and eventually hated by many of his colleagues within his own party, Mayer never feared to take strong actions or to arouse controversy. With his deep knowledge of the business world, he represented a state of mind that is far removed from that of the *radicaux classiques*. But *sui generis* is a state that many Radicals can be said to have attained, at least in varying degrees. There is little doubt that, relatively speaking, Mayer had more in common with the *néo-radicaux* than with other members of the party. His membership in the party symbolized the alliance between the Radical party and powerful business interests, and his political success coincided with the halcyon days of neo-radicalism.

*
* *

How did the *néo-radicaux* set out to 'revitalize' the Radical party? What were the ideas that they advanced?

Some of the most articulate—and frank—expressions of their ideas and aspirations were enunciated during the party's 'great debate' after its crushing electoral defeat in October 1945, a debate that culminated in the formation of the RGR in the spring of 1946. In its conception, its evolution and its objectives, the RGR may be said to have symbolized the outlook of the *néo-radicaux*, as well as embodying their hopes. A study of the conception, evolution, and objectives of the RGR may be considered, therefore, as of a prime relevance in an attempt to understand the role of the *néo-radicaux* during the post-war years.

After the shock of their defeat at the polls (among their prominent leaders who failed to win seats were Daladier, Mendès-France, and Queuille), Radicals were faced, more than ever, with an urgent need to find new supporters, and the RGR was the outgrowth of this need. A desire for new supporters and new allies was, of course, no sudden whim on the part of a group of men devoted to winning elections—the post-war flirtation with the Communists may be cited as an extreme example of the willingness of Radicals to co-operate with other segments of the political spectrum. But their early post-war efforts to find new allies had proved to be insufficient—one contemporary critic described the Radicals' plight by saying that 'they sleep with everybody but no longer reproduce'.[6] The degree of pessimism varied among Radicals (Herriot, who had been re-elected by his faithful *Lyonnais*, remained a pillar of strength), but there was no doubt that the October elections had inspired most Radicals with a renewed willingness to make concessions to potential partners.

The *néo-radicaux* were in the vanguard of those Radicals who called for new policies, new leaders, and new allies. The party's *Assemblée générale* of 12–13 January 1946, a meeting unprecedented in the history of the party, provided a scene for much soul-searching and self-diagnosis. Those present agreed that the situation was grim. One orator compared the party to an old store.[7] In early 1945, at the congress of the *Fédération du Sud-Ouest* in Bordeaux, it was clear that a new coat of paint was needed; in August at the party's congress in Paris, the building was rotting; by the time of the elections entire new pieces were needed; but after the elections the entire building had collapsed. It was now a question, he concluded, of rebuilding and of deciding which pieces should be used again and which should be replaced.

Such questions aroused vigorous, and at times brutal, suggestions by the *néo-radicaux*. Maniglier, the ebullient delegate from the Ivory Coast, was among those who were the most outspoken. After noting that two days previously he had been 'in tropical forests' and less than a month earlier had been hunting

---

[6] Cited by Gordon Wright, 'The Resurgence of the Right in France', *Yale French Studies*, vol. 15, Winter 1954–5, p. 6.

[7] M. Guillon.

elephants, he went on to voice his first impressions of the solutions that most of his colleagues had been offering: 'In France people do not bury corpses, they embalm them! (commotion).' Proclaiming that the time for action had passed and that the time for revolution was arriving, he proceeded to upset at least a few of the basic tenets of radicalism by pleading with his listeners not to embalm the 'corpse', but to bring it back to life— 'Lazarus was brought back to life by a young fellow about whom much has been written in the history of the world.'

Several of those present lamented the preponderant position of old men in their party. Laffargue complained that the party's *bureau* was too encumbered with former presidents and secretaries-general and with honorary presidents and vice-presidents who had been elected 'in the enthusiasm and euphory of certain congresses'. Another speaker remarked that theirs was a *vieux parti*, and added that *les vieux* do not father many children.[8] Maniglier, remarking that it was not a *vieux parti* but a *parti de vieux*—'which is not exactly the same thing'—concluded that, although it was necessary to keep the older members, their role should be limited to indicating the policies to be followed and should not include the responsibility for carrying them out.

The major solution that was advanced by the *néo-radicaux*, however, was the idea of a broad *rassemblement* in which diverse forces would be united under a single electoral banner. The *néo-radicaux* were not alone, of course, in advancing this tactically logical step. What distinguished their proposals was the broad scope and the diversity of the organization that they envisaged and the persistence and skill with which they worked towards its realization.

The idea of a new *rassemblement* was officially launched at the January meeting, but it had been a subject of particular concern to many Radicals ever since the October 1945 elections—especially to those who had been defeated. At a meeting held shortly after the elections, one defeated candidate even went so far as to say that the title 'Radical-Socialist' was out-dated.[9] This charge was echoed in January, one orator stating that young voters considered the word 'Radical' as a scarecrow or as an obsolete and aged title.[10] Although the suggestion that the party should

[8] M. Mortier (Seine-et-Marne).

[9] Cited by Charles Martinetti, *I.R.S.*, October 1954.   [10] M. Ribera (Gard).

change its title did not arouse enthusiasm, it became clear that there was little open hostility to the idea of participating in a new *rassemblement* which, it was hoped, would attract youth and women. According to the supporters of the new project, the Radical party would be the centre of an alliance that would unite all those Frenchmen who wanted 'unlimited social progress', but only to the point beyond which 'there would no longer be any liberty of individual property'.[11] Amidst general agreement as to the advantages—ideological and electoral—of such an organization, it was decided that the necessary negotiations would be undertaken and proposals submitted at the next Congress.

The negotiations were long and laborious, both within the party and between the party and its potential allies. The *Ligue de la République*, a new organization that was composed of Radicals (including Mendès-France and Gaston Monnerville) and members of the *Jeune République* and the UDSR, issued a manifesto on 6 February 1946, calling for an entente between its members' respective parties and addressed letters to Herriot setting forth their arguments.[12] During the same period a *Comité d'Initiative en vue de Rassemblement Républicain*, with Jean-Paul David as secretary-general and including Lafay and several important Radicals among its members, was organized and also solicited Herriot's support; the title that they originally proposed was *Front de la République*.[13] The latter group, animated by *néo-radicaux*, provided the nucleus around which the RGR was eventually formed.

Much of the strongest opposition to these proposals came from within the Radical party. The *radicaux de gauche* were, of course, the bitterest opponents of those who advocated union with parties to the right of the Radicals. Kayser's strong opinions have already been noted. At the party's congress in April 1946, he stressed his concern as to the new 'colleagues' and, belittling the supposed advantages of the new alliances, noted that he had not

[11] *Le Monde*, 12 January 1946.

[12] Radical party archives. For information and documentation concerning the evolution and activities of the RGR, I am indebted to M. Christian Loyauté, long the administrative secretary-general of the RGR. Interview, Paris, 5 December 1955. Along with several other leaders of the RGR, M. Loyauté was expelled from the Radical party on 9 December 1955.

[13] Radical party archives. Letter from Jean-Paul David, secretary-general, to Édouard Herriot, Paris, 8 March 1946.

been able to find the addresses of their parties in the Paris telephone book—along with the Radical party, the RGR was originally composed of the UDSR, the *Alliance démocratique*, the *Parti républicaine et social de la réconciliation française*, the *Parti socialiste démocratique*, and the *Parti républicain socialiste*.[14] Stressing their doubts as to the republican character of certain of their proposed allies, the *radicaux de gauche* also argued that the leaders of the UDSR, most of whom had served as ministers under de Gaulle, had never been favourable to Radicals or their policies.

Of greater importance was the attitude of Herriot, who was too influential to be either absorbed or by-passed: no plan could succeed without his approval. In a speech before a group of his constituents in March 1946, he declared that he was 'not about to give my daughter in marriage to just anybody'.[15] By the time that the party's crucial congress took place in April, however, he was ready to grant his rather grudging approval. Although noting that he had been 'a little hurt that people offered to come near us but not with us' and remarking that he did 'not understand too well why the same people who had insulted, despised, scorned, and reviled us in October suddenly found us interesting, useful, and almost charming', he went on to say that the decisions of the congress would be carried out. Assuring his listeners that he could be counted on not to give up the principles of radicalism, he added that he was glad to see the word *gauche* in the title of the new organization.

The arguments of the *néo-radicaux*, therefore, had won the day. Herriot's approval had been won; the *radicaux de gauche* were forced out of the party; and the *néo-radicaux* had a new vehicle for the advancement of their ideas and ambitions—one of which of course, was the restoration of the Radical party as a strong political force.

Certain Radicals—particularly Paul Anxionnaz, who as secretary general of the party had played a vital role in the negotiations—had emphasized the contribution that the other member parties notably the UDSR, could make in permeating radicalism with the spirit of the resistance. The *néo-radicaux*, in *their* arguments

[14] For a description of the small formations that belonged to the RGR, se Philip Williams, *Politics in Post-War France*, London, 1958 ed., pp. 147–8.

[15] Speech at Arbresle (Rhône), 31 March 1946. Cited by Jacques Kayser, *Congr extraordinaire*, 1946.

took a much broader view. If the crux of the position of the *radicaux de gauche* may be said to have been their insistence on a policy of 'No enemies on the left', that of the *néo-radicaux* may be described as a willingness to win friends on the right.

In regard to those located on the left of the political spectrum, they were staunchly anti-Communist, distrusted the Socialists, and, above all, were strongly opposed to any mention of a new Popular Front—'in this alliance between Radicals and Socialists, the latter had all the advantages of marriage and all the pleasures of adultery'.[16]

At the same time, it was their stated objective to group all those who would co-operate with them. At the *Assemblée générale*, Maniglier told his listeners that France had been *pétainiste*—'All of you probably were (protests and laughter). When I say all, I am speaking of all of France.' Now France was all *gaulliste*, but Radicals, he said, must learn how to find the middle way, 'the way of measure, the Cartesian way'. To do this they must group all those in the country who were 'republican and liberal, without limitations based on words or personalities'. At a meeting of the executive committee in March, Laffargue warned his colleagues not to ostracize anyone. 'You will never be too numerous to win victories.' The following month, at the April congress, Lafay declared that the RGR was the last hope of the forces of liberty against those of economic collectivism, and described the new organization as the last rampart of a civilization that had been made by Christianity and latinity. There was no doubt that those being sought were expected to share such viewpoints.

The *néo-radicaux* also made it clear, on a more practical level, that they were interested in both men and money. The first headquarters of the RGR was at 5, Avenue de l'Opéra, an address it shared with the powerful and influential *Comité républicain pour le commerce l'industrie et l'agriculture* (known as the CRCIA or *Comité Mascuraud*), an organization with which many Radicals had long been affiliated. Marcel Astier, a Radical senator who had been one of the earliest supporters of the RGR, pointedly asked his listeners at the April congress if they did not agree that it would be useful to have, 'along with the 30,000 dues-payers on whom you count, the 100,000 dues-payers who belong

16 M. Mortier (Seine-et-Marne), *Assemblée générale*, January 1946.

to the economic organizations in question?' Declaring that 'these people are not hesitating to compromise themselves with us,' he concluded: 'Must we reject them automatically and send them to right-wing groups when they clearly want to place themselves on the left? (commotion).' To *néo-radicaux* such questions were clearly rhetorical. They were glad to have the assistance of the CRCIA, as well as that of other economic groups less in the Radical tradition.

Although the *Comité Mascuraud*'s relationship with the Radical party manifestly had not begun with the RGR, it did serve to symbolize an attitude that had long been opposed by many of the party's more left-wing members who hoped that new habits would prevail after the war. By the time of the party's congress at Nice in 1947, however, the Radical party's close relationship with the CRCIA was again taken for granted. 'In the same way that it is impossible to conceive of a Good Friday without gloom,' wrote one observer, 'there is no Radical congress without the traditional and inevitable banquet of the Comité Mascuraud.'[17]

The subsequent evolution of the RGR was to be marked with serious vicissitudes, and in many ways was to parallel that of the *néo-radicaux*. Instrumental in the conception and in the development of the RGR, the *néo-radicaux* were to participate in its establishment as a political party in late 1955. Not having been able to remain in control of the Radical party, they maintained their possession of the RGR and, after their exclusion by the *radicaux mendésistes*, made it into a party of their own. Even if it were not to be the last rampart of Western civilization, the RGR was to serve as the last rampart of the *néo-radicaux*.

As an electoral alliance, the RGR was subject to all the problems and pressures inherent in the task of trying to win elections. It was to be judged, moreover, by the harsh standards of electoral success—with each candidate or prospective candidate inevitably inclined to judge it from the vantage point of his own particular situation. The task of maintaining peaceful relations among the member parties of the RGR was a particularly thorny one. There is room for only one man at the top of each electoral list, and if an alliance is to be operative, there is room for only one list in each constituency. On a national level, the necessity

17 *Le Canard enchaîné*, 24 September 1947.

of sharing the more promising electoral possibilities was clear. At the local level, where potential candidates are primarily concerned with their own destinies, this necessity was less evident. The RGR, therefore, was at the centre of many bitter controversies—both ideological and tactical. Many Radicals bitterly questioned the electoral value of their new allies. 'There are those,' one critic remarked, 'who bring us their parties as dowries—parties which, in the civilian world, correspond to what the Haitian army is in the military.'[18] Certain of the other parties were also attacked on ideological grounds, particularly *Réconciliation française* and the *Alliance démocratique*—this latter, under the leadership of Pierre-Etienne Flandin, a former premier who had held office under Vichy, eventually left the RGR. Even the UDSR was not immune to Radical attacks. 'In it,' one Radical senator charged, 'fascists are grouped with clericals and with authentic socialists. Let the Republicans leave this monster, we will know how to recognize them! (applause).'[19]

Electoral periods were particularly fruitful in providing new occasions for disputes. In June 1946 the choice of Claudius-Petit —a prominent resistance leader and a member of the UDSR— as the RGR's *tête de liste* in Loire was strenuously opposed by local Radicals who reproached him for having voted in the Consultative Assembly for the maintenance of subsidies to church schools and for having belonged to the minority in the Constitutional Assembly that, with the MRP, had asked for the inscription of freedom of education in the Declaration of the Rights of Man.[20]

Another ideological and tactical struggle was waged in Seine-et-Oise, where another UDSR deputy, Edouard Bonnefous, wanted the RGR label and local organizations to take precedence over those of the Radicals. Led by Radical deputy Maurice Bené, the Radicals vigorously defended their position as members of the largest party in the RGR and protested against attempts to force them to accept a secondary role. The annual banquet held at Versailles to commemorate the anniversary of General Hoche, one of the Radicals' favourite Revolutionary heroes, long gave rise to an annual outbreak of incidents, as both

[18] Marc Rucart, later senator from Côte d'Ivoire and Haute Volta, *Congrès extraordinaire*, 1946.

[19] Auguste Pinton, senator from Rhône, *ibid.*

[20] Radical party archives. Letter from Jean-Paul David, secretary-general of the RGR, to Henri Queuille, vice-president of the Radical party, Paris, 8 May 1946.

groups felt they should have the honour of sponsoring the event. Their differences reached a peak in 1949 when Bonnefous prevailed upon Queuille, then premier, not to accept an invitation to the banquet that had been proffered by the president of the Radical *comité* at Versailles.[21] Such quarrels between the RGR and the Radical party in Seine-et-Oise—whether resulting from invitations to banquets or choices of candidates in cantonal and municipal elections—long served to enliven and envenom the local political scene.

Of much greater import, however, was the bitter struggle that took place in Rhône where Léon Chambaretaud, a prominent Radical who was also the local secretary-general of the RGR, undertook to use the latter organization to challenge the position of Herriot. The party's president was able to bring about the exclusion of Chambaretaud and his principal colleagues from the Radical party in May 1951; but in the general elections held in June of that year, the rebel leader ran as an independent candidate and managed to win enough votes to prevent the government coalition from securing an absolute majority and all the constituency's seats.

The relationship between the RGR and the Radical party did not improve with time, and those who opposed Radical participation in the RGR became more and more outspoken. In a speech at the party's 1953 congress, one delegate provided a particularly sombre historical summary of the first seven years of the RGR—'we were compelled to participate in shocking promiscuities'—and concluded that Radicals had become dupes and cuckolds.[22]

Such charges, however, did not mean that all Radicals were willing to forgo the advantages offered by the existence of the RGR. One structural factor was to be of particular significance the over-representation of the small parties within the RGR made it convenient as a weapon of political power for influential groups or individuals within the Radical party. Daladier, for example, greatly advanced his post-war political comeback when with the aid of the smaller groups, he won a surprising election

---

[21] Radical party archives. Letter from Léon de Riedmatten, president of the *Comité Radical-Socialiste de Versailles*, to Léon Martinaud-Déplat, administrativ president of the Radical party, Versailles, 24 May 1950, with enclosures.

[22] Charles Martinetti.

to the presidency of the RGR in May 1950. Herriot, provided with one more reason for regretting his grudging approval of the RGR in 1946, resigned as honorary president four days later.

Daladier's election as president of the RGR coincided with the most conservative level of his post-war political fluctuations; he was to use the RGR as the central instrument for the advancement of his hopes to form a conservative 'Fourth Force' to supersede the governmental 'Third Force' in the 1951 elections. Such hopes were, of course, in complete accord with the objectives of the *néo-radicaux*. Daladier's subsequent leftward migration was paralleled by a decline in his RGR activities. His role as president of the RGR ended in August 1954, when the office of presidency was replaced by a *délégation permanente* of six members.

After their defeat by the *radicaux mendésistes* at the tumultuous special congress of 4 May 1955, the *néo-radicaux* were able to profit—as had Daladier five years earlier—from the structural vagaries of the RGR. In a move that was to intensify the desire of the Radical party's new leaders to alter the composition of the predominantly *néo-radical* delegation to the RGR, the *Bureau national* of the RGR asked Premier Edgar Faure to accept the presidency of the *délégation permanente* on 23 June. In this way, Faure was provided with a haven that was to be of useful service after his exclusion from the party a few months later on 1 December 1955. The subsequent refusal of the majority of the members of the Radical delegation in the RGR to obey their party's direct order to resign their positions provided the official grounds for the most spectacular of the Radical party's exclusions of December 1955. Faced with the necessity of choosing between a 'renovated' Radical party and an RGR that they had helped conceive, organize, and lead, Lafay, Laffargue, Martinaud-Déplat, Jean-Paul David, and René Mayer were among those who chose the latter alternative.

*

* *

What may be said, in retrospect, concerning the role that the *néo-radicaux* played within the party before they were relegated to the status of ex-Radicals at the end of 1955? To what degree, and in what ways, did they attempt to enunciate a new and revitalized doctrine of radicalism?

First, it is undeniable that the *néo-radicaux* did make a significant contribution towards the revival of the Radical party as an important political force during the years that followed the Liberation. At the same time, it must be noted that there were several basic factors—independent of any one group or individual—that facilitated the political comeback of the Radicals. These included their strategic position at the centre of the political spectrum, their great tactical skill, and the prestige and ability of their many leaders. The role of the *néo-radicaux*, like that of most of their colleagues, was not limited to any single sphere of activity. Their contribution included not only new money and new supporters, but also new leadership and new ideas.

Of particular significance was the fact that the aid brought by the *néo-radicaux* was primarily *new*. This enabled the Radicals to profit, once again, from their skill in remaining faithful to the stomach theory of political parties—'the main task of a great party is the same as that of a good stomach, not to reject but to assimilate'.[23] By living up to this rule, Radicals were able to utilize the support and advice of their new members, and at the same time found it possible to continue to enjoy the co-operation of most of their traditional followers.

Like nearly all of their fellow Radicals, the *néo-radicaux* had a strong interest in tactics. Their desire to have the Radical party work in unison with the political forces on their right already has been stressed: this central feature of neo-radicalism found its most vivid illustrations in the controversial formation and evolution of the RGR. Another basic *néo-radical* objective must also be mentioned: they were in the vanguard of those Radicals who manifested a fervent desire to have their party participate in the exercise of power.

The latter objective met with approval and enthusiasm on the part of most of the other members of the party and was in complete accord, in particular, with the desires of the *radicaux de gestion*. The period of the *néo-radicaux'* rising importance within the party coincided with the party's remarkable return to power after the war, a feat for which the *néo-radicaux* must be given a measure of credit. Active in the party's administration, they

23 See above, p. 9.

did not hesitate in putting all their influence on the side of those of their colleagues who were willing and able to assume high government positions.

There was no lack of Radicals who had these qualities. Several Radicals participated in the government formed by Ramadier in January 1947. Herriot was elected president of the National Assembly during the same month, and in March of the same year Gaston Monnerville began his long reign as president of the *Conseil de la République*. As Minister of Finance under Schuman, René Mayer was able to orient French economic and financial policies during the latter part of 1947 and the first half of 1948. The Radicals' political comeback was consecrated in July 1948 when André Marie, a pre-war Radical deputy who had been deported to Buchenwald during the war, became the first post-war Radical premier. Although they only had forty-three deputies in the 1946–51 National Assembly, the Radicals were able to wield more influence than the Communists could with their 163 deputies.

In the opinion of the *néo-radicaux*, an opinion that they shared with the *radicaux de gestion*, participation in power was not just a matter of wielding influence or gaining tactical advantages. It was a primary mission of the Radical party, they argued, to be a governmental party. It was also the party's duty to help carry out—and if possible attenuate—even those policies that it did not approve.

Such a task required skill; it also required a willingness to make concessions. Addressing his fellow Radicals in a speech at the party's special congress before the 1951 elections, Laffargue declared that those in the party who opposed participation in the successive post-war governments were right to fear that the country would not understand why the party supported policies whose principles it opposed, and added that the same Radicals were also correct in fearing that government by parties with contradictory principles could only end in impotence. He went on to conclude, however, that those Radicals who advanced contrary arguments were *also* correct and that 'our chiefs were right to take no notice of the voice of logic and to put the interests of the nation above those of their party'. In a speech shortly after the elections, Martinaud-Déplat argued that the advantages inherent in such an attitude far outweighed the disadvantages—both from the party's point of view and from that of the nation.[24] After remarking that it would have been easier 'to remain during five years in a sterile opposition', he explained that by taking part in governmental responsibilities, Radicals had 'put an end to the mad nationalization policies', had slowed down the plundering of newspapers, and had 'loosened the vice of a mischief-making and bureaucratic *dirigisme*'. Adding that it was the duty of all Frenchmen to unite in support of a convalescent Republic, he paid a tribute to Henri Queuille by noting that, when the Republic had been gravely ill, it was *'le bon docteur* that the Radical party had furnished who had brought about its recovery'.

To fulfil such a role it was necessary, above all, that Radicals be realistic. 'If republicans,' Martinaud-Déplat warned, 'split among themselves, if they are fickle, if they reason in the name of doctrines that ignore realities, they will lead the Republic once more to the edge of the abyss.' The historic mission of radicalism was to be the party of the *juste milieu*; it was the duty of Radicals to continue to represent *le bon sens français*.

Speaking before a group of his fellow Radicals at a banquet in January 1955, Martinaud-Déplat provided his listeners with a particularly revealing and significant account of his views concerning what he described as the unique nature of the Radical party[25]—a uniqueness that found a more active expression in the fall of Mendès-France's government nine days later. The series of actions involved in the latter event—a Radical premier overthrown largely through the efforts of one Radical colleague and subsequently replaced as premier by another—was to provide a severe test for the 'realism', if not the *bon sens*, of many Radicals. Speaking during a preparatory stage of the new crisis, however, Martinaud-Déplat betrayed no sign of dismay or pessimism. After referring to the presence of so many contrasting personalities and opinions within the party, he spoke of 'the mysterious attraction' that was responsible for inducing Radicals to remain faithful to their party and went on to offer an explanation for this phenomenon. 'It is perhaps due to the fact that it is not a party like the others.'

[24] *I.R.S.*, 28 June 1951.

[25] Léon Martinaud-Déplat, *Discours de M. Martinaud-Déplat, prononcé le 31 octobre 1953 devant la Fédération de la Seine*, Paris, 1954.

Maurice Thorez once attributed this same quality to *his* party, but the Radicals' administrative president had a different variety of uniqueness in mind. There was once a time, he explained, when people highly praised groups of men who based their unity on a body of statutes and on a programme—'a sort of calendar that was never followed but was always venerated'. Radicals, however, who were often reproached for not having a programme, were intimately united by a 'common philosophy', which he defined as 'the love of democracy, the love of liberty and the constant search for progress'. If in the latter search Radicals happen to diverge, 'or if it happens that we do not even meet on the same route', Radicals are tolerant, and this latter characteristic was 'still another of the Radical virtues'. Even in their disagreements, Radicals knew how to remain affectionate friends, and a moment would always come when their paths would come together again.

There is no doubt that this was an outlook that was shared in varying degrees by many other Radicals. From the vantage point of history, however, it must be concluded that the *néo-radicaux*, in their actions during this period, were making excessive demands on the much vaunted Radical *état d'esprit*, and in this way facilitated the rise within the party of their increasingly bitter rivals, the *radicaux mendésistes*.

*
* *

It is undeniable, in any case, that the opinions of the *néo-radicaux* concerning the proper role of the party often coincided with those of other Radicals—in particular the *radicaux de gestion*. Their attachment to certain of the basic characteristics of the traditional Radical *état d'esprit*—tolerance, willingness to compromise—was marked, if anything, by too much enthusiasm. Before proceeding to a discussion of fundamental issues on which the *néo-radicaux* were often conspicuous for their differences with other segments of Radical opinion, it must be observed that an additional Radical characteristic also was shared by many *néo-radicaux*: the ability to wield a staunchly republican vocabulary.

Although certain of the *néo-radicaux* belittled the style of oratory dear to many of their colleagues ('these exegetical discussions

concerning the Republic'),[26] others derived much profit from
their ability to handle, in a traditional manner, the traditional
themes of radicalism. This was particularly true of those *néo-
radicaux*—notably Laffargue and Martinaud-Déplat—who had a
background of experience in the Radical party and who almost
effortlessly were able to hold their own with the most eloquent
of the *radicaux classiques*. In a speech at the party's congress in
1948, Martinaud-Déplat even went so far as to present himself as
a spokesman for his party's faith in its old slogans. 'We remain
faithful to the old formulas. They are ancient but they cannot
become old, because they are eternal. . . .' In the last editorial
that he was to write for the party's official newspaper, he eloquently proclaimed his party's objectives. 'Turned towards the
future of the country, the Party must defend the French Union,
the peace of the world, the bread of the workers, and all the
liberties that it has won for the respect and the dignity of
humanity.'[27]

It was not difficult to arouse approval, if not vigorous enthusiasm, for such a 'programme'. But the *néo-radicaux*, priding
themselves on their realism and vitality, did not hesitate to
enunciate and to work towards the implementation of more
concrete goals. Unlike certain of their colleagues, they did not
limit themselves to oratorical and tactical activities, but took
strong stands on critical problems. They were particularly explicit and ambitious in their pronouncements on economic and
social questions. Their concern with the destiny of the French
Union and with the dangers of international Communism never
waned. They were strong supporters of European unification.
And although less emphasized, their views and actions regarding their country's perennial problem of Church–State relations
were of a particularly significant interest—especially when viewed
in the context of their party's ideological background.

As we shall see, the viewpoints of the *néo-radicaux* on these
issues often merged with those of their colleagues. In many in-
stances, of course, there is no clear line between neo-radicalism
and contemporary radicalism. A consideration of the issues on
which there was a degree of unity of opinion between *néo-
radicaux* and their colleagues, as well as those questions on which
differences of opinion were to become insupportable, constitutes

[26] René Mauclair, 1945 Congress.   [27] *I.R.S.*, December 1948.

an important feature of a study of the Radical party during the post-war years.

*
* *

The *néo-radicaux* were eloquent and insistent in emphasizing the high priority that they attached to economic questions. Of all their preoccupations, their interest in their country's economic problems was probably the one that was closest not only to their pocketbooks but also to their hearts and minds. This interest in economics was one of the few characteristics that they shared with Mendès-France, and with a persistence rivalled only by that of their future rival, they never ceased to proclaim and defend the great importance that they attributed to economic matters.

As early as 1945, in his report on the party's economic and financial policies at the first regular post-war congress, Laffargue stressed the transcendental nature of France's economic problems. 'We apologize for being repetitious,' he said, 'but it is on the French economy, on the manner in which it will assert its strength in the world, that the grandeur of France will depend.' Laffargue again emphasized this theme at the party's next congress when, making a distinctly non-Radical literary allusion, he drew an analogy between the 'vanity of vanities' of which Bossuet spoke in his funeral oration on Henrietta Maria of England and the desire to have France win prestige without first curing her economic problems. Laffargue and his fellow *néo-radicaux* were forceful concerning the magnitude of the latter. At a meeting of the party's executive committee in 1947, after telling his colleagues that all their debates would be dominated by France's economic situation, Laffargue explained that there were 'in 1940, 1,778 tons of gold in the vaults of the *Banque de France*; last 11 April, 678 tons; when the recently voted financial measures are applied, 400 tons'.

In addition to the primacy that they accorded France's economic problems, the *néo-radicaux* shared another belief with Mendès-France. In their opinion, as in that of the co-author of *La Science économique et l'action*,[28] economics was a science, one

28 Pierre Mendès-France and Gabriel Ardant, *La Science économique et l'action,* Paris, 1954; *Economics and Action*, London, 1955.

that necessitated study and respect. 'You will excuse me for giving no credit to slogans or improvisations,' Laffargue once declared, 'economics is a science, it has its laws, and they do not allow themselves to be jostled with impunity.' Laffargue, who made this statement at his party's congress in 1945, and who during the succeeding years was to be the major Radical spokesman for neo-liberal economic principles, did not always find support or agreement even among his Radical colleagues. The elevation of a subject to the rank of a science is not always accompanied, unfortunately, with unity of opinion among the new scientists.

On economic issues, however, the *néo-radicaux*' primary enemies were outside their own party. This was particularly true during the years following the war, when nearly all Radicals were joined in a staunch and bitter opposition to their country's new economic policies and methods. Laffargue was expressing a general Radical attitude when, in an article published on 20 April 1946, in *La Dépêche de Paris*, he stated that 'a revolutionary wind has swept over this country since the Liberation, a tempestuous wind that has devastated everywhere'. Adding their voices to those of Herriot and other Radical spokesmen, the *néo-radicaux* eloquently criticized the new nationalization programme and ridiculed the activities of the *dirigistes*. In Laffargue's words, the latter had 'transformed a nation of builders into a team of functionaries'.[29] Private industries, he added, were run by men whose mission it was to hand down the property that they hold; nationalized ones were administered by officials whose futures were not connected to enterprises whose destinies were 'constantly bandied about in the changing whims of politics'. At the party's congress in 1948, Martinaud-Déplat provided his listeners with a summary of the misdeeds of the *dirigistes*. 'Our imports have been thrown into confusion, our production costs heavily augmented, our production capacity stifled by the consequences of mad financial methods, the number of officials increased beyond the limits of reason and the means of the state, and the inexorable law of budgetary equilibrium treated with scorn.' Thanks to the malice of some and the inexperience of others, inflation in all its forms had resulted.

Firm in their faith in economics and in the primacy of their

[29] 1949 Congress.

country's economic problems and eloquent concerning the causes and scope of the latter, the *néo-radicaux* were also forceful in advancing remedies. In their minds, the abolition—or at least the reorganization—of the economic apparatus that had been erected since the war was a basic prerequisite of any improvement of their country's economic situation. In October 1946 Martinaud-Déplat made a thundering radio speech, entitled 'On the Edge of the Abyss', in which he declared that 'the state lives like the lord of the manor and abandons the nation to misery' and charged that '*dirigisme*, the creator of the Black Market and the generator of scandals, constitutes a permanent obstacle to production'.[30]

All *néo-radicaux* were emphatic in denouncing this state of affairs and in stressing the primordial need for increased productivity. In a manifesto published before the 1951 general elections, the RGR's newspaper, *L'Unité française*, declared that the RGR's economic and financial programme was 'inspired entirely by the only remedy that has ever existed and will ever exist for combating the misery or the mediocrity of the standard of living: produce more at lower cost'.[31] The dilemma was clear. 'There is no solution to France's problems if French production does not increase.'

Increased productivity, then, was the central economic objective advanced by the *néo-radicaux*. The 1951 economic programme proposed by the RGR contained a list of twelve 'urgent measures' that were designed to encourage employers and workers to 'modernize their businesses in order to produce more at less cost and during the same period of work'.[32] The first measure listed was one that was particularly dear to the *néo-radicaux*: the need to have a more flexible scale of salaries. As early as the *petit congrès* of December 1944, Lafay had approvingly cited the wide range of salaries in the Soviet Union and had concluded that if France's rulers wanted collectivism, they should at least have it in a workable form. At the party's congress in 1945, Laffargue, pointing out that 'Russia taught us Stakhanovism as America taught the Taylor system', declared that France would have to revise her salary scale in order to encourage the recruitment of her elites. It was all right, he agreed, to have a minimum

---

[30] *La Dépêche de Paris*, 29 October 1946.
[31] *L'Unité française*, May–June 1951.   [32] *Ibid.*

salary, but high salaries should be allowed to those worthy of them—'In Russia there are differences that range from one to eight between labourers and specialized workers.'

The authors of the RGR's economic programme also called for the abolition of all social security deductions for overtime work and for the spread of bonus systems to encourage high productivity. Among other urgent measures listed were an expanded housing programme, a simplification of the tax system, a massive increase in medium term credit at low interest rates, and a massive reduction in inheritance taxes. Such measures, it was felt, would encourage all producers, both employers and workers, and would promote initiative and the creation of wealth.

The *néo-radicaux* did not limit their economic studies to a diagnosis of their country's economic problems and the compilation of 'urgent measures' but also ventured into the field of general ideas. It was in the latter endeavour, in which 'neo-radicalism' may be said to have merged its forces with 'neo-liberalism', that the *néo-radicaux* made what was undoubtedly their most significant contribution to the ideological corpus of radicalism. While not hesitating to extol the ancient virtues of property and liberty or to warn of the dangers that inevitably accompanied any infringement of these historic rights, they also claimed the right to use a more contemporary vocabulary and to ally the wisdom of the past with the needs of the present. The traditional tenets of radicalism, they argued, were not sufficient to contend with the problems of the mid-twentieth century. Or, as Laffargue explained in his controversial speech at the party congress in 1945, the political thought of Léon Bourgeois and Camille Pelletan 'is certainly present in our minds, but I have the right to say that it would be overtaxed by contemporary events'.

In presenting their economic ideas, the *néo-radicaux* were more inclined to group them under the banner of liberalism than that of radicalism, but as has been noted, the modern forms of these two terms came to be used interchangeably. Radicalism had found still another synonym. At a meeting of the party's executive committee in March 1947, one delegate flatly declared that 'the modern liberals are represented in France by the Radicals'.[33]

The *néo-radicaux* made it clear that the accent was on modernity, both in regard to the liberalism and the radicalism involved. At

[33] M. Maniglier.

the party's *Assemblée générale* in January 1946, Laffargue was categorical in disavowing 'total economic liberalism', which he said had committed two grave errors: it had not only neglected the great social problems, but had also permitted trusts and cartels to upset the system of free competition. He then went on to declare his allegiance to a new and revitalized form of liberalism. 'I belong to a school whose principles are spreading in numerous countries and which believes that it is by the end of controls and the return to liberty that we will save not only the world's economy, but with it will rescue the essential values of Western civilization.'

This ambitious undertaking required a consideration of broader principles than those contained in a list of measures designed for the specific use of one country. In this challenging task, probably the most significant contribution made by the *néo-radicaux* was a rousing call to arms—'Arise liberals!'—presented by Laffargue in a much-heralded speech at the party's congress at Toulouse in 1949. Along with offering 'practical solutions', he told his listeners that it was also his ambition to show them that 'we have an economic doctrine, that it goes back to the very fountainhead of liberalism, and that we can oppose it with pride and confidence against the errors of a collectivism whose bankruptcy displays itself far beyond our frontiers and constitutes the obstacle to the recovery of Europe'.

There was still much profit to be drawn, Laffargue argued, from the basic teachings of the great liberals of the past, who showed that 'it is not the State that regulates prices, but the market that sets them by the law of supply and demand and by the workings of free competition'. Laffargue went on to ask for an end of attacks on 'what is called our lack of logic'. There was, he proclaimed, 'no incoherence in our doctrine. We say: freedom of prices in a system of free enterprise.' In order to lower prices it was first necessary to increase supply, and 'if our fiscal law *polytechniciens* would only get away from their theories and embrace the great horizons of economics, they would subscribe to the ideas that we have never ceased to defend'. Although opposed to total economic liberalism, Laffargue did not hesitate to stress the continued relevance of the basic economic laws enunciated by the great liberals of the past. Contemporary France, by scorning these laws, was reduced to living on loans and on gold reserves that had been built by the work of generations of Frenchmen. It was dependent on outside aid for its indispensable imports—'only the Marshall Plan today insures us against asphyxia'.

Liberalism, therefore, was a source of eternal truths. It was also a dynamic doctrine. And, in Laffargue's words, the 'great progressive revolution of liberalism' provided a proper framework for the Radicals' economic doctrine. This great revolution of liberalism, he went on to explain, had staggered the civilized world; in 150 years it had transformed small autarkic communities into specialized members of a vast economic system. The division of labour and continuously expanding markets had made this evolution possible. The open market had become the great regulator and with the mechanism of supply and demand had determined the movement of capital and labour. No economist had ever invented a way to decide what men should produce; the classical economists had only tried to describe how the system worked. This free economy had permitted such a great amelioration of the standard of living of those countries that adopted it and had brought about such a great influx of material wealth, that even Marxists, he noted, no longer insist on their master's original thesis that capitalism inevitably leads to increasing poverty for the masses.

Such a vast revolution, however, had upset 'both interests and habits'. Free exchange had provoked a rapid and violent dislocation of the established interests of capital and labour, and 'that is why for eighty years we have seen in the world an organized revolt of collectivism against a free economy'. Labour asked for laws against immigration; both labour and capital called for protective customs. Trusts, pools, and cartels came into being. The sum result of all these measures was to prevent the division of labour from operating in the cadre of a free market.

The Second World War, Laffargue continued, had accentuated these tendencies. The *dirigisme* of the war period had been advanced as an economic system. The legitimate need for plans, for guidance, gave birth to a cult of planism. 'Everywhere bright prophets equipped with their slide rules and logarithm tables sprang forth determined to organize the market.' Their misguided efforts had led to the establishment of the wasteful economic apparatus and the stifling controls that Radicals had done so much to oppose. Costly mistakes had been made. The forces of collectivism had exacted a heavy toll.

Laffargue illustrated his sombre picture of the problems of the contemporary world by citing a passage written before the war by Walter Lippmann, 'a great American, one of the most open minds of our era'. In his book *The Good Society*, Lippmann had posed an agonizing dilemma. The liberals are the inheritors of the science which truly interprets the progressive principle of the industrial revolution, but they have not been able to carry forward their science; they have not wrested from it a social philosophy which is humanly satisfactory. 'The collectivists, on the other hand, have the zest for progress, the sympathy for the poor, the burning sense of wrong, the impulse for great deeds, which have been lacking in latter-day liberalism, but their science is founded on a profound misunderstanding of the economy at the foundation of modern society and their actions, therefore, are deeply destructive and reactionary.'[34] Men, in Lippmann's words, were being offered impossible choices. 'They are asked to choose between the liberals who came to a dead stop—but stopped on the right road up to wealth and freedom and justice —and the collectivists who are in furious movement—but on a road that leads down to the abyss of tyranny, impoverishment, and general war.'

The tragic years that followed the publication of Lippmann's book provided Laffargue with additional documentation for his indictment of the collectivists. The world had gone even further down the road of collectivism, but the collectivists, unfortunately, 'were able to comprehend neither the errors nor failures of their system'. Liberalism, on the other hand, was being reborn everywhere. 'It has again found its writers and philosophers: in all the parliaments of Europe and under diverse titles it is regaining its position after a long eclipse.' The Radicals, with 'the support of other liberal elements', had returned to power in France—Queuille had just completed a year as premier—and this had constituted an important step in the liberal renaissance. The banners that brightened the hall in Toulouse where the *congressistes* were meeting—'A year of Radical arbitration, a year of French stability'—vividly described the Radicals' achievements.

---

[34] Walter Lippmann, *An Inquiry into the Principles of the Good Society*, Boston, 1938, p. 204.

I

The fears of Lippmann concerning the future of liberalism, Laffargue went on to say, were not being implemented. 'No,' he declared, 'liberalism had not been stopped, as Lippmann feared, on the right road up to wealth and freedom and justice; it is already on the move again.' Liberalism, Laffargue continued, was not the doctrine of facility. 'Free competition and free enterprise are dominated by the law of effort.' Liberalism was not the *laissez-faire* régime. 'It is the equality of the law for all in a regained liberty for each; it is the interest of the nation above the interest of the various syndicates.'

Ripened by war and by common ordeals, the 'new liberalism' had also become 'impregnated with humanity and had acquired the sense of solidarity, this suffering of injustices that had been lacking in old liberalism'. The new liberalism had studied the problems of the modern world that its ancestors had done so much to bring into being. It knew the difficulties of the task ahead; it was now time for liberals to arise and continue their crusade. It was impossible to compromise. 'There is no halfway mark,' Laffargue said, 'between a collectivist system and a liberal régime.' The Czechs had tried to compromise (Laffargue had been reading the memoirs of a former Czech minister), and when the last compromise had been reached, it was too late to save their country from servitude.

Laffargue's exhortations were welcomed with approval and enthusiasm by his listeners, and the themes he advanced were used on other occasions. A résumé of his ideas—'Georges Laffargue, *Sénateur de la Seine*, defends the thesis of liberal radicalism'—was published the following year in a semi-official history of radicalism.[35] In this presentation he particularly emphasized the role that the Radicals had played in the new rise of liberalism—'neo-liberalism, we are tempted to write'.

Other Radicals joined Laffargue in disavowing certain of the theories advanced by their liberal precursors and, like Laffargue, tried to define more tenable positions. In a speech in 1947 before the National Assembly, the president of the RGR, Gabriel Cudenet, pointed out that 'we are not fetishists of the old liberalism based on the Manchester school; we are not what might be called the legitimists of economics; but we believe that there is still room for a vast sector where a free economic system can

[35] Albert Milhaud, *Histoire du radicalisme*, Paris, 1951, pp. 404–406.

eign'.[36] He chose to ignore a contribution offered by André Philip, the Socialist Minister of the National Economy: 'You are not the legitimists but the *Orléanistes* of economics!'

The social ideas of the *néo-radicaux* were closely related to their positions on economic matters. Their economic doctrine was explicit in assigning a limited role to the State, and the latter precept found a logical expression in their position on social issues. In a speech in 1951, Martinaud-Déplat agreed that 'certainly, in the twentieth century, the State is obliged to orient and control', but added, 'there its role must end'.[37] In a joint article published in 1947, Laffargue and Lafay were more specific. 'The essential role of the State is to assure respect for the laws of commerce by protecting the legitimate interests of all, producers, merchants, and consumers, against the abuses of monopolies. It must arbitrate and prevent abuses but at the same time refrain from introducing vexatious rules into the operation of daily life.'[38]

Those who held these views concerning the proper functions of the State found much to attack in France's post-war social legislation. The *néo-radicaux* joined other Radicals in citing the long list of social measures that their party had helped to implement in the past, but they were quick to denounce what they considered to be the abuses and the scandals of France's new social measures. The generous post-war social security legislation was a subject of particular concern to *néo-radicaux*. Although they were willing to support the *principle* of social security—'a generous idea to which none of us can refuse his support when it is envisaged as a principle of solidarity among men of the same Nation'—they were less enthusiastic as to its *implementation*—' . . . but which must be managed intelligently and which must not be weighted down with a bureaucracy that renders it onerous'. This statement, made by Martinaud-Déplat at a meeting of the party's executive committee in May 1949, may be cited as indicative not only of *néo-radical* opinion but also as expressing a traditional Radical attitude. 'Human progress is infinite, on condition that it be carried out in stages.'[39]

Laffargue, who never ceased to denounce the 'gigantism' of social security, was emphatic in arguing that social progress had to be viewed in the context of economic realities. At the party's

[36] *Journal Officiel*, 20 February 1947, p. 404.   [37] *I.R.S.*, 28 June 1951.
[38] *Paris-Ville*, 22 September 1947.   [39] See above, p. 6.

congress in 1948, in a speech devoted to castigating 'an imbecile *dirigisme*, preface to an obsolete Marxism', Laffargue noted that the goal of social security—'to guarantee to all Frenchmen, in all periods of their existence, including diarrhoea, headaches, and haemorrhoids, security in all the acts of daily life'—was 'infinitely nobler' than that of other measures advanced by the collectivists and declared that social security was 'a great work', but went on to conclude that the basic problem was 'whether the nation had the means of offering itself this great work'.

France's social security system, therefore, was not only an example of 'monstrous statism'. In the opinion of the *néo-radicaux*, it was not economically viable. The great expenditures required to finance it were, in Laffargue's words, unmercifully added to net prices. Social security, therefore, 'under the pretext of insuring the working class, imposed enormous sacrifices on it'.[40]

While combating the evils of France's new social security system, the *néo-radicaux* also made suggestions for its amelioration. It was essential first that it be decentralized. In a speech at the party's congress in 1946, Lafay pointed out that under France's earlier social security systems participants had been able to choose the funds with which they wished to be affiliated, and employers had been insured against accidents by the company of their choice, but now, he declared, 'there is no freedom for anyone, the State seizes everything'. Social security should also be rendered more personal. 'Childbirth,' Lafay complained, 'submerged in the midst of other categories of social insurance, is considered by the administration as a misfortune on the same order as tuberculosis or the loss of a limb crushed by a machine.' Along with the need for far-reaching internal reforms, it was also necessary, he noted, that the social security system be administered by independent men who were not indebted to any party.

The *néo-radicaux* prided themselves on the practicability of the social measures they advanced. In an article published in 1949 Lafay was able to cite thirty specific measures sponsored by the Radical party during the previous two years.[41] These included legal authorization for the grafting of corneas, obligatory vaccination of all children against tuberculosis, and diverse measures

[40] *L'Unité française*, October 1950. Speech at *Salle Wagram*, Paris, during an RGR meeting, 13–14 October 1950.

[41] *I.R.S.*, September 1949.

elating to housing, school cafeterias, and the adoption of abandoned children. Other political groups could use extravagant
ocial programmes to further their political ambitions, but the
néo-radicaux were on the side of those men of experience and
wisdom who want 'social progress to be evolutionary, and not
o take place in disorder and revolution'.

*
* *

Another basic pillar of neo-radicalism was anti-communism.
The *néo-radicaux* were categorical on this point. In an article
published shortly before the 1951 elections, Laffargue, after
rhetorically asking 'what is our objective?', went on to answer:
'To assure the defeat of the Communists.'[42] The latter goal was,
in the hierarchy of priorities, of the greatest importance'. 'Italy
has just voted, and voted well; the free world is now waiting
or word from France.'

The *néo-radicaux* did all in their power to fight communism
and those who supported it. Jean-Paul David, described by some
of his opponents as 'the agent of America', played a central
role in this effort as secretary-general of *Paix-et-Liberté*, an
organization devoted to spreading anti-Communist propaganda.
Martinaud-Déplat, as Minister of Justice in the Faure, Pinay,
and Mayer governments of 1952 and 1953 and as Minister of
the Interior under Laniel in 1953–4, became known by his detractors as '*le McCarthy français*', particularly after the 'pigeon
episode' of the 28 May 1952, demonstration against General
Ridgway. Found near the scene of the rioting, the Communist
leader Jacques Duclos was arrested for 'conspiracy against the
safety of the state' after a loaded pistol, a truncheon, a wireless
transmitter, and two carrier pigeons had been found in his car.
After much publicity had been given to this episode, it was
determined that the pistol and truncheon belonged to his body-
guard, the transmitter was an ordinary car radio, and the two
pigeons were dead—according to Duclos, they had been destined
to be eaten *aux petits pois*.

The *néo-radicaux* also carried on their anti-Communist activities within the Radical party. They were, of course, in the vanguard of those who had fought the *radicaux de gauche* when the

[42] *I.R.S.*, June 1951.

latter were still in the party. In March 1952 the party's *Commission exécutive* issued a circular to all departmental federations asking that action be taken against any Radicals who participated in or supported organizations that were 'manifestly inspired or directed by the Communist Party'.[43] In a postscriptum, the circular noted that the organizations involved included the *Jacobins*.

Although certain of their colleagues may have been dubious of the efficacy of some of their methods and opposed the direction taken by some of their attacks, all had to agree to the sincerity of the *néo-radicaux'* anti-Communist sentiments. The same comment may be made concerning another pillar of neo-radicalism: the defence of the French Union. The latter 'defence', however, was to arouse even more difficulties within the party than the offence against the forces of communism.

The differences between Radicals on questions relating to the French Union did not become extreme until the latter part of the *néo-radicaux'* sojourn in the party. During the early post-war years the old Third Republic Radicals and the new Fourth Republic Radicals presented a relatively united front on issues concerning the organization and the operation of the new French Union. As was noted in an earlier chapter, virtually all Radicals, led by Herriot, had strongly opposed the constitutional proposals made in the two Constituent Assemblies, which in Herriot's much-quoted words would have made France 'a colony of her colonies'.

During the following years, this dire possibility continued to arouse the concern of Radicals who feared, in particular, the 'colonization' of their familiar parliamentary scene by new overseas deputies. The narrow political margins of the early post-war assemblies contributed to Radical misgivings. In the Second Constituent Assembly, for example, the deputies for metropolitan France were evenly divided between Marxists and non-Marxists.[44] The deputies from overseas France, many of whom were willing to ally themselves with the Communists, were therefore in a very strategic position. In September 1946, after a cherished Radical amendment had been defeated by a vote of 275 to 273

[43] Radical party archives. Circular of 3 March 1952.

[44] Among the deputies from metropolitan France in the Second Constituent Assembly, there were 146 Communists and 115 Socialists, making a total of 261 Marxists. There were 160 MRP deputies, 39 RGR, and 62 Moderates, making a total of 261 non-Marxists.

in the National Assembly, a leader of a right-wing party wryly exclaimed to his fellow deputies: 'The Malagasy are making the laws!'[45]

A more spectacular example of this paradoxical form of 'colonization' was provided by prognostications and preparations made prior to the January 1947 presidential elections. In his pre-election calculations, Vincent Auriol, the Socialist candidate, counted on having the support of slightly less than the absolute majority necessary for his election, and in order for his victory to be certain, he was hopefully awaiting the arrival of eleven coloured parliamentarians whom Jules Moch, the Socialist Minister of Transport, had promised to have brought from Equatorial Africa in a special plane. Pacing in the corridors of the Palais-Bourbon during the night before the election, one Radical deputy expressed his dismay at this state of affairs by repeatedly declaring: 'When I think that the choice of the first magistrate is going to depend on eleven Negroes dropped from the sky!'[46]

The *néo-radicaux* did their best to lessen the recurrence of such situations by vigorously advocating the establishment of the double electoral college system in overseas territories. In the eyes of its supporters, the major virtue of this system was that, by relegating the bulk of the native populations to the second college, the white elements would not be submerged under the weight of superior numbers. In a speech at the party's congress in 1946, Maniglier was particularly forceful in denouncing proposals for a single electoral college in 'Black Africa'. There was not an appreciable difference between Berbers and whites, he argued, but the African Negro, he went on to exclaim, 'does not know the meaning of the words "democracy", "proportional representation", "bicameralism"—words that cannot even be translated into his language—and it is to him, to the man who goes about naked all day long, that you wish to accord equality in electoral matters!' Calling for an end to demagogy, Maniglier asked that more schools be constructed.

Radicals also provided strong support for the successful campaign in the Second Constituent Assembly to establish a separate Algerian Assembly; the alternative plan would have doubled

---

[45] *Journal Officiel*, 11 September 1946, p. 3657. Jean Legendre, then a member of the conservative PRL, later a member of the RPF.

[46] Roger Priouret, *La République des partis*, Paris, 1947, pp. 11–12.

Algerian representation in Paris. They also favoured the formation of the Assembly of the French Union. When compared to
the National Assembly, the new assembly provided an im-
measurably less influential forum to which the bulk of France's
overseas representatives could be assigned and at the same time
constituted a not-to-be-neglected haven for politically ambitious
Radicals—including those who had been or were to be defeated
in attempts to become members of the National Assembly.

In the formulation of the Algerian Statute in July and August
1947, Radicals were once again in the vanguard of those who
opposed any abandonment or limitation of French sovereignty.
by threatening to leave Ramadier's government, they won a series
of concessions insuring the maintenance of close ties between
Algeria and metropolitan France and the continued predominance of the latter. Socialists had attempted to substitute a single
college for the double college; Radicals were instrumental in
foiling this attempt. René Mayer, who served as the party's
principal spokesman in the long series of debates in the National
Assembly that preceded the final vote, was eloquent and insistent
in expressing France's right to be proud of her record in Algeria. [47]

Stalwart support for the system of two electoral colleges in
Algeria and in the territories of the French Union must be added,
therefore, to any list of the tenets of post-war neo-radicalism.
Faced with the opportunity of faithfully following the principles
of 1789 and the hallowed doctrine of universal suffrage, the *néo-
radicaux*, along with nearly all Radicals, chose to align themselves
with the more adaptable Radical tradition that placed primary
emphasis on realism, logic, and progress by stages. Speaking in
the name of the Radical party in a debate in the National Assembly
on 24 April 1951, Henri Caillavet forcefully defended this position against the attacks of Fily-Dabo Sissoko and Léopold-Sédar
Senghor, coloured deputies from French Sudan and from Senegal.
In answer to Senghor's remark that 33 per cent. of France's
population was illiterate when universal suffrage was introduced,
Caillavet pointed out that France's cultural heritage, inspired by
the Greeks and the Romans, was nearly 2,000 years old and that
'in 1789 France was already a highly evolved country'. Majority
rule was admissible for an ethnically unified state, but not for

---

[47] *Journal Officiel*, 10 August 1947, pp. 4199–200; and 22 August 1947, pp.
4534–40. See also *L'Année politique*, 1947, p. 139, pp. 148–52.

a territory composed of men who were of different races and very dissimilarly evolved. 'I say it frankly, M. Senghor,' said Caillavet, 'the conception of the modern world is inconceivable at the level of the tribe.'

In the years that followed the establishment of the French Union, the *néo-radicaux* continued to eulogize France's past achievements in her overseas territories and were in the forefront of those who called for firm measures against secession movements. On learning of the outbreak of hostilities in Indo-China in December 1946, *La Dépêche de Paris*—directed by Martinaud-Déplat—declared, in an editorial published on 22 December and entitled 'The Flag Is Engaged', that the situation required firmness. 'One does not argue with assassins and rebels.' Along with Moderates and members of the MRP, Radicals argued that it was necessary to break the insurrection in Indo-China with force and upheld the viewpoint that France should not undertake negotiations that were doomed to failure. During subsequent years, the *néo-radicaux* saw no reason to alter this viewpoint.

Of much closer concern to most *néo-radicaux* was France's position in North Africa. In a speech at the 1946 Congress, Auguste Rencurel, who served as deputy from Algiers in the two Constituent Assemblies and in the 1946–51 legislature, expressed his shock at the idea that people could even discuss the question of whether Algeria could remain French. Algeria, he said, 'this admirable province which we are happy to call France's oldest daughter and which is the keystone of all our colonial Empire', had been built by the 'heroic efforts of our soldiers, of our farmers, of our officials, of our religious and laic missionaries, of our workers, of all these sons of France'. France had not destroyed the natives, but in one century had increased their numbers from one to eight million. French colonists had created and equipped twenty-one great ports, had built 80,000 kilometres of roads, had drained swamps and irrigated plains. To Rencurel, an ex-army officer who had led overseas troops in battle and who had been wounded five times, the only course to follow was that of continued close association between Moslems and European French, 'with the French element never losing its absolutely normal role of tutelary leadership in an area that we consider specifically French'.

Similar arguments were also advanced in regard to Morocco

and Tunisia. The *néo-radicaux* were particularly adamant concerning the latter. In a speech at the party's congress in 1946, Robert Scemama, president of the Radical Federation of Tunisia, declared that France had the right to say that Tunisia is 'as French as it is Tunisian'. He went on to explain that Tunisia, 'the crossroads of races', had been the 'ancestral land of Latin and Christian civilization before becoming Arab', but that the mixed Mediterranean races that had lived there 'had been subjected to the violent and tyrannical influence of the Arabs who had colonized them'. France had brought order and progress to Tunisia; no Frenchman worthy of the name could allow France's sovereignty to be put in question.

There were other ingredients in the *néo-radicaux*' Tunisian programme. In 1952, the RGR newspaper *L'Unité française* proclaimed that 'The RGR has long since taken its position on the Tunisian question: it is for firmness and justice, for order and for reforms; by acting on these principles one is certain of following the right road.'[48] Their primary emphasis, however, was on the maintenance of French sovereignty. Their fury was great after Mendès-France's spectacular visit to Tunis on 31 July 1954. By proposing that a new Tunisian government be formed to negotiate new conventions with France, Mendès-France had prepared the way for the internal sovereignty of Tunisia.

In both the National Assembly and the *Conseil de la République*, the bitterest opposition to this plan came from the ranks of the *néo-radicaux*. On learning of Mendès-France's trip to Tunis, Borgeaud immediately called a meeting of the RGR group in the *Conseil de la République* where, joined by his fellow senator, Antoine Colonna of Tunisia, he strongly denounced Mendès-France's actions. Martinaud-Déplat led the attack in a meeting of the Radical party's group in the National Assembly and in subsequent parliamentary debates. In a violent exchange with Mendès-France in the National Assembly on 10 August, he declared that there was 'a direct and evident connexion' between Mendès-France's trip to Tunis and the 'events of Fez and Petitjean' in which many French residents of Morocco had been murdered by terrorists. After painting a grim picture of the Tunisian Néo-Destour movement and castigating the activities of its leader, Habib Bourguiba, Martinaud-Déplat warned that if

[48] *L'Unité française,* February-March 1952.

Léon Martinaud-Déplat

France, 'instead of defending itself, negotiates with assassins, new crimes will succeed old ones, and France, *Monsieur le Président du Conseil*, one day bloodless, will find itself reduced to its metropolitan size, too small in a modern world to permit it to play a role of a great power'.

Later in the same debate, when Mendès-France noted that there were several nuances in Bourguiba's party, he was greeted with 'laughs and exclamations on the right' and was interrupted by a Socialist deputy who interjected: 'Like the Radical party!' In retrospect, however, it is clear that at least as far as the Radical party was concerned, more than controllable nuances of opinion were involved: a new turning point in the party's evolution had been reached. Mendès-France's actions in Indo-China and his lack of support for the European Defence Community had earned for him the bitter dislike of the MRP. His actions in North Africa, and in particular Tunisia, were to win him the enmity of the *néo-radicaux*. Bitterly hated for his actions in Tunisia and for his presumed projects in Algeria and Morocco, Mendès-France was to reap the harvest of the *néo-radicaux*' opposition when the National Assembly, after listening to an aroused René Mayer, voted him out of office in February 1955.

The *néo-radicaux*, in turn, were to reap *their* harvest after Mendès-France gained control of the Radical party's administrative machinery three months later. Issues relating to non-metropolitan France were long ignored by most Radicals during the Third Republic. During the Fourth Republic, however, they not only had constituted a major source of concern but had provided an ideological and political gulf that contemporary Radicals found impossible to bridge.

*
* *

After the elections of 1951 France's political parties were confronted with yet another source of bitter discord: German rearmament. The latter issue, particularly when viewed in the total context of the European unification movement, was to constitute an important new criterion of neo-radicalism.

It can be argued that the *néo-radicaux*' support for the successive projects that were designed to promote European unity constituted a logical continuation of their ideas on economic and political questions. In their eyes, and according to their conceptions, the construction of a 'new' Europe would provide the wide scope necessary for the implementation of their economic ideas and at the same time would constitute a bulwark against communism. The challenge and the magnitude of the task of creating the new Europe was in keeping with the *néo-radicaux'* desire for new and dynamic solutions for their country's problems. In the forefront of those who were becoming impregnated with a European *mystique* ('We are the promontory of a small peninsula, but we remain the beacon of a civilization whose light still sweeps over continents'),[49] the *néo-radicaux* saw the creation of a new and unified Europe as a necessary condition for the survival and propagation of their most fundamental beliefs.

Along with most of the exponents of a unified Europe, the *néo-radicaux* accorded highest priority to economic unification. They were eloquent in support of the first major step that was taken towards this end: The European Coal and Steel Community. In a speech at the party's congress at Bordeaux in 1952, Laffargue—who was a member of the new organization's Assembly—decried those who wanted political unity to precede economic unity. 'Ah! I beg of you,' he exclaimed, 'let us not always go against the current of history. All national units were born from economic communities. The War of Secession was a tariff war. The political unity of England followed long after its economic union. When Bismarck wanted to create Germany he created the Zollverein.'

At a meeting of the party's executive committee five months later, Laffargue went so far as to advance the creation of Europe as a central object of radicalism. 'Old party of the end of the nineteenth century,' he proclaimed, 'you can become the great party of the end of the twentieth century if you are able to seize the magnificent opportunity that is offered to you.' After describing the attributes of the new Europe (an open and free market, free competition, the free movement of riches, capital and men, and the free convertibility of money), Laffargue went on to ask his listeners: 'Do you not hear ascending in the night of history the voices of your illustrious predecessors?'

The great majority of Laffargue's contemporary Radicals were willing to join him in supporting the creation of the European Coal and Steel Community. In the three crucial votes in December

[49] Georges Laffargue, *Congrès extraordinaire*, May 1951.

1951 by which the National Assembly granted its approval of the new project, no Radical had cast a negative ballot.[50] This degree of unity, however, did not survive the addition of German rearmament to the agenda of the proponents of European unification. The European Defence Community, dedicated to the cause of unity and co-operation among its proposed member nations, was to distinguish itself in France for causing bitter disunity among Frenchmen. And, in the long controversies that ensued, the Radical party was to remain, more than ever, faithful to its traditional task of reflecting French opinion.

None of the Radical party's deputies in the National Assembly voted against an order of the day passed on 25 October 1950, in which France's representatives, accepting the eventuality of German rearmament, specifically noted their determination 'not to permit a German army and general staff to be recreated'. On 19 February 1952, the National Assembly, in a confidence vote sponsored by the Faure government, approved the principle of the EDC but attached many reservations. In the latter vote, seven Radicals, including Daladier, were among the opposition. In October of the same year came the 'bomb' of the Radical party's congress at Bordeaux: Herriot and Daladier, in eloquent and moving speeches, voiced their strong opposition to the proposed project. The unity of their appeal was particularly striking in view of the many years of differences of opinion between '*les deux Edouards*' on foreign policy questions. Noting that the Radical party had to be given credit for opening a debate that had been 'haunting the consciences of all of us', *Le Monde* expressed the general relief that the problem was now before the public.[51] During the nearly two years that followed before the EDC was rejected by the National Assembly on 30 August 1954, Radical spokesmen were to provide what were probably the most eloquent arguments for each side.

In this 'great debate', the *néo-radicaux* played a prominent role among the pro-EDC forces. One of their major tasks was to rise in defence of the EDC in the often stormy and hostile atmosphere of Radical party congresses. René Mayer was conspicuous

---

[50] *Journal Officiel*, 11 December 1951, pp. 9048–9; 13 December 1951, pp. 9142–4. The votes were 376–240, 377–235, and 377–233. All Radicals voted in favour in the first vote, and two abstained in the latter two.

[51] *Le Monde*, 21 October 1952.

for his skill and perseverance in performing this service. Speaking after Herriot and Daladier at the Bordeaux congress, he was forceful in presenting the reasons for which he was 'not entirely in accord' with 'the two men who are the chiefs of our party'. Stressing the need for France to admit new ideas, Mayer stated that if there were not a change in the relationships between the countries of Western Europe there could be no permanent peace. Germany, he argued, could not be occupied indefinitely. Mayer had recently seen a field in Yugoslavia where the Germans had tied and shot 7,000 people in one twenty-four-hour period during the war, but Yugoslavia's leaders, he noted, considered German rearmament as inevitable and necessary. Germans were needed for the defence of Europe. Americans were also necessary, and the defeat of the EDC project, Mayer warned his listeners, might lead the United States to change to a peripheral defence strategy.

At the same dramatic congress, Laffargue, too, supported the EDC and also was eloquent in stressing the need for new ideas. Noting that England and France had long been opposed to each other on battlefields and were now bound together in close friendship, Laffargue stressed the great service that had been rendered by 'those who lifted the mortgage that so long had burdened their relationship'.

The *néo-radicaux* continued to speak in defence of the EDC until the bitter end, and then joined those who reproached Mendès-France for the role that he played in the treaty's defeat. The latter attitude may be cited as an additional characteristic that differentiated *néo-radicaux* from most of their more benevolent fellow Radicals. In the critical vote of 30 August 1954, twenty-nine Radicals voted in favour of the motion—for which Herriot was one of the sponsors—that signalled the end of the EDC. Thirty-one Radical deputies, including Jean-Paul David, Lafay, Martinaud-Déplat, and Mayer, had supported the EDC by voting against the motion. Eight had abstained, and one was absent. Six weeks later, in discussing the manner in which the EDC had 'passed directly from the refrigerator to the coffin', one orator at the party's congress at Marseilles noted that the party's deputies had split down the middle, but more tolerant on this point than most of the *néo-radicaux*, he went on to conclude that despite their differences of opinion all had been guided by 'the same passionate desire to serve the Republic and our liberties, France, and peace.'[52]

After the defeat of the EDC, the *néo-radicaux* continued to support European unification projects, and the latter continued to provide a source of discord for Radicals. The end of the EDC did not mean a return to the unanimity that prevailed at the time of the Coal and Steel Community vote. On 11 July 1956, the French National Assembly voted 332 to 151 in favour of Euratom, a new major step towards European unity. Twenty-eight Radical deputies were in favour, twenty-six were opposed, and two abstained. All members of the new RGR group, except Faure who was absent, voted in favour. Several months earlier, Mayer, who was not a deputy in the 1956 legislature, had replaced Jean Monnet as president of the European Coal and Steel Community. Whether inside or out of the Radical party, the men who have been described as *néo-radicaux* remained in the vanguard of those who were devoting themselves to the arduous task of 'creating Europe'.

*

* *

In a poll taken in France in September 1951 to find which problems were causing the greatest concern to the French public, investigators reported that second place was shared by German rearmament and the Church schools—both were well behind 'the price of meat' and slightly ahead of 'events in Korea'.[53] During the same month the National Assembly found it necessary to devote thirty-five sessions to debating two bills that were designed to provide financial assistance to Church schools. There was no doubt that in mid-twentieth-century France the old problem of Church and State relations could still arouse deep and bitter emotions. The separation of Church and State had been the Radical party's greatest victory in the early part of the century, and laicism long was considered to be the central feature of radicalism. What was the attitude of the party's *néo-radicaux* concerning this venerable and persistent problem?

[52] Henry Laforest, deputy from Dordogne.

[53] *Sondages*, 1951, no. 3, p. 11. The percentages were as follows: price of meat, 33 per cent.; German rearmament and Church schools, 15 per cent. each; events in Korea, 14 per cent.; social security deficit, 9 per cent.; Iranian oil, 5 per cent. The poll was taken 20–30 September 1951.

A study of the public statements and parliamentary votes of contemporary Radicals reveals that many of them have been, at most, lukewarm in supporting anti-clerical policies. And, of all Radicals, the most half-hearted supporters of laicism were found among the *néo-radicaux*. Some of the latter, indeed, had 'pro-clerical' voting records that could match those of the most devout MRP deputies. It must be noted, however, that Radicals who supported legislation favoured by the Church did not do so for religious reasons. Their motivations were not doctrinal, but electoral. Those Radicals—most notably the *néo-radicaux*—who represented right-wing constituencies found it eminently natural to vote in keeping with the desires of their electoral supporters, both past and potential.

During the post-war years the most faithful adherents of strict laicism were certain of the *radicaux de gauche* and the bulk of the *radicaux classiques*. Along with the *radicaux gaullistes*, the *néo-radicaux* were at the opposite end of the spectrum. Most of the latter preferred not to make an issue of a problem that they considered as out-of-date in modern France. More outspoken than most of his colleagues, Maniglier bluntly expressed this opinion when he pleaded with his listeners at the party's *Assemblée générale* in January 1946 to forget these 'questions of exclusions and personalities, these questions of Freemasonry, of radicalism, etc.' Although he was a freethinker, he added, he did not care if his wife went to church. Maniglier concluded his remarks by reminding his fellow Radicals that the French Union included Buddhists, people who obeyed God or Allah, and fetichists. 'Certain of those who voted for me,' he noted, 'have four wives and four concubines.'

At the same meeting, a woman delegate from the south-western *département* of Charente-Maritime presented a contrary opinion.[54] After noting the party's lack of feminine supporters, she explained: 'But, *Messieurs*, if the women are not with you it is your fault. Why? It is because you do not have *la foi laïque*! How many of you have I seen who have sent their wives to mass, who have had their children baptized and who were married in church? (applause). If you do not fight against the Church,' she warned, 'it will fight against you (applause).' 'I have had in my hands a history book used in Church schools; it treated the

54 Madame Gresse.

French Revolution as ignominious,' she added, and then went on to conclude: '*Messieurs*, the Church is, after all, superstition. Believe me that in the countryside there is a great task to be carried out.'

During the years that followed, most Radicals made it clear that they were willing to leave this 'great task' to others. Along with Communists (who found in laicism an excellent issue with which to drive a wedge between the Socialist party and the MRP), Socialists were to become the primary champions of the old Radical war-cry. Basing their attitudes primarily on their personal electoral situations, Radicals were increasingly inclined towards moderation and indifference.

The lack of Radical unity concerning this early basic tenet of radicalism was to become particularly evident when Radical deputies were confronted in the National Assembly with issues involving Church–State relations. It was on the latter occasions that the *néo-radicaux*, joined by many colleagues who did not share certain of their other attitudes, were to provide the most striking evidence of their lack of concern for what had been the issue closest to the hearts of most of their predecessors.

The first major post-war parliamentary vote concerning Church schools took place on 14 May 1948, when by a vote of 297 to 267 the National Assembly decided that twenty-eight Catholic schools which had belonged to nationalized mining companies should be brought under the State system. Nineteen Radical deputies voted in favour, seven abstained, and sixteen, including Jean-Paul David, Edgar Faure, Emile Hugues, and Gabriel Cudenet, were opposed. The line of division in the voting had passed through the middle of the Radical party. Embittered in their defeat, members of the MRP had been separated from their Socialist colleagues. This pattern of behaviour was to become familiar with the passage of time and the repeated efforts of both sides to advance their respective causes.

After the 1951 elections parties favourable to the demands of the Church schools for financial assistance had, for the first time since the Liberation, a majority in the National Assembly. In their election campaigns, MRP, RPF, and Moderate candidates had been insistent in stressing their desire that public funds should be granted Church schools—in 1941 Pétain had given a substantial state subsidy to Church schools, a subsidy which de

Gaulle's provisional government had let lapse in 1945. After
their success at the polls, the supporters of State grants were
determined to press their advantage. In a speech on All Saints'
Day, Paul Antier, who had just been appointed Minister of Agriculture, noted that 'for the first time a Government is being
formed with a majority favourable to Church schools', and said
that 'all my zeal and that of my friends will be, as it has always
been, at the service of this cause'.[55] He concluded by asking his
listeners 'to pray to the Virgin Mary to enlighten and bless the
politicians who are determined to carry to a successful conclusion
the reforms necessary to give at last to France *la justice scolaire.*'

In the ensuing *mêlée*, in which Socialists and Communists bitterly opposed the MRP, the RPF, and the Moderates, the Radical
deputies—in the words of the reporter on National Assembly
activities at the party's congress in Lyons later that year—'tried
to conciliate, rightly or wrongly, the categorical imperatives of
doctrine with governmental exigencies and the necessity of avoiding a governmental crisis whose consequences could have been
grave'. This task of conciliation proved to be an onerous one.
Two bills were advanced for consideration by the embattled
deputies. The first one, a governmental bill sponsored by André
Marie, the Radical Minister of Education, extended the granting
of State scholarships to students attending private secondary
schools. After long and stormy debates, this bill was adopted
on 4 September 1951, by 361 votes to 236. Twenty-eight Radicals were opposed, twelve abstained, and twenty-five, including
Jean-Paul David, Emile Hugues, Lafay, Martinaud-Déplat, and
René Mayer, voted in favour.

Of much greater significance was the famous Barangé law,
which was passed on 10 September 1951. Sponsored by an
MRP deputy, Charles Barangé, and an RPF deputy, Edmond
Barrachin, this bill provided for quarterly grants of 1,000 francs
for each student attending primary school, whether public or
private; in the case of students attending private schools, the
grants would go to parents' associations which would admini-
ster their usage. In the tumultuous debates that followed the
introduction of this bill in the National Assembly, Radical
spokesmen stressed the need for moderation. On one occasion,

---

[55] Published by the Catholic newspaper, *La Croix*. Cited by Maurice Deixonne,
Journal Officiel, 29 August 1951, p. 6577.

Canon Kir, a Catholic clergyman serving as Mayor of Dijon and deputy from Côte-d'Or, pointed out that in a secular grammar the phrase 'the soul is immortal' had been replaced by 'the donkey is patient'—a laic '*âne*' being preferred to a clerical '*âme*'. Speaking in the name of the Radical party, René Billères noted that the authors of the grammar had not written 'the soul is not immortal' and observed that the patience and gentleness of a donkey 'would not be superfluous in our Assembly'.[56] To Billères the Assembly was engaged in a 'great debate' ('This dialogue between Voltaire and Pascal which, incidentally, is carried on sometimes in the depths of each of us'), but in his opinion it was also an archaic one. 'It resuscitates old oppositions and hostilities, dead passions, buried quarrels.'

The strongest initiative taken by the Radicals during the debate on the Barangé law was an attempt to postpone it. Speaking in the name of his party, the veteran Radical deputy Alfred Jules-Julien, who was a close friend and colleague of Herriot, advanced a motion that would have adjourned the debate until the end of the following month. The intensity of Radical support for this measure was illustrated by a rare occurrence: the party decreed that, except for ministers, *discipline de vote* would be required. This Radical initiative was defeated, however, on 5 September by 333 votes to 267. Four Radical members of the government abstained, two Radicals—including Lafay—were 'excused or absent on leave', and two, ignoring the *discipline de vote*, voted against the measure. Five deputies, *apparentés* to the Radical party, joined their two colleagues who voted in opposition.

The Barangé law was finally passed on 10 September 1951, by a vote of 313 to 255. Forty-four Radicals voted against it, fifteen abstained, and six Radicals voted in favour. Those who voted in favour had earned the undying enmity of those Radicals who were still militant anti-clericals, but the latter phenomena were not of great concern to the six Radical supporters of the Barangé law. Two of them, Lafay and André Hugues, were deputies from Paris; another, Jean-Paul David, represented the neighbouring *département* of Seine-et-Oise. None of their constituencies was noted for anti-clericalism, nor were those of

[56] *Journal Officiel*, 6 September 1951, p. 6988. A practising Catholic, Billères is also 'a sincere laic Radical', in the words of a later Radical opponent, Charles Hernu. *Le Jacobin*, 12 July 1954.

Menouar Saiah, a deputy from Algiers, and Pierre Bourdellès, a deputy from Catholic Brittany.[57] René Mayer, Faure, Marie, Queuille, and Bourgès-Maunoury were among those Radicals who abstained. Martinaud-Déplat, from Bouches-du-Rhône in the anti-clerical *Midi*, was among the forty-four Radicals who voted in opposition. It was evident that the 'categorical imperatives of doctrine' were not of primary concern. Voting was regional more than doctrinal, with deputies' attitudes reflecting their personal electoral situations.

The subsequent parliamentary votes on Church and State issues were not enveloped with the great symbolic significance that was attached to the Barangé law, but they continued to be a fertile source of controversy. In November 1952 the examination of a National Education budget gave the National Assembly another opportunity to discuss state aid to Church schools: Article Six in the proposed budget extended state grants for higher education to students in private schools. Once more Socialists led the battle against the clericals, and once more Radicals were reticent and divided. Violently denouncing the measure in a speech in the National Assembly during a debate late in the night of 8 November 1952 ('this early morning hour propitious to all crimes'), Maurice Deixonne, a fiery Socialist spokesman, thundered that the next morning the taxpayers would be astounded to learn that, 'while sleeping the sleep of the just', they had once more been the victims of the 'famous de Léotard–de Tinguy–de Pouët gang of gentlemen-bandits'. The 'hold-up', he declared, amounted to 177 million francs. There was no money for war veterans or reconstruction, but 'for the *curés*, all that they want!' Deixonne was particularly bitter regarding André Marie, the Radical Minister of Education. 'And, you, *Monsieur le Ministre, grand maître de l'université*,' he asked, 'is not your conscience troubled by the work on which you are made to collaborate?' Citing the precedent of a Socialist Minister of Education who, abandoned by his premier, had walked back to the Socialist benches in order to show that 'if clericalism prevailed, he

[57] Radical deputies from Brittany are a rare phenomenon, but the sixth Radical deputy who voted for the Barangé law, Jacques Ducreux, from Vosges, was an even rarer one. After the latter's death in an automobile accident in February 1952 it was discovered that his real name was Jacques Tacnet. A fugitive from justice he had served as an agent for a Nazi propaganda organization during the war *L'Année politique*, 1952, p. 29.

preferred to give up his portfolio rather than retain it dirtied', Deixonne told Marie that he missed two opportunities to leave and was now missing a third. After stating that 'my heart tightens when I happen to cross columns of children led by priests or nuns', the Socialist spokesman concluded by proclaiming to Marie 'the celebrated expression that has not reverberated within these walls for a long time: *"Le clericalisme, voilà l'ennemi!"* ' The old Radical slogan, however, did not arouse much emotion among contemporary Radicals. The measure was passed by a vote of 355 to 240. Twenty-three Radicals voted in favour, thirty-four were opposed, and eight abstained. Lafay, Jean-Paul David, Martinaud-Déplat, and René Mayer were among those in favour.

It was undeniable that Radicals in the mid-twentieth century were no longer militant concerning an issue that had been the touchstone of existence to many of their predecessors. The mantle of anti-clericalism had clearly passed to their colleagues on the left. The latter, it must also be noted, had also inherited many of the followers of the early Radicals. The *néo-radicaux* were in the vanguard of the Radical movement away from anti-clericalism, but they were not alone. Additional evidence for the latter point was to be provided in the new 1956 legislature—when the *néo-radicaux* were no longer in the Radical party. In two votes in February 1956, the National Assembly expressed its will that a debate of the abrogation of the Barangé law be postponed. The first vote, on 17 February, was passed by 288 to 279. Seventeen Radicals were in favour, thirty-one opposed, and five abstained. On 24 February, when the margin was 294 to 281, sixteen Radicals favoured a postponement, thirty-three were opposed, and four abstained. In both votes all the members of the new RGR party—ten full members and four *apparentés*—voted in favour of delaying the debates. It was a group of young *radicaux mendésistes*, however, who by voting with the pro-clericals had been instrumental in bringing about a postponement. Although they were hostile to the Barangé law, they felt that before the Assembly took up the problem it was 'necessary to have a calming of spirits'.[58]

---

[58] *Le Monde*, 26–27 February 1956. Some *radicaux mendésistes* were to declare later that it was a great mistake not to have forced a vote on the Barangé law in 1956, as this would have led to a split between Guy Mollet and the Right. The attractiveness of such a prospect, they argued, would have justified the use of laicism as a *cheval de bataille*.

Whether in or out of the party, the *néo-radicaux* varied from grudging approval to stalwart opposition to anti-clerical stands —their spectrum ranged from Martinaud-Déplat's vote against the Barangé law to Lafay's unfailing allegiance to a strict 'pro-clerical' line. None of the *néo-radicaux*, certainly, may be described as a doctrinaire anti-clerical. Of all of the characteristics of neo-radicalism, however, it may be said that a lack of strong feelings on laicism is the one that has found the most general acceptance among all contemporary Radicals.

*

* *

What general conclusions may be reached concerning the ideas of the *néo-radicaux* and the role that this group of men played in the Radical party? What was their significance in the contemporary evolution of radicalism?

We have seen that many of the *néo-radicaux*' characteristics and opinions were shared, in varying degrees, with other members of the Radical party. The viewpoints of the *néo-radicaux*, whether concerning economic questions, foreign policy, the French Union, or Church schools, often coincided with those of other Radicals. And, moreover, lack of unity could often be attenuated by enveloping controversial issues in the familiar shrouds of republican oratory. There were, of course, occasions when differences of opinion were spectacular, but this too was another characteristic tradition of radicalism.

What made the *néo-radicaux*' position unique was the degree to which they advanced their ideas and, in addition, the methods that they employed in their support. A third crucial factor was the emergence on that Radical scene of an unprecedented phenomenon: Pierre Mendès-France.

Although the *néo-radicaux* had much in common with many of their fellow Radicals, they had at least as much in common with political groups on the right of the Radicals. There was no doubt that Martinaud-Déplat was thinking primarily of his own brand of radicalism when he wrote, in 1949, that Reynaud had not been mistaken in declaring that there was 'a nearly complete identity of opinion concerning doctrine between his Independents and our Radicals'.[59] A predilection for forming political

59 *I.R.S.*, 2 June 1949

friendships outside the Radical party was probably inevitable for those who occupied the extreme positions on the wide Radical spectrum. It was, however, by too enthusiastically following this natural predilection that the *néo-radicaux*, like the *radicaux de gauche*, contributed to their own fall from Radical grace.

The *néo-radicaux*' desire and ability to win right-wing friends had found a particularly graphic expression in the *Rassemblement des Gauches républicaines*—an organization that, despite its name, was primarily devoted to gaining allies on the right. The devotion of the *néo-radicaux* to promoting unity with the political forces on their right did not decline with the advancing years. Laffargue was expressing a typical *néo-radical* viewpoint when, speaking of the leaders of right-wing political groups in a speech at a banquet given by *Réconciliation française* in 1950, he proclaimed that, 'in the name of the entire RGR, I extend my hand to you, my friend Duchet, on one side, and my friend Betolaud, on the other'. [60]

A particularly significant point in the evolution of such friendships was reached after the beginning of the 1951–6 legislature. Prior to this date, Socialists had participated in France's successive governments, but after 1951 Radicals constituted the left side of subsequent governmental coalitions. The Radical party, traditionally a link between the Right and the Left, was now faced almost exclusively towards the former. By deflecting their party away from its traditional role as a link between Socialists and the Right and by extending their hands only to the latter, the *néo-radicaux* facilitated the rise of the *radicaux mendésistes* and, at the same time, their own downfall.

The *néo-radicaux* also went too far afield in the methods that they utilized. There is no doubt that Radicals have never distinguished themselves for a puritanical attitude towards their party's statutes. The flexibility of the party's doctrine has traditionally been rivalled only by the flexibility of its structure. Towards the end of the *néo-radicaux*' reign, however, even the most understanding of their colleagues began to rebel at certain of the methods being employed.

Dissatisfaction with the methods of certain of the *néo-radicaux*

---

[60] *Le Rhône Républicain. Journal mensuel du* R.G.R. *pour la région rhodanienne*, Lyons, May 1950. Roger Duchet was secretary-general of the *Centre National des Indépendants et Paysans*; Robert Betolaud, a member of the conservative PRL.

was greatly augmented by the actions of the latter at the party's congress held at Marseilles in October 1954. This congress was a great personal triumph for Mendès-France: the delegates gave him great ovations, and Herriot, in a gesture that was completely unprecedented, reverently bowed before him 'my person and my past'. At the same congress, however, Martinaud-Déplat—whose virulent attack in the National Assembly a few weeks earlier against Mendès-France's North African policies was only one example of the differences between the two Radicals—was able to retain his position as the party's administrative president in a bitter electoral struggle with Daladier.

The congress had been carefully prepared by Martinaud-Déplat, who in addition to his long period at the helm of the party's administrative machinery, was also able to draw on his experiences as Minister of the Interior. Marseilles, the site of the congress, was the centre of his personal political fief. He controlled the party's machinery and was a close friend of Vincent Delpuech, the party's affluent treasurer. Federations that were under his control received a large influx of members shortly before the congress took place. The *rapporteurs* were chosen from among Radicals not favourable to Mendès-France. It was clear that Daladier, when he announced his candidacy for the post occupied by Martinaud-Déplat, was confronted with a task of considerable proportions. In addition to the resources of his opponent, he also had to face the neutrality of Mendès-France and the personal hostility of many of the younger delegates who found it difficult to accept the former premier as a symbol of their party's renovation.

The ensuing election was marked with confusion, controversy, and charges of irregularities. Many delegates voted on behalf of absent colleagues, and there was minimum of verification of credentials. When the results were announced (Daladier had lost by only fifty-seven votes, receiving 689 votes as compared to Martinaud-Déplat's 746), there was a 'violent tumult' during which, in *Le Monde*'s words, 'the re-elected president remained undisturbed at his place and tried to smile'.[61] Shortly afterwards, Marcel Perrin, a close friend and colleague of the defeated candidate, issued a communiqué to the press denouncing the result of 'a vote falsified by the massive use of the membership cards

[61] *Le Monde*, 19 October 1954.

of delegates absent from the congress'.[62] The victor answered
that the voting method used was the same as that which had
been employed when Daladier was elected president of the party
in 1927 and when Herriot had defeated Daladier for the presidency in 1949. This explanation, however, did not suffice to
assuage the feelings of his aroused and outraged opponents.

The latter were to get their revenge at the party's special congress on 4 May 1955. In the meantime, Mendès-France's fall
from power had removed him from a position of neutrality to
that of an embittered leader of the opposition. He had wanted
to maintain a modicum of unity at Marseilles, but it was clear
that subsequent events had greatly modified his situation and his
objectives. The Radical party had been allotted eighty-nine
minutes in the National Assembly to discuss the fifteen inter-
pellations on North Africa that were to lead to his fall. Fifty-
three minutes of this time was devoted to René Mayer's bitter
and influential indictment of his fellow Radical. In the dramatic
roll-call in which he was defeated by 319 votes to 273, seventeen
Radicals voted against him and four abstained. Mendès-France's
desire to prevent such occurrences in the future marked the
turning point in the role of the *néo-radicaux* in the party. For
Mendès-France and his supporters, a basic prerequisite for the
renovation of the Radical party was the eviction of the *néo-
radicaux* from the party's administrative machinery.

The competing conceptions of radicalism clashed head-on at
the tumultuous meeting on 4 May 1955. Martinaud-Déplat and
his friends did their best to delay the special congress, but finally,
after the intervention of Herriot, they had to agree to a confrontation with their opponents. As at Marseilles, Martinaud-
Déplat did his best to arrange propitious conditions. Unable to
prevent the congress from taking place, he tried to limit its
duration and its scope, but did not succeed in either of these
objectives. He arranged for it to be held in Paris's *Salle Wagram*
on a day when this meeting place was available only until 6 p.m.,
but after this time limit had expired, the debate was transferred
to the *Salle de la Mutualité*. He wanted the discussion to be devoted primarily to the coming senatorial elections, but by a
narrow margin a meeting of Federation presidents and secretaries-
general voted to put a discussion of the party's organization on

[62] *Ibid.*

the agenda of the special congress. What were described by his opponents as irregular efforts to add to his voting strength were effectively countered by what many observers described as the equally irregular methods of his enraged rivals. Neither side was reticent in advancing its charges. A woman delegate from Martinaud-Déplat's home *département* rose to declare that the party's administrative president was able to dispose of as many membership cards as he liked and that in her town of Arles 'their number grew from 100 to 450 and then to 1,000 in the weeks that preceded the congress'.[63]

Painting an even blacker picture, *L'Express* charged, after the congress, that the party's headquarters had sent 2,000 cards to the Radical *comité* at Arles and went on to observe that in the previous elections the Radical candidate had only received 1,200 votes in that town.[64] *L'Express* also charged that the party's headquarters had sent 2,120 membership cards directly to Martinaud-Déplat's own *comité* at Aix-en-Provence without working through the departmental federation as required by party regulations. At a meeting of one of the party's commissions the following month, André Maroselli, an influential former minister who was supporting the *radicaux mendésistes*, produced an 'official list' that showed that '12,000 membership cards had been withdrawn on the eve of the congress by federations reputed to be favourable to the former administrative president'.[65]

Martinaud-Déplat's preparations, however, were of no avail. After ten hours of the most violent debates in the history of the Radical party, the congress adopted the *motion du Doubs* by which the administrative presidency was abolished and replaced by a seven-member *commission d'action*. Martinaud-Déplat had tried in vain to have a vote that allowed the use of mandates, but his opponents, vociferously calling for a vote by show of hands, were able to carry the day. Prior to the final vote, Mendès-France made a frank appeal to his rival to resign without waiting for a vote. 'I turn towards Martinaud-Déplat and ask him to facilitate the work of unification by making the gesture that many are expecting of him.' (*Le Monde*: 'The clearness of this declaration carried the tumult to a point hitherto unattained.') A subsequent appeal by Martinaud-Déplat to the *congressistes* had no

63 *Le Monde*, 6 May 1955. 64 *L'Express*, 14 May 1955.
65 *I.R.S.*, 23 June 1955.

more success: 'During seven years I have worked only for you' ('A large part of the crowd howls'). Wearied by ten hours of tumult, Herriot finally pronounced the closure of the debates, but not without making an unexpected observation. 'The parti-sans of voting by mandate,' he remarked, 'have the regulations in their favour, but the partisans of voting by raised hands have in their favour the facility and rapidity of counting the votes' ('The crowd roars at this declaration'). In a last effort to state his case, Martinaud-Déplat mounted once again to the tri-bune but was unable to make himself heard. 'He goes back to his seat, closes his brief-case and leaves the hall in the midst of increased howling and jostling.' Mendès-France's supporters waved their cards; Martinaud-Déplat's partisans did not parti-cipate in a similar test of their number; and Herriot, despite his earlier statement, proclaimed that the Doubs motion had passed.

A new era in the history of the Radical party had begun. The *radicaux mendésistes* did not consolidate their control of the party until the regular congress held in Paris six months later, but with the *Place de Valois* in their possession, their task was greatly facilitated. There were many Radicals who were not entirely in accord with the methods that had been used, but many of these were also willing to agree that the objectives of the *radicaux mendésistes*—and the methods of their predecessors—had justified their means. In an editorial published after the controversial vote, an editorialist in the influential *La Dépêche du Midi* noted that the party's former leaders had not begun as soon as the congress opened to verify the delegates' mandates, but went on to observe that, 'and yet, for all that, there were irregularities, as there were irregularities at Marseilles'.[66] Other observers were more opin-ionated in their views. A new era had begun, but old battles continued to rage.

After their exclusion from the party in December 1955, the *néo-radicaux* carried on their attacks from outside the Radical party. The RGR, transformed into a competing political party, provided a headquarters from which to launch these attacks. The changed character of the RGR had also provided the new leaders of the Radical party with grounds for expelling their rivals, and at their party's congress in November 1955 Radicals voted to withdraw their delegates from the RGR. After Faure was

[66] Cited by *Le Monde*, 7 May 1955.

expelled from the Radical party on 1 December, following his abrupt dissolution of the National Assembly, the leaders of the RGR pointedly confirmed him as their president and, proclaiming their decision to make the RGR a political party, began to distribute investitures to candidates for the forthcoming elections. They refused to reply to an ultimatum from Radical headquarters in which the latter had demanded compliance with three conditions: Radicals must be represented in the RGR by a new delegation; Radical investitures should have priority over those of the RGR; and there should be consultations between the two organizations before decisions were made concerning the political situations in individual *départements*. A final ultimatum gave those Radicals who had remained as leaders of the RGR twenty-four hours to choose between the RGR and their old party. Among those who chose the RGR were René Mayer, Georges Laffargue, Léon Martinaud-Déplat, Jean-Paul David, and Bernard Lafay. After declaring that they would 'remain Radicals true to an ideal that we are convinced we are serving', the latter concluded, in a letter of protest, that 'our bitterness is tempered by the certitude that common sense, moderation, and friendship will recover their rights in this party where such obvious excesses break with its traditions and its *esprit*'.[67]

The *néo-radicaux* were henceforth able to pursue their objectives in a cadre that was of their own construction. With fourteen deputies of whom four were *apparentés*, the RGR was able to constitute a group in the new legislature. With time erstwhile *néo-radicaux* were also able to envisage and to construct new cadres and new organizations. In the spring of 1956, Laffargue became president of an 'autonomous' Radical Federation of the Seine. During the same period, Lafay undertook the organization of the *Centre Républicain*, which during the following years was to become one of France's more successful new centre groupings. At the end of 1956, Jean-Paul David was active in working towards the organization of a '*groupe libéral*' in the National Assembly and, in competition with Lafay, was trying to unite members of the UDSR and the RGR with *radicaux dissidents* and Moderates.

In the meantime, the new leaders of the Radical party, occupied in confronting other rivals from within the party, were able

[67] *Le Figaro*, 10–11 December 1955.

to consider the *néo-radicaux* as a Radical phenomenon of the past. Certain *radicaux mendésistes*, indeed, did not wait for the exclusion of their rivals from the party before speaking of them in the past tense. A particularly concise description of the reign of the *néo-radicaux* was provided by a writer in a summer, 1955, issue of the *Bulletin des étudiants radicaux*. 'A veritable colonization, finally, disfigured the party after the Liberation. It was led by frankly reactionary elements whose domination, more and more impatiently tolerated, came to an end in the night of 4 May.'[68] Less than ten years after the Lyons congress that had marked the end of the *radicaux de gauche* in the party and the rise of the *néo-radicaux*, the victors of 1946 were being presented not only with ultimatums, but also with an epitaph.

The *néo-radicaux* were, manifestly, no longer '*néo*', and in the eyes of their rivals they had never been true '*radicaux*'. In the context of the history and traditions of radicalism, however, it was undeniable that they had many characteristics in common with their conservative predecessors within the party. Their differences with the latter were largely of degree and of environment. The *néo-radicaux'* conservative predecessors had never had to contend with *radicaux mendésistes*. At the same time, they had never carried their convictions, and methods, to the extremes attained by the *néo-radicaux*. No group of Radicals had ever been as frank as were the *néo-radicaux* in identifying themselves with right-wing political groups. And, paradoxically, it may be said that it was by becoming ex-Radicals, by carrying their differences to a point where a break was rendered possible, that the *néo-radicaux* most convincingly earned the prefix '*néo*'.

[68] Pierre Avril, 'Le Radicalisme', *Bulletin des étudiants radicaux*, 1955 (mimeographed). Later published in pamphlet form, with the title *La Tradition radicale* on the cover and *La Doctrine radicale* on the title-page. (Issued by the Radical party, Paris, 1956.) (Unsigned.)

VI

The Radicaux Gaullistes, 1947-51

*'Pour moi, je sais ce que pense Charles de Gaulle. Je parle en son nom. Je ne
suis que son micro.'*

JACQUES CHABAN-DELMAS, Deputy from Gironde and Mayor of Bordeaux,
in a speech at Bordeaux, October 1947. (*Le Monde*, 17 October 1947.)

On 7 April 1947, speaking from the balcony of Strasbourg's
city hall, General de Gaulle called on his countrymen to unite
in a new political movement, the *Rassemblement du peuple français*.
Among those with him on the balcony were Paul Giacobbi and
Jacques Chaban-Delmas, two Radical deputies. A few months
later, on the afternoon of 20 August, the formation of an RPF
'intergroup' in the National Assembly was announced by André-
Jean Godin. A Radical deputy from the Somme, Godin was the
new organization's secretary-general and, with Giacobbi, was
one of the five deputies who were members of the intergroup's
comité d'initiative. Of the forty-one deputies who were listed as
charter members, four were Radicals: Chaban-Delmas, Giacobbi,
Godin, and Maurice Bourgès-Maunoury. On the same day that
the intergroup was formed it was also announced that the RPF
would present candidates in the forthcoming municipal elections,
and in a speech on 24 August de Gaulle further declared that the
RPF's electoral lists would include 'men and women of diverse
political tendencies'.

This call had a strong appeal to many Radicals, and in particular to those who were seeking office. By the time that the elections began three weeks later, 25 per cent. of the Radical candidates
had formed joint electoral lists with the RPF and, ensconced on
the Gaullist bandwagon, went on to participate in one of the
most spectacular landslides in French post-war history.[1]

*
* *

[1] The RPF won approximately 40 per cent. of the votes in the large cities. The
Communists won 30 per cent., and the centre parties, the remaining 30 per cent.
L'Année politique, 1947, p. 143.

It was clear that a new species of Radical was now in existence: the *radical gaulliste*. It was equally clear, however, that the bearers of this new title varied both in seniority and in motivations. Although most of the *radicaux gaullistes* had appeared on the scene in answer to the 'call' of 24 August 1947, there were others who had answered an earlier call—that of 18 June 1940.

The latter, however, were a small minority, and for most of them their Gaullist allegiance antedated their Radical affiliation. Jacques Chaban-Delmas, who was only twenty-five years old when France fell, became a general in the *Forces françaises de l'intérieur* during the war and in 1944 was de Gaulle's *délégué militaire* responsible for military co-ordination in France. 'Perspicacious and skilful', in de Gaulle's words,[2] he was active in the liberation of Paris and played a prominent role in preventing the destruction of the city. In addition to bearing the title 'general', Chaban-Delmas was also an *inspecteur des finances* and a rugby player of international status. After the war, he was to achieve fame both as a dynamic deputy-mayor of Bordeaux and as a respected force on the national political scene. A member of the Radical party from 1946 to 1951, Chaban-Delmas combined his faith in radicalism—'you know that, no matter what, I am a Radical by nature, essence and disposition'[3]—with an even stronger faith in de Gaulle, and, after the latter dissolved the RPF in 1953, became the leader of the larger of the two groups that succeeded it.[4]

Chaban-Delmas was the most prominent *radical gaulliste* who, when forced to choose between the Radical party and the RPF, chose the latter. Others who also made this choice included Jean-André Godin, who was elected deputy from the Somme as a Radical in 1946 and as a member of the RPF in 1951, and Michel Debré, who was elected senator from Indre-et-Loire in 1948. Godin's pre-war background was administrative rather than political: his posts included two years as *chef de cabinet* for Tardieu when the latter was Minister of the Interior in 1928–30,

---

[2] Charles de Gaulle, *Mémoires de guerre*, vol. 2, *L'Unité 1942–1944*, Paris, 1956, p. 293.

[3] *Comité exécutif*, 14 March 1951.

[4] The *Républicains Sociaux*. Chaban-Delmas was elected president of the first National Assembly of the Fifth Republic in December 1958.

and several years of service in the Prefecture of Police. During the war he was active in the resistance. Debré, born in 1912, was a *chargé de mission* in Reynaud's government in 1938–9 and went on to play a very active role in the resistance. After the war he distinguished himself by writing a series of political studies that reflected a strong Gaullist point of view.[5]

Bourgès-Maunoury was in an entirely different category. One of the original members of the RPF intergroup that was formed on 20 August 1947, he took a very non-Gaullist step only three months later by accepting a post in the Schuman cabinet that succeeded Ramadier's government. Like Chaban-Delmas, Bourgès-Maunoury was only twenty-five years old in 1940, and like his contemporary had had a distinguished wartime career—in 1944 he was de Gaulle's *délégué militaire* in south-western France. As deputy from the Radical stronghold of Toulouse, however, he chose to make his political career as a member of the Radical party. Chaban-Delmas's first cabinet post was under Mendès-France in 1954. Bourgès-Maunoury, who had already served under Schuman, Marie, Queuille, Faure, and Mayer, was also a member of Mendès-France's government and after the fall of the latter went on to attain new ministerial heights as Minister of the Interior under Faure and Minister of National Defence under Mollet. He reached the summit of French political power sixteen months later when he succeeded Mollet. Despite his early allegiance to de Gaulle, Bourgès-Maunoury manifestly does not belong among the *radicaux gaullistes*: he was one of the more successful of the younger generation of *radicaux de gestion*.

The most notable example of a *radical gaulliste* who could claim seniority both as a Radical and as a Gaullist was Paul Giacobbi. Giacobbi began his long political career in 1922 when, already an active Radical, he was elected mayor of Venaco, the Corsican town in which he had been born twenty-six years earlier. The youngest mayor in France, he later became Corsica's youngest *conseiller général* and in 1938, France's youngest senator. After voting against Pétain at Vichy in July 1940, Giacobbi returned to Corsica and founded a resistance movement. Subsequently imprisoned by the Italians, he later escaped and played an important role in the liberation of Corsica. He then joined de Gaulle

[5] Debré was invested as the first premier of the Fifth Republic in January 1959.

in Algiers, became a member of the Consultative Assembly, and in April 1944 was appointed Commissioner of Agriculture, Food, and Industrial Production. After the liberation of France, de Gaulle made Giacobbi his Minister of Colonies. Elected to the first Constituent Assembly in the general elections of October 1945, Giacobbi served as Minister of Education until de Gaulle's resignation on 20 January 1946.

*
* *

In any attempt to analyse the ideological tenets of the *radicaux gaullistes* a prominent role must be accorded to the calendar. Giacobbi's long record both as a Radical and as a Gaullist was to be characterized by his strong attachment to both allegiances, and the long extent of his Radical background was to be instrumental in his final choice of his first allegiance. Most of the other early *radicaux gaullistes*, who were Gaullists before becoming Radicals, were to remain faithful to *their* early allegiance. Their major ideological contribution to the corpus of radicalism was a determined attempt to equate their newly acquired radicalism with their enthusiastic Gaullism.

Although those Radicals who flocked to de Gaulle in 1947 did not distinguish themselves for their interest in doctrinal matters, they did constitute the numerical preponderance of those who shared the title of *radical gaulliste*. The Radicals who formed this vintage of the *radicaux gaullistes* were guided more by opportunism than by conviction. Their 'Gaullism', as well as their 'radicalism', was strongly dependent on tactical needs and was to vary with the fluctuations of political history.

As long as de Gaulle was in power, most Radicals found little to their liking in either his methods or his policies. After the Radicals began their return to power, those of them who led the return were instrumental in obstructing de Gaulle's new political projects. During the intervening period, however, when both de Gaulle and the Radicals were out of power, there were periods of relative unity based on a common opposition to those who were in power and a willingness to co-ordinate their tactics in order to remedy the situation.

Giacobbi's career as a minister under de Gaulle fell in the first period. Other Radicals—Mendès-France, for example—had served

as ministers under de Gaulle, but none of them for as long a
period as Giacobbi. The latter's continued presence in the government did not please many of his party colleagues and gave rise
to much bitterness. After the formation of the new de Gaulle
government in November 1945, Herriot declared that Radicals
would vote for the government even though they were not represented in it.[6] Giacobbi, in Herriot's eyes, was not a *Radical*
Minister of Education.

Dissatisfaction with Giacobbi's anomalous position reached a
peak at the party's *Assemblée générale* in January 1946. After noting that he had made 282 speeches in his *département* during the
recent electoral campaign, one delegate declared that he had often
been reproached by people who told him: 'There is a Radical
Minister in power and you share the responsibility.'[7] To say that
Giacobbi was in the government '*à titre personnel*' was a 'mockery';
it was necessary to make it clear to voters that Radicals were
really in the opposition. Other delegates echoed these charges.
Speaking in his own defence, Giacobbi said that 'a systematic
attitude in the present movement of opposition to the government is something that the country, despite what you may think,
or despite what you may say here, will not understand (loud
exclamations and protests)'. Giacobbi noted that he had always
been a Radical, as had his father before him, but added that it
was only natural to want to remain with resistance colleagues—
Meunier had remained with Thorez, *he* wanted to remain with
de Gaulle.[8] Despite his arguments, the delegates proceeded to
pass a motion 'inviting *le citoyen* Giacobbi to leave the government immediately, and if he does not do so, his exclusion will
be asked at the next congress'.

The latter drastic step, however, did not prove to be necessary. A week later the government that Giacobbi was reproached
for joining no longer existed: de Gaulle, exasperated with the
conditions under which he was trying to rule, had startled his
compatriots by withdrawing to private life.

Now that Radicals and de Gaulle both were out of power
there was little cause for controversy. During the following
months, however, there was also no basis for common action.

---

[6] *Le Monde*, 25–26 November 1945.   [7] Robert Chautemps (Indre-et-Loire)

[8] Pierre Meunier, a *radical de gauche*, was Thorez's *chef de cabinet* when Thorez
served as Vice-Premier under de Gaulle after the war. See above, p. 63.

While the Radicals vigorously opposed the first Draft Constitution, de Gaulle did not even cast a vote. After de Gaulle's Bayeux speech on 18 June 1946, however, he became the most influential force among those who opposed the second Draft Constitution.

Thus, for a time, the Radicals and de Gaulle were to share certain common objectives. Both, along with the Moderates, strongly opposed the constitution on which the Fourth Republic was to be based. And, unable to prevent the enaction of the new constitution, both opposed the political system that resulted. Although they were allied in opposition, they differed, however, in the solutions they proposed. Both opposed the rigid system of parties that characterized the new régime; but while the Radicals wanted a return to the Third Republic, de Gaulle envisaged a presidential system.

Common criticism of an evolving political situation was, at best, a tenuous basis on which to base an alliance. Common criticism, however, did allow many Radicals to board the Gaullist bandwagon in the October 1947 municipal elections and enabled them to remain on it at least long enough to be elected. Other Radicals performed a similar feat in the November 1948 senatorial elections. In the eyes of many of the new *radicaux gaullistes*, tactical advantages more than made up for the lack of a common doctrine.

The 1947 municipal elections constituted a particularly striking example of a Gaullist electoral triumph and of Radical tactical skill. With the aid of Gaullist labels and co-operation, Radicals went far towards rebuilding their strength in the country and helped to make up for their electoral defeats of 1945 and 1946. Joint Radical–RPF lists were formed in many localities, and in many others it was agreed not to run competing candidates. Radicals, who had demonstrated their electoral dexterity by permitting certain of their candidates to ally themselves with Communists in the preceding elections, did not limit their attentions, however, to their new friends. Although the highest proportion of their joint electoral lists—25 per cent.—were formed with the RPF, 15 per cent. of the candidates were allied with the MRP, 10 per cent. with the Socialists, and 15 per cent. with both the MRP and the Socialists.[9]

[9] *Le Monde*, 9 October 1947. These figures apply to the first ballot only.

When the final results had been tabulated, the RPF was able to claim that their candidates had received 38 per cent. of the votes cast, a figure that included votes cast for their allies. Official listings, issued by the Ministry of the Interior, credited Radicals with 20.5 per cent. of the total number of votes. A year later, in the senatorial elections of November 1948, the RPF went on to win fifty-six seats. The RGR increased its representation from forty-four to seventy-nine, of whom twenty-six were among the 130 members of the RPF senatorial intergroup. Aided by their RPF alliances, by the predominance of rural voters, and by the use of a voting system based on single-member constituencies, the group of which the Radicals formed the core had become the largest in France's second chamber.

There was no doubt that the Radical party had profited by the electoral achievements of the new *radicaux gaullistes*, but it was to become increasingly clear that alliances based largely on opportunism could not long endure. Other Radicals, who had already been elected to office, were being offered new and attractive opportunities. With the rapid evolution of the French political scene, a revived and flowering radicalism came to constitute the antithesis of Gaullism. And, although Radicals have often vaunted their great assimilative powers, the architects of this revived radicalism had neither the desire nor the ability to 'digest' the intransigent general who wished to replace a régime that was becoming more and more to their liking.

Although both historical forces and doctrinal contradictions were to be arrayed against the continued survival of the *radicaux gaullistes*, expediency and tactics constituted additional factors that were not to be ignored. Radicals did not bring about a synthesis between radicalism and Gaullism, but they were able to demonstrate, once again, their great skill in deriving all possible benefits from an alliance before recognizing the need for a rupture.

*

* *

It did not take long for the evolution of history to complicate the doctrinal position of the early *radicaux gaullistes*. The high point of doctrinal compatibility between Radicals and Gaullists had been reached in the latter part of 1946 when both opposed the new constitution. This compatibility continued during the early part of the Fourth Republic, but only to the extent that the Radicals continued to oppose the régime that resulted from the constitution. It had not taken long, however, for Radical attitudes to diverge on the subject of governmental participation. After having been unsuccessful in their attempts to prevent the new régime from being born, many Radicals became reconciled to joining it. The hallmark of the early *radicaux gaullistes* was to oppose this trend. It was indeed more than a hallmark: it came to constitute the central feature of their radicalism.

Chaban-Delmas played a particularly active role in the challenging task of trying to persuade Radicals not to accept high political office. For the young deputy from Bordeaux, opposition to those who had succeeded de Gaulle in governing France was the crux not only of Gaullism but also of radicalism. And, for him, such opposition was also a matter of personal integrity. After returning to civilian life in 1945, Chaban-Delmas served as secretary-general of the Ministry of Information and in this position had strongly opposed the controversial post-Liberation press policies that favoured the MRP, the Socialists, and the Communists, often at the expense of the Radicals. Shortly after Félix Gouin succeeded de Gaulle as premier in January 1946, Chaban-Delmas resigned in protest when Gouin's Socialist Minister of Information insisted that the property of newspapers that had been acquitted for their wartime activities should be confiscated along with those that had been condemned. The surprise of the Minister and of Gouin when they were faced with Chaban-Delmas's decision was, in the words of the latter, 'total'. 'I regret to say that I was the only official in a position of authority who gave up his career for reasons of conscience.' After recalling this episode in a long speech at a meeting of the party's executive committee on 14 March 1951, Chaban-Delmas went on to describe and defend his later political activities. 'And then? Well, then, as I like public affairs, I joined the Radical party.' He entered political life, he added, with the objectives of 'reconstituting the true republican and democratic condition of the State', of 'dislodging the political influences that were rotting the administration', and of 'restoring to France its administrative machinery'.

Elected as a Radical deputy in November 1946, Chaban-Delmas

was designated by the party's *Comité Cadillac* to negotiate with Léon Blum when the latter was undertaking to form a government the following month. On meeting Blum, he was both charmed and stupefied, 'charmed by all that you know of him, but stupefied that the destiny of France could be held, in such difficult hours, in hands that were so fragile'. Blum told him that the MRP would participate in his government only on condition that the Communists also participated; the latter were willing to participate only on condition that they be given the Ministry of the Interior, the Ministry of Foreign Affairs, or the Ministry of Defence. Blum had decided to give them the latter. Chaban-Delmas reported back to the *Comité Cadillac* where, despite 'the eloquence of President Herriot, according to whom there was no major obstacle to entering this government in these conditions', it was decided by a large majority to refuse to approve or join a government that was willing to give the Ministry of Defence to the Communists.

In December 1946, therefore, Radicals had been faithful to the position that they had upheld during the electoral campaign a month earlier. In January 1947, however, when a new government was being formed by Ramadier, Radicals contradicted their earlier position by agreeing to participate. 'For reasons that have remained mysterious to me, it turns out that in six weeks the majority had completely reversed itself, and that which was refused six weeks earlier was granted six weeks later.' For Chaban-Delmas, speaking from the vantage point of 1951, the Radicals' decision to enter Ramadier's cabinet was 'the crucial point that constitutes the pivot of all France's parliamentary and political history for the past five years'. It was, he argued, a decision as tragic as it was important. 'On that day the Radical party had tied its hands, had tied itself entirely to tripartism; from that day onward it was never again able to recover its freedom of action.'

Chaban-Delmas went on to illustrate this argument. Four months after the formation of Ramadier's government, Communists were no longer in his cabinet, and the Socialists and the MRP no longer had the support of the 180 Communist deputies in the National Assembly. The Radicals could have required a very high price for their support of a new government; many concessions could have been won and much damage repaired.

This great opportunity had been lost, however, on the 'fatal day of January 1947 when we agreed to make this accursed entry in this accursed Ramadier government'.

The year 1947 was clearly a turning point in the post-war evolution of the Radical party, but many of their number, including the early *radicaux gaullistes*, were recalcitrant about turning— or in any case, disagreed as to which direction they should turn. A critical year for the Radical party, it was also, of course, a critical year both on the national and international scene. Worsening relations between East and West were accompanied in France with the eviction of the Communists from the government, social and economic strife, and the rise of the RPF. To many worried Frenchmen, the RPF was a particularly potent attraction. Chaban-Delmas had joined the RPF parliamentary intergroup because he considered that 'the line, the objectives, the goals presented by this RPF corresponded with the essential objectives of the Radical party'. Many voters, not concerned with the relevancy of the Radicals' 'essential objectives', flocked to de Gaulle in the belief that he constituted the best defence against the Communist menace and the only effectual answer to France's problems. Many of the *radicaux gaullistes*, in turn, were attracted to de Gaulle not only by their concern for their country's woes, but also by their desire to represent those who shared this concern.

France's political situation continued to evolve, however, and many *radicaux gaullistes* did not hesitate to adjust their positions accordingly. After having reached their high point of doctrinal compatibility in late 1946, Radicals and Gaullists had gone on to attain the peak of their electoral unity in the municipal elections of October 1947. By 1949, however, most of the *radicaux gaullistes* had returned to the Radical fold.

This return was facilitated by an easing political situation, by a spectacular Radical return to political power, and by increasingly bitter divergences between Radicals and the RPF.

*

* *

Radicals did not hesitate to link the easing political situation with their rising governmental role. Others could contest the validity of this argument, but the magnitude of the Radical return to power was beyond denial. The disintegrating effect of this on the *radicaux gaullistes* was also undeniable. While the RPF continued to oppose the Third Force, Radicals became an integral part of it. The path from opposition to participation had been a short one, but the one from participation to leadership was not much longer. In July 1948 André Marie succeeded Schuman and became the first Radical to form a government since Daladier succeeded Blum in April 1938. Marie served as premier for only a month, and after a two-day Schuman government and the third governmental crisis in six weeks, another Radical came to power: Henri Queuille.

Queille's long premiership put an end to the Gaullists' hopes for achieving an early success. It also put an end to the Gaullist vocations of most of the *radicaux gaullistes*. With the return of the Radicals to governmental power, only the most enthusiastic of the *radicaux gaullistes* remained steadfast in their opposition to the régime. When Marie formed his government on 28 July 1948, none of his Radical colleagues had voted against him, but five Radicals had 'abstained voluntarily'; these included Chaban-Delmas, Giacobbi, Godin, and Jacques Chevallier, all *radicaux gaullistes*. Jean Masson, another *radical gaulliste*, joined the same four in abstaining when Queuille was voted in as premier on 10 September 1948. The following year, when René Mayer formed an ephemeral government on 20 October 1949, five of his Radical colleagues—including Chaban-Delmas, Godin, and Lucien Bégouin, another *radical gaulliste*—were among those who abstained voluntarily. Thirty-four Radicals had voted in support of Marie, and thirty-five had voted in support of Queuille and Mayer. Most Radicals were finding that the régime that they had joined Gaullists in opposing was now becoming, under Radical leadership, more and more likable both in spirit and in practice. Radicals were still free to belong to the RPF parliamentary intergroup, but the delights of 'double membership'—or, to use the usual Radical term, 'bigamy'—were becoming less and less attractive to those of them who had rushed to join de Gaulle in 1947.

Encouraged by their party's rising political position, more and more Radicals began to speak out against contradictions inherent in their colleagues' political bigamy. Herriot was the major spokesman for this point of view. The veteran leader had never hidden his distaste for de Gaulle's political objectives, nor had he ever disguised his scepticism concerning the RPF. In a speech at the party's congress in December 1948 he warned his followers against the wiles of the Gaullists. 'They are telling our Radical friends "Come with us, little ones. We won't hurt you, you will see how nice we are. Come work with us, all together." One for all, all for one. I know the story.' To Herriot, the dangers of Gaullism were evident—'I read speeches besides those that I give.' On questions of foreign policy, Gaullists were speaking of *la France seule*, 'but at the present time I think that the best form of patriotism is modesty'. On domestic questions, Gaullists were crying 'Dissolution! Dissolution!', but 'at the present time, dissolution is only possible by a *coup d'état*, do you understand me?' After Herriot's speech, Giacobbi rose to defend those who refused to renounce their support of de Gaulle. For Giacobbi, there could be no true parliamentary régime in an Assembly with 184 Communists. De Gaulle, he declared, did not want a policy of *la France seule*, and the Radical party had never been noted for rigorous party discipline. Not only was Giacobbi in favour of allowing 'double membership', but he felt that to do so was to defend the interests of the Radical party as well as those of the Republic.

Despite Herriot's eloquent warnings, no decision was reached at the party's congress in 1948 concerning the 'bigamy' issue. Too many Radicals were still favourable to de Gaulle, and it was too profitable to remain at the crossroads. The problem of 'double membership', therefore, was allowed to remain on the shelf—a position that it continued to occupy, indeed, until it was no longer of great import. By the time that the party's executive committee met on 9 February 1949, faithfulness to the Radical allegiance was much more marked. Queuille was given a warm reception, and an order of the day was voted praising him for his actions as France's premier. In January, Jean Masson, a Radical deputy from Haute-Marne, had resigned from the RPF intergroup declaring that the RPF now deserved the criticism of monolithism that it directed at the parties. Two months later, in March 1949, he was re-elected *conseiller général* by a comfortable majority against an RPF candidate.

A more spectacular resignation was tendered in July 1949. A series of incidents had given rise to much ill feeling between members of the RPF parliamentary intergroups and the Gaullists who ran the RPF central office. The displeasure of the former at what they considered the authoritarian methods of the central office reached new heights after a bitter dispute during a cantonal election held in June at Melun, in Seine-et-Marne. Confronted with the problem of choosing a potential *conseiller général*, the Gaullist members of parliament from the *département*—three RPF senators and Lucien Bégouin, a Radical deputy—supported a different candidate than the one named by the RPF's central office.[10] Their candidate was elected, but the three senators were reprimanded by the RPF, and Bégouin was expelled. These disciplinary actions were greeted with strong protests by members of the RPF intergroup, and in particular by its president, Giacobbi. A few weeks previously Giacobbi had written to de Gaulle asking him to give the RPF back to its first vocation. 'The RPF', he declared, was 'killing the *Rassemblement*'.[11] In July he repeated this remark, and further expressed his dissatisfaction by resigning from the intergroup, from the presidency of the intergroup, and from his membership in the RPF's executive council.

By the summer of 1949, therefore, it was clear that the disintegration of the *radicaux gaullistes* was nearly complete. In January 1946 Giacobbi had been threatened by expulsion if he did not leave de Gaulle's cabinet. In July 1950 Radicals made his presence in an ephemeral government led by Queuille a *sine qua non* of the end of a long governmental crisis. The interval between these two dates had seen a striking evolution of the régime, the Radical party, and the *radicaux gaullistes*.

*

* *

It was not until 1951, however, that the final hard core of *radicaux gaullistes* were required to make a choice between their two allegiances. By then it was clear to most Radicals that continued tolerance of this particular form of political bigamy was no longer profitable. Increasing tactical differences between Radicals and Gaullists had been accompanied with growing doctrinal divergencies. Like the régime it opposed, the RPF also had undergone its own evolution. It had become a party in everything but name. Its leaders were finding it increasingly necessary

[10] See *L'Année politique*, 1949, p. 101 and p. 123; and *Le Monde*, 7 July 1949.
[11] *Le Monde*, 8 July 1949.

to stress the need for cohesion and discipline among its parliamentary members—concepts distasteful to most *radical gaullistes* Influenced by its right-wing members, the RPF was becoming more and more clerical. Radicals had not been unaware of such developments prior to 1951, but by the latter date most Radicals felt that the time for decision had come: 1951 was an election year. Electoral imperatives, too, had evolved since 1947.

The central roles in the final scenes between *radicaux gaullistes* and the Radical party were played by Chaban-Delmas and Herriot. The former was the most prominent of the *radicaux gaullistes* who had continued to proclaim his loyalty to both allegiances. Most of the 1947 vintage of *radicaux gaullistes* had long since returned to the Radical fold. Of the other early *radicaux gaullistes*, Giacobbi had resigned from the RPF, and Godin, after having aroused the ire of his Radical colleagues in early 1950 by supporting an RPF list against a Radical one in a municipal election in Calais, had resigned from the Radical party.[12] Herriot, who had long symbolized the distrust of the older Radicals for de Gaulle and who had never ceased to put his vast political power and experience on the side of those who opposed the RPF's objectives, took the lead in forcing the last of the *radicaux gaullistes* to choose between their two affiliations.

In the final *dénouement* of the drama of the *radicaux gaullistes*, tactical and doctrinal factors were generously blended with personal considerations—a typically Radical mixture that had characterized most of the *radicaux gaullistes'* activities. Herriot had long served as a target for certain of the more extreme Gaullists. In January 1949, for example, an RPF newspaper in Bordeaux printed a picture of Herriot having dinner with Laval and a third person whose head had been replaced with a sketch of Otto Abetz, Nazi ambassador to occupied France.[13] Entitled '*Les déjeuners de Matignon*', it was the newspaper's way of reconstructing Herriot's controversial visit to Paris in August 1944. The picture was published on the front page of the newspaper, a position it shared with an article written by Bordeaux's deputy-mayor, Chaban-Delmas. Herriot was also the subject of other attacks that were equally biting, if less crude. In the heat of

[12] *Le Monde*, 8 June 1950.

[13] *Le Rassemblement du sud-ouest, hebdomadaire du Rassemblement du peuple français*, Bordeaux, 2 January 1949.

political struggles, prominent Gaullist leaders—including André Malraux, Gaston Palewski, and Jacques Soustelle—were not adverse to berating him for his role at Vichy in 1940.[14]

It was on the basis of party discipline, however, that Herriot was to make his successful stand against the *radicaux gaullistes*. As early as the latter part of 1950, it was becoming evident that the RPF had chosen Lyons as the constituency in which its secretary-general, Jacques Soustelle, would run in the forth-coming elections. On 12 November 1950, Soustelle made a significant step towards his eventual candidacy by presiding over a political banquet at Lyons. One of the distinguished guests who attended was Chaban-Delmas. By coming to the political fief of his party's president in order to participate in a meeting presided over by one of Herriot's potential electoral rivals, Chaban-Delmas had committed a grave act of *lèse-majesté*. Although Chaban-Delmas maintained that he had notified Herriot of the meeting and argued that 'nothing was said that was contrary to the essential ideas of the Radicals',[15] Herriot proceeded to open '*l'affaire* Chaban-Delmas' by addressing a complaint to the party's discipline committee. After the committee decided on technical grounds to take no action, Herriot utilized his ultimate weapon: he resigned as president of the party on 15 February 1951. The party's *commission exécutive*, after noting that only a congress was qualified to accept the resignation, proceeded to convoke a meeting of the executive committee.

The latter meeting took place on 13 March 1951. After listening to eloquent arguments from both sides, the delegates voted by a large majority—543 to 128—to force the remaining *radicaux gaullistes* to choose between their two loyalties. Herriot, once again, had carried the day, and on 17 March he withdrew his resignation. Most of those who spoke at the meeting of the executive committee supported his position. Aroused delegates cited examples of *radicaux gaullistes* who had supported RPF lists against Radical ones. Godin's actions in the municipal elections in Calais were recalled. Roger Gaborit, a Radical deputy from Charente-Maritime, noted that an official in his department's Radical federation had gone so far as to lead an RPF list that had opposed the official Radical list in the recent senatorial elections. For Gaborit, such a situation was impossible. 'We con-

[14] *Le Monde*, 22 May 1951, 10–11 June 1951.   [15] *Ibid.*, 16 November 1950.

sider,' he proclaimed, 'that there must not be two categories of Radicals, but only one, that which made the great Radical family of the Third Republic.'

In a long speech in which he spoke as the party's administrative president, Martinaud-Déplat made it clear that there was a limit beyond which even the flexible Radical doctrine could not extend and argued that those Radicals who had remained in the RPF had now passed this limit. The party had long been tolerant towards the *radicaux gaullistes*, he observed, but now that the RPF was clearly a party the tolerance of an earlier period could not be maintained. After noting that the Radical party had long 'closed its eyes on deviations that seemed to us perhaps incompatible with Radical doctrine', Martinaud-Déplat argued that such a policy had been a good one. 'It is necessary to try to bring back stray sheep when one has a small flock, and it is necessary to try to keep the flock complete and to enlarge it if possible.' The *radicaux gaullistes*, however, had gone too far in their deviations. After referring to the Calais incident and noting the existence of other 'grave conflicts', the party's administrative president went on to offer his listeners some alarming observations. 'I tell you, you are no longer a party organization, you are only a band that is trying to win places (loud applause), you are no longer anything but a friendship gang that works for the advantage of some one or another, without concern for doctrine or for conviction, but only for luncheons eaten together or for participation in Parisian *salons*, and in that case you are no longer a party!'

Michel Debré and Chaban-Delmas were the major spokesmen for the defence. Debré argued that Radicals had originally taken part in governing France in order to defend their programme, but that now they were defending the programmes of others. In an eloquent speech, Chaban-Delmas advanced his point of view that it was the *radicaux gaullistes* who had remained faithful to the true beliefs of radicalism. The delegates admired Chaban-Delmas for his eloquence and for his other personal qualities, but were not willing to accept his thesis that the tenets of radicalism had become crystallized in the latter part of 1946. After a final intervention by Herriot in which the old leader told his listeners that their vote would constitute a 'decisive moment for the future of the Republic and of the *patrie*', the members of the

Radical party's executive committee proceeded to vote the condemnation of double membership.

*

* *

The *radicaux gaullistes* were now part of past history. They
had joined the *radicaux de gauche* in the Valhalla of rejected Radicals. Unlike the latter, however, most of them had been reab-
sorbed before the final battle. The executive committee gave the
small group that remained three weeks to make their final choice.
On 31 March 1951, Chaban-Delmas, who was the only Radical
deputy affected by the new ruling, reluctantly declared that he
was 'on leave from the party'.[16] Debré, the last of the *radicaux
gaullistes* in the Senate, refused to accept the executive committee's ultimatum, but resigned before the elections three
months later.[17]

The latter elections—the critical parliamentary elections of
June 1951—had never been far from the thoughts of those who
had debated the fate of the *radicaux gaullistes*. After the vote on
13 March, Chaban-Delmas had observed that the executive committee's act would 'cost five hundred thousand votes in the elections', and went on to add that 'we will leave, but it will only be
au revoir'. Before the members of the executive committee had
voted, however, Herriot had assured them that to condemn
double membership did not mean that certain federations could
not ally themselves with the RPF if local circumstances made
this desirable. The traditional freedom of federations to make
their own electoral alliances was not to be affected by the new
measure: they were being asked to condemn bigamy, but not
alliances. In the ensuing elections, however, few candidates
availed themselves of this liberty to form alliances with the RPF.
Of seventy-eight Radical and allied members who were elected
for French constituencies, fifty-eight were elected in alliance with
the Third Force, three in alliance with the RPF, and seventeen
in opposition to both.[18]

In conclusion, it may be said that the *radicaux gaullistes* had
constituted only a temporary phenomenon in the evolution of
radicalism. Those Radicals who were Gaullists by conviction

---

[16] *L'Année politique*, 1951, p. 71.　　　[17] *Le Monde*, 18 May 1951.
[18] Williams, p. 94.

had been unable to equate their two allegiances. Those who had joined the RPF from opportunism had not hesitated to leave for the same reason. A key role in both cases was played by the evolution of the French political scene, an evolution that had heightened doctrinal contradictions and had provided new electoral opportunities.

Subsequent developments served to confirm the necessity— or at least the logic—of the final break. The 1951 electoral alliances had shown the closeness of the Radicals' relationship with other Third Force parties. Led by Herriot, Radicals devoted much of their electoral efforts to fighting de Gaulle. Official party propaganda castigated the General for his past actions and for his current projects. 'De Gaulle left the Government when the Communists were still in it. The Radicals entered it when the Communists had left.' 'It is because we have seen de Gaulle and Thorez together that we want neither de Gaulle nor Thorez.' 'De Gaulle promises us forty divisions, why not! He has already achieved the division of the French.'[19]

Such charges were echoed again and again by Radical orators. At a meeting of the party's executive committee held shortly before the elections, Martinaud-Déplat particularly stressed de Gaulle's treatment of Thorez after the Liberation. Almost as soon as de Gaulle had returned to France, he had, in Martinaud-Déplat's words, amnestied 'the deserter Thorez', made him a vice-premier and allowed him to 'organize the poisoning of our administrative services'. In a speech that closed the 1946–51 legislature, Herriot castigated both the Communists and de Gaulle. After decrying the actions of the latter, he went on to say that he was more disappointed than irritated. 'We would have wished that the protester of the hours of distress would have remained above us and our divisions like a living symbol of the *patrie*.'[20] A few days earlier, after stressing the need in politics for 'a certain amount of experience, a certain amount of practice', Herriot had also voiced this disappointment and had gone on to echo the traditional Radical distrust of military men in government. 'Why did an evil spirit have to incite him to enter politics, like a certain number of other generals?'[21]

[19] Radical party archives. Slogans suggested in party circular issued June 1951.
[20] *Journal Officiel*, 22 May 1951, pp. 5775–6.
[21] *Congrès extraordinaire*, May 1951.

De Gaulle, however, *had* entered politics. He had attracted a great number of supporters. Certain of his objectives had coincided with those of the Radicals. Given these conditions, it was virtually inevitable that a new species of Radical—the *radical gaulliste*—would rise to meet the occasion. Radicals had never been adverse to having representatives in other political camps, and the appearance of the RPF on the French political scene in 1947 was too advantageous an opportunity to be missed. In a party in which some members had been able to equate themselves with Communists on the left and in which others were willing to equate themselves with Independents on the right, it was only natural for still other Radicals to make the attempt—whether sincere or not—to equate themselves with the political movement led by the hero of their country's darkest years.

VII

The Radicaux de Gestion

'Nous ne sommes pas de ceux qui proclament: Périsse la France plutôt qu'un principe.'

FRANÇOIS DELCOS, Deputy from Pyrénées-Orientales, at Toulouse Congress, 1949

A few days after the general elections of 21 October 1945, Edgar Faure spoke frankly of his political problems while having lunch with an old friend.[1] Along with many of his fellow Radical candidates, Faure had been defeated in France's first major post-war elections. It had been Faure's first attempt to become a deputy, and in his negotiations prior to the elections he had been able to choose between representing the Radical party in either of two Parisian constituencies or the Roman Catholic MRP in Vaucluse.

In making his choice, Faure had not been overly concerned with doctrinal issues. In the words of his friend, written shortly after their luncheon conversation, Faure's 'natural scepticism had inclined him neither more nor less towards one or the other conviction'. His choice had been based, rather, on tactical considerations. 'With prudence, Faure had felt that radicalism had remained rooted in the mentality of the voters, and that on the other hand it would be madness to espouse the MRP in Vaucluse, where people always vote to the left, and to let oneself be caught between the Communists and the traditional majority of Daladier.' Declining the MRP's offer, 'Edgar therefore ran in Paris, but his carefully pondered calculations were frustrated'. The MRP candidate who replaced him at Avignon had won. Daladier had been badly defeated, 'and Faure has been left holding the bag in Paris'.

[1] Jacques Dumaine, who served as *chef du protocol* at the Quai d'Orsay, 1945–51. Dumaine died while serving as ambassador to Portugal. His voluminous diary, *Quai d'Orsay, 1945–1951* (Paris, 1955), was published posthumously. The comments cited concerning Faure are from the entry for 27 October 1945, pp. 27–8.

M

Faure's status in 1945 was temporary. Ten years later, when an account of his luncheon conversation unexpectedly appeared in print, he was serving his second term as premier of France —and was completing his ninth year as a very firmly implanted Radical deputy from Jura, a rural *département* bordering Switzerland. In terms of his objectives, there was no doubt that Faure had done brilliantly since his early electoral defeat. He had become one of the most successful *radicaux de gestion* of the postwar years.

*
*   *

Unlike the *radicaux gaullistes*, the *radicaux de gestion* were not a species of Radical that had waited until the end of the Second World War before making an appearance on the Radical horizon. They represented a tradition as old as the party itself. Faure was one of the most spectacular contemporary examples of those Radicals who have placed a very high priority on keeping their governmental abilities at the service of the Republic, but this preoccupation is one that has been shared by nearly all Radicals. As has been the case with most other categories of Radicals, the title *radical de gestion* is one that must be awarded on the basis of degree, and not kind.

Although no *radical classique*, for example, would ever have considered using the Roman Catholic MRP as a route to the National Assembly, few old-school Radicals have exhibited any great disinclination towards sharing in the exercise and fruits of power. In their deeds, if not always in their words, the *radicaux classiques* never distinguished themselves for drawing sharp lines between doctrinal objectives and more immediate aims. Their ambivalent attitude may be said to have found an apt expression in the venerable political slogan, 'Justice for all, and jobs for friends!'

Other Radicals have shared the *radicaux de gestion*'s sincere conviction that it was their party's duty to play an active role in governing France, even when sharing governmental responsibilities could mean supporting policies contrary to certain of their party's official objectives. After the founding of the Fourth Republic, Herriot was forceful in putting his great influence at the service of this argument. In his view, it was necessary to accept collaboration in office in order to create, little by little, a new balance of power. For the *néo-radicaux*, the necessity for such a policy was even more obvious. The implementation of their basic aims, as well as the logic of their membership in the Radical party, was contingent on the exercise of political power.

After their epic period of opposition during the immediate post-war years, Radicals had gone on to establish a remarkable record as a governmental party. Radicals headed ten of the twenty-one governments that were formed in France under the Fourth Republic and were present in all of them. Although the early *radicaux gaullistes* felt that the party had made a tragic decision when it decided to enter Ramadier's government, this decision was one that Radicals never failed to emulate during the formation of subsequent governments. The arguments of the *radicaux gaullistes*, even when combined with those of an equally intransigeant Edouard Daladier, were never able to carry the day in any major Radical gathering. Daladier and his followers came closest to winning general approval for their arguments at the party's congress at Toulouse in November 1949, but Herriot, aided by Queuille, Mayer, Faure, Martinaud-Déplat, Laffargue, and an increasingly conciliatory Giacobbi, was able to unite a large majority of the delegates behind his name—and a smaller, but still sufficient, majority behind the policy of governmental participation.

Even those Radicals who were most vociferous in decrying their party's willingness to participate in all governments often did so for tactical rather than doctrinal reasons. Most of those who supported Daladier at Toulouse saw opposition to the government as the most effective path to electoral success—and an opportunity to have *their* turn at managing the affairs of their country. Once in power, however, most Radicals have succumbed to the almost irresistible desire to remain in positions of authority, even at the risk of sacrificing their original electoral support.

The danger of losing electoral support by winning power, however, must not be exaggerated. The most successful *radicaux de gestion* have been fortunate enough to enjoy the support of voters who have been more influenced by political power than by political programmes.

There is no doubt, in any case, that a loyal and faithful constituency is a basic prerequisite for a *radical de gestion*. Having won the firm allegiance of understanding and admiring voters, the ambitious *radical de gestion* is then free to participate in the administration of a broad variety of policies. A willingness and ability to perform this function is the mark of the true *radical de gestion*. The Radical party has always been able to provide leaders for conflicting programmes, but when a true *radical de gestion* is already in office, the search for a new leader is greatly facilitated: the incumbent is the logical choice. Some Radicals, including Herriot, have stressed the advantages that participation in power could bring to basic Radical objectives. Other Radicals have found more negative reasons for joining successive governments. 'But my dear friends, is it not also true that our presence in the governments has prevented the other parties, too, from applying their programmes?'[2] For the true *radical de gestion*, however, such considerations are not fundamental. In their opinion, the opportunity to share in the exercise of political power constitutes a sufficiently convincing incentive.

Although the most typical characteristics of the *radicaux de gestion* are not the exclusive property of any limited group of Radicals, it is possible, by introducing the factor of degree, to isolate a few of the more significant examples. All aspiring *radicaux de gestion* must accomplish specific tasks. The obvious habitat of the *radicaux de gestion* is the National Assembly, or as an alternative choice, the Senate. A *radical de gestion*'s first major step, therefore, is to become a deputy or a senator. Now a representative of the people, his next objective is to become a member of an important committee. After winning his first cabinet position, he must then become a *ministrable*, a proven leader whose name is always among those to be taken into consideration when new governments are being formed. The measure of his success is the regularity with which he is able to win election to high office, and of course the importance of the positions that he fills.

There has been no lack of Radicals who have brilliantly fulfilled these qualifications, but two men, representing different generations and in many respects very different outlooks, may be cited as of particular interest. A veteran minister of the Third

Roger Gaborit, deputy from Charente-Maritime, *Comité exécutif*, 14 March 1951.

Republic, Henri Queuille reached new heights of governmental glory during the Fourth Republic. With much in common with the *radicaux classiques*, Queuille represented many of the old traditions of radicalism. Edgar Faure, on the other hand, who began his political career after the war, had much in common not only with the *néo-radicaux*, but also—to a lesser but still visible degree—with the *radicaux mendésistes*. It was as *radicaux de gestion*, however, that Queuille and Faure were most remarkable.

*
*   *

Henri Queuille was invested premier three times during the Fourth Republic, a feat unequalled by any other French politician. His first government made history by remaining in office thirteen months, from 11 September 1948 to 6 November 1949, a record that was to stand until 1957. His second government was virtually stillborn: it lasted only two days, from 2 July to 4 July 1950. His third government, the last one of the 1946–51 legislature, was in office from 3 March to 7 July 1951.

The full measure of Queuille's ministerial durability can only be seen, however, in the light of his complete governmental record. During the Third Republic he served twenty times as a minister. He was Minister of Agriculture, for example, under Herriot, Poincaré, Paul-Boncour, Daladier, Sarraut, Chautemps, and Doumergue. Interrupted by Vichy, his governmental career resumed after he joined de Gaulle in 1943. De Gaulle appointed him *commissaire d'état*, and in his new chief's absences from Algiers in 1943 and 1944, Queuille served as acting president of the *Comité Français de la Libération Nationale*.

During the Fourth Republic, Queuille established a memorable record by serving as either a minister or as premier without a break from July 1948 to June 1954. Minister of State under Marie in July and August 1948, he was Minister of Public Works in Schuman's two-day government in September, and the following month for the first time formed his own government. He was his own Minister of Finance until January 1949. After he resigned as premier on 6 November 1949, he served as vice-premier under his successor, Bidault, until February 1950, when Bidault appointed him Minister of the Interior. Queuille then proceeded to serve as Minister of the Interior from 7 February 1950 to 10 July 1951, in four successive governments, two led by Bidault and Pleven and two led by Queuille himself. After the resignation of his third government at the beginning of the 1951–6 legislature, Queuille served as Minister of State under Pleven until January 1952, as vice-premier and Minister of State in the cabinets formed by Faure and Pinay in 1952, and as vice-premier in the cabinets formed by Mayer and Laniel in 1953. He was not a member of the government that Mendès-France formed in June 1954.

From a quantitative point of view, Queuille's record was undeniably a staggering one. From a qualitative point of view, he was the subject of considerable criticism. Charged with being the father of *immobilisme*, of having made a fine art of delay and inertia, Queuille came to personify for many critics those characteristics which they most severely condemned in French post-war politics. For others, however, he represented a much needed element of stability in a régime that was threatened from more than one side. In any case, Queuille never attempted to misrepresent himself or his objectives. When presenting his governmental programmes, he always insistently stressed their limited character.

Queuille's lack of political aggressiveness was matched by his patience and personal modesty. He cannot be numbered among those Radicals who distinguished themselves for precocious brilliance. Born in 1884, he was sixty-four years old when he became premier for the first time. Before entering the Chamber of Deputies in 1914, Queuille began his long local political career by being elected mayor of Neuvic d'Ussel, the small town in southwestern France in which he was born. Queuille soon combined his duties as mayor with those of *conseiller général* of Corrèze. Throughout his long career, he never ceased to reflect the outlook of his rural constituents. A country practitioner, *le bon docteur* Queuille never succumbed to the flattery of the dreaded Parisian *salons*. Unpretentious and astute, he continued to enjoy the loyal support and respect of the people among whom he was born. It is illustrative of his personality that the only aspect of Queuille's appearance that differentiated him from most of his followers—he carries a cane—was a result of a very democratic accident—a fall from a bicycle.

Queuille's retiring personality had a strong influence on the way in which he exercised power. Always moderate and polite, he made very few enemies during his long years of parliamentary and ministerial apprenticeship. Lacking strong views on controversial subjects, he became admirably qualified in the arts of conciliation and temporizing. His skill in these arts, as well as his able mastery of parliamentary manœuvre, was to reach its apogee during his thirteen months as premier in 1948 and 1949.

The veteran Radical's 'great year' did not begin auspiciously. Coming to power after what had been the longest governmental crisis since the Liberation, Queuille had to face the open hostility of many of the rank and file of his own party. Although his willingness to attempt to form a government had been approved by all those present at a meeting of the party's *Comité Cadillac*, many local *comités* and federations passed resolutions expressing their opposition to having a Radical accept the responsibilities of the premiership when there were so few Radicals in parliament and when the new government would have to face critical problems that had been caused by other parties.

From the beginning of his premiership, however, Queuille made it clear that party considerations were not his primary concern. 'I hope that my Radical friends will excuse me: it is not as a representative of their party that I mean to take over the government.' Speaking before the National Assembly on 10 September 1948, he went on to tell his listeners that France's situation required 'an empiricism that must strip the man of government of his partisan armour.' It was his duty, he argued, to be 'the man of all those who, understanding as I do the hard necessities of the present, will be willing to follow me in the effort that I am undertaking for the good of the country'. As a more tangible sign of his desire for widespread support, he had already agreed to bestow cabinet rank on an unusually large number of those who were to be his followers: among the thirty-two members of his cabinet were nine members of the MRP, eight Socialists, and a minority of seven of his fellow Radicals.[3]

During his thirteen-month premiership Queuille demonstrated great skill in keeping his coalition together. And, although he may have limited his activities to a minimum, a minimum of

---

[3] *L'Année politique*, 1948, p. 156. His cabinet included a Minister of the Merchant Marine.

action can be far from negligible during turbulent times. In attempting to bring a degree of stability to his country's régime, Queuille was forced to contend with two extremely active organizations: the Communist party and the RPF. His period in office coincided with serious reverses for both of these formations and a resultant rise in authority of the beleaguered Third Force.

The effect of Queuille's long premiership on the Gaullists' hopes for an early success, as well as its effect on the Gaullist vocations of many of the *radicaux gaullistes*, has already been noted. Queuille's role in this process was not limited to a disinclination to vacate his office, nor was it based only on his skill in avoiding being forced to leave. A week after coming to power, he deprived de Gaulle of his 'guard of honour' after a bloody riot at an RPF rally at Grenoble in which several Communists had been wounded and one killed. This strong action marked an important step in the decline of the RPF and the rise of the authority of the Third Force. A few days later, on 23 September, Queuille accomplished a more characteristic feat by engineering the postponement of the forthcoming cantonal elections. By a majority of only five votes (twenty-five Radicals voted in favour, fifteen in opposition, and two abstained), the elections were adjourned until the following spring —and the RPF was deprived of the opportunity of winning many electors for the senatorial elections scheduled for November. This strategem helped prevent what could have been a major Gaullist landslide and provided a much-needed respite for the government.

Queuille's government was equally firm in opposing the activities of the Communists. Like many other Third Force leaders, Queuille did not hesitate to link the two opponents of the régime in the same approbrium. After attacking the RPF in a speech in the National Assembly on 15 March 1949, Queuille went on to express this viewpoint by telling his listeners that 'as for the Communists, you know well that no matter what we do, we will always have them against us, because they, too, have for a goal not the interests of the country, but the success of a vast political enterprise'.

One of the Communists' most violent attempts to achieve their political ends in post-war France took place soon after Queuille became premier. A particularly bitter miners' strike, begun on

4 October 1948, soon brought violence to many parts of France. Certain areas in the north and a few villages in the southern *département* of Gard were temporarily dominated by Communists. At a meeting of the Socialist party on 10 October, Jules Moch, Queuille's Minister of the Interior, dramatically declared that shortly before his death Zhdanov had ordered the French Communist party to sabotage the Marshall Plan by all possible means.[4] Faced with the need to take action, Queuille demonstrated his ability to make difficult decisions. A year later, after hearing his record in office belittled by Daladier at the Toulouse Congress, Queuille recalled with pride his role during this period. Despite the insurrectionary nature of the strikes, he had remained calm. 'At the most critical moments, I did not pound my fist on the table, and I thought, M. Daladier, that it would not suffice to wear a mask of authority.' To illustrate the way in which he had done his difficult duty, Queuille recounted one of his experiences. At the height of the crisis, the Minister of the Interior had telephoned to inform him that a prefect in central France was surrounded by 3,000 Communists. Protected only by a few policemen, the prefect wanted to know whether he could have his men threaten to fire. Faced with this 'dreadful question', Queuille replied in the affirmative. 'We do not have the right to leave a representative of the government at the mercy of rioters.' Queuille concluded his anecdote by noting that Gabriel Cudenet, the president of the RGR, had been present in his office when the call was received and, overhearing the conversation, had told him: 'I congratulate you for your courage; I understand that you will now want to be alone; I will leave.'

Queuille had shown his ability to take firm defensive measures in opposing the designs of those who fought the régime, but his tenure in office was not marked by actions of a more positive nature. He reacted to events more than he moulded them. Aided by a good harvest and the influx of the Marshall Aid, his premiership coincided with increasing stability in France. Basic economic difficulties and bitter social agitation continued, however, and Queuille finally resigned in the face of Socialist demands for wage increases to compensate for the rise in the cost of living.

---

[4] *L'Année politique*, 1948, p. 182. Moch also added that he was certain that French Communist agents had been given 100 million francs 'to lead their campaign of disorganization against our economy'.

Supported by his conservative Finance Minister, Maurice Petsche, Queuille refused to accept the Socialist programme out of fear of reopening the inflationary cycle. The ministerial crisis that followed his premiership was even longer than the one that had preceded it.

In his thirteen months as premier, Queuille had not dealt vigorously with the fundamental problems facing France, but he had provided the régime with an interlude of comparative respite. His lack of dynamic action was not surprising, however, in the light of the conditions under which he was governing. As a leader of a divided coalition, most of his energies were inevitably devoted to keeping his coalition together. Inaction was often the price of survival. At the same time, the limited nature of this method of government was in keeping with Queuille's aptitudes and personal inclinations. The new and the unknown were never attractive to Queuille. In a speech in the National Assembly on 5 April 1949, mid-way in his first year in office, he expressed his nostalgia for the calmer ways of the past by telling his listeners that the country was asking for 'a normal régime, analogous to that which it knew under the Third Republic'. Queuille could be decisive when it was absolutely necessary, but he usually found it advisable to temporize and to let situations evolve by themselves. In a speech that he made to his fellow deputies on 30 June 1950, prior to his investiture as premier the following month, he was frank in stating his faith in the latter principle of government. 'In a period when the course of events can give a different form to a problem tomorrow than that which it had the day before, honesty requires prudence and even the acknowledgement of certain doubts.'

In his attempts to meet problems one at a time, Queuille found it preferable to be guided by the 'national interest' rather than by 'Radical doctrine', and never hesitated to advance this argument before Radical audiences. In a speech at the party's congress at Toulouse in 1949, after the end of his thirteen-month premiership, Queuille told his listeners that when he formed his coalition government, he knew that he would be reproached later for not having followed 'strictly Radical policies'. 'Strictness in doctrine', however, had been impossible in the circumstances, and he reminded his party colleagues that he had never ceased to proclaim that his government's policies 'would be inspired only by

Henri Queuille, Emile Roche, and Edouard Daladier at party's
congress in Paris, November 1955

Edgar Faure, speaking at party's congress in Paris,
November 1955

the national interest as it could be defined by the majority of the coalition that supported the government'.

A *radical de gestion*, Queuille never considered himself a Radical premier. During his third premiership, from March to July 1951, his major task was to concoct an electoral law that would limit the success of the Communists and the RPF, and at the same time be acceptable to the parties that formed the Third Force. These objectives, and not the long proclaimed Radical desire to return to the electoral system used during most of the Third Republic, guided Queuille in his calculations and negotiations.

Queuille was provided with an opportunity to expound his governmental and party philosophy at a meeting of the presidents and secretaries-general of Radical federations held in Paris shortly after he became premier in March 1951. His first step was to clarify the reasons for his presence: Martinaud-Déplat had introduced him by saying that the new premier had wanted to be present in order to bring his listeners any explanations that they might wish.[5] Queuille said that, in reality, he had only come to give them a friendly greeting and also—'it is almost a tradition for me'—to 'ask you to agree that I am henceforth on leave from the party'. He then reminded his listeners that when he had taken office in 1948, he had made it clear that he 'no longer would be the Radical faithful to the party's doctrine, rules, and directives', but that as the leader of a coalition he could not follow policies other than those of the majority of his cabinet. 'When one is premier, one must not carry out party doctrine.' In order that France may have a government, he noted, it was often necessary to search for a way to conciliate opposites, and it was this thankless task that he was obliged to undertake. Queuille then assured his listeners that, although on leave from the party, if he did his duty 'as a premier who raises himself above doctrines in order to deal with reality and prevent disaster', he would be remaining 'no less faithful to this party to which I have been attached for forty years'. In a final statement, he observed that if in the course of his premiership he had 'difficulties with my conscience and with a doctrine that I will not forget completely', he would be forced to compromise, and if no compromise were possible, he would resign. 'I will do my best,

---

[5] Radical party archives. *Conférence des présidents et secrétaires généraux de Fédérations*, 14 March 1951. Stenographic record, pp. 4–19.

the least harm possible; you can pass judgement afterwards; France must have a government.'

France must have a government, the régime must be protected: these were Queuille's major concerns. He was *not* among those Radicals who liked to equate the Radical party with France. His country's leaders, in his opinion, had always had more serious preoccupations than party doctrine. On 5 April 1949 he told his fellow deputies that 'in the course of our parliamentary history, the régime has been able to function because the men who sit on these benches knew that above their parties there was the national interest to serve'. There were times in all parliamentary assemblies when party interests must give way: 'This is the case whenever the régime is in danger.'

Six weeks later, on 24 May, in one of his most memorable speeches, Queuille told those deputies who had been voting for him that they were condemned to remain united in their support. 'You must serve together; this is a necessity to which you are condemned.' This announcement was greeted first by 'laughs on the extreme left and on certain benches on the left, in the centre, and on the right', and then by 'applause on the left, in the centre, and on the right'. After André-Jean Godin, the stalwart *radical gaulliste*, had interrupted to note that this was 'a terrible punishment', Queuille again repeated his conviction that they must remain together and warned that the only governmental majority possible in the Assembly was the one that had been supporting him.

Mid-twentieth-century France provided a particularly large scope for a politician specializing in conciliation and compromise. Queuille may not have brought solutions to the fundamental problems that his country was facing, but given the nature of the problems and the conditions under which he governed, this was not surprising. It is undeniable, in any case, that many of those whom he opposed could have done much more 'harm'.

Political leaders in other democracies also have not been exempt from having to work hard in order to remain relatively stationary. In attributing this quality to the leadership of the industrious Harry S. Truman (who was directing the destinies of the United States during the same periods that Queuille served as premier of France), an American observer once made a remark that would be equally applicable to Queuille. 'There is much to be said, after all, for the mariner who, knowing that he cannot quiet the storm, contrives somehow to stay afloat until the storm has died down of itself.'[6]

Queuille, however, had to face problems of a more basic nature than those faced by any of his American or English contemporaries. Truman did not have to contend with an electorate in which a fourth of the voters supported Communist candidates, nor was he dependent on a representative body in which nearly half of those participating advocated a new system of government. Under such conditions, minimum objectives could be of major importance.

Under virtually all conditions, however, Queuille remained on the side of those who counselled moderation and restraint. In later years, when other members of the Radical party were in the forefront of those advocating stern measures of reform, Queuille remained hesitant and doubtful. At the end of 1956, when most of his fellow countrymen were calling for new answers to their numerous problems, Queuille was still able to argue that 'one must never let oneself be carried away by the desire to do something new'.[7] Queuille had won the gratitude of many of his compatriots for his defence of the régime in 1948 and 1949, but by 1956 more and more of them were insistent in demanding more positive measures.

*

* *

Queuille's three premierships all took place during the 1946–51 legislature. In the following legislature, a younger and more dynamic *radical de gestion* emerged from the ranks of France's aspiring politicians and established a similar record: Edgar Faure was the only one of the new legislature's premiers who formed more than one of its governments.

Faure had risen far since his electoral defeat in Paris in 1945. Unlike Queuille, he did not pass through a long period of apprenticeship before reaching the summit of French political power. Elected a deputy in November 1946, Faure became a '*demi-ministre*' in February 1949, when Queuille appointed him

[6] Samuel Lubell, *The Future of American Politics*, New York, 1952, p. 22. Chapter II, entitled 'The Man Who Bought Time', is devoted to Truman.

[7] At a banquet of the dissident Radical party, 12 December 1956. *L'Express*, 21 December 1956.

secrétaire d'état in the Ministry of Finance. He continued to occupy the same post when Bidault succeeded Queuille and then enjoyed full cabinet rank as Minister of the Budget in the next three governments—led successively by Queuille, Pleven, and Queuille—that preceded the opening of the 1951–6 legislature.

A proven expert in financial matters, Faure enlarged his ministerial horizons by becoming Minister of Justice in the government formed by René Pleven in August 1951. On 20 January 1952, after three years of service in seven consecutive cabinets, Faure made parliamentary history by becoming premier. Only forty-three years old, he was France's youngest premier since Armand Fallières succeeded Gambetta after the latter's death in 1881. Fallières had only remained in office for three weeks before being replaced by Jules Ferry. Faure's government did not last much longer; he fell on 29 February, after forty days as premier.

Faure was not a member of the Pinay and Mayer governments that followed. After eighteen months without a cabinet post (during his final six months of ministerial isolation, he served as chairman of the National Assembly's important Foreign Affairs Committee), Faure made his governmental *rentrée* in June 1953 when Laniel chose him as his Minister of Finance. Faure remained in control of the same ministry after Mendès-France succeeded Laniel a year later. Shortly before his government was overthrown in February 1955, Mendès-France moved Faure to the Ministry of Foreign Affairs. After Mendès-France fell, Faure succeeded him as premier and remained in office until the end of the legislature.

Faure's spectacular rise to political eminence was in keeping with his educational and professional background—in all his activities he had demonstrated great determination and ability. He had also distinguished himself for his desire to please others. The latter characteristic, along with his determination to win a loyal electoral following, was to cause difficulties of an unexpected nature after he began his political career. It is proverbially useful for a politician to share his origins with his constituents. Therefore, in order to win popular acceptance as a native son of Jura, Faure attempted to conceal the name of his birthplace.[8] Noting his persistent discretion on the latter subject, certain of

[8] Jean Sarrus, *Edgar Faure*, Paris, 1955, pp. 13–19.

his adversaries mistakenly concluded that he was of Jewish and foreign origin.

In order to silence his opponents' conjectures, Faure was obliged to undertake two libel suits. Although he had wanted people to think he was born in Jura, he had actually been born at Béziers—in 1908—in the southern *département* of Hérault. The son of an Army medical officer and the grandson of a viticulturist of Hérault and a schoolteacher of the neighbouring department of Aude, Faure had as much seniority as a son of France as had the most vitriolic of his legal opponents, Pierre Poujade.

Faure did not spend all his childhood at Béziers. Although depriving him of the benefits of having a fixed residence, the inevitable moves of an officer's family were to provide Faure in later years with the politically advantageous honour of having been a student at an imposing number of schools. After studies at Verdun, Narbonne, Paris, Fontainebleau, and Orléans, he completed his *baccalauréat* at Paris's *Lycée* Voltaire. Continuing his studies in Paris, Faure went on to earn a *licence* and a law doctorate at the *Faculté de Droit* and a diploma for Russian language studies at the *École des Langues Orientales*.

As a student, Faure's primary interests were politics, literature, and law: in later years he was to remain faithful to all three. While studying in Paris, he wrote for several student reviews. On one occasion, after noting the seemingly inevitable ephemeral nature of such publications, Faure produced a typically ingenious suggestion: in order to profit from the curiosity that a new review aroused, each issue should have a new name. His favourite review—*The Shaggy Bear*—having recently expired, Faure proceeded to found *The Cockroach*. As planned, the new review only appeared once, but despite the manifest logic of Faure's scheme, the publication did not have a further reincarnation.

At nineteen, while still a student, Faure became a lawyer and a member of the Bar. In 1928 he won a coveted position as secretary of the Paris *Conférence des Avocats*, the youngest lawyer to win this distinction since Raymond Poincaré. While writing his doctoral dissertation, *Oil in Peace and in War*, he worked in the office of a prominent business lawyer. By the time war broke out in 1939, Faure was a solidly established lawyer—and, in his spare time, the author of detective novels which he published under the name Edgar Sandé.

Although it interrupted his legal career, the war opened new horizons to Faure. On one occasion, while engaged in a resistance mission, he narrowly escaped meeting a particularly unpleasant fate. By inadvertently failing to catch a train, he missed arrest and deportation to Germany.[9] In November 1942, shortly before the Allied invasion of North Africa, Faure went to Tunisia. Six months later, he joined de Gaulle in Algiers.

After holding two administrative posts under de Gaulle during 1943 and 1944, Faure was provided with a new opportunity for advancement by his old friend and future rival, Pierre Mendès-France. After his appointment as Minister of the National Economy by de Gaulle in September 1944, Mendès-France brought Faure into his personal cabinet as a *chargé de mission*. The two colleagues had known each other since their student days and had shared many experiences. In 1932, when Mendès-France was twenty-five and Faure twenty-three, the former won his first election to the Chamber of Deputies, and the latter won the hand of *Mademoiselle* Lucie Meyer. After his election and his friend's marriage, Mendès-France accompanied the young couple on their honeymoon, an adventurous Intourist trip to the Soviet Union which was marred when the travellers became ill with food poisoning—Mendès-France's case was so severe that a worried official in the French Embassy went so far as to order a lead-lined coffin in which to return the remains of the young deputy to France.[10]

When Mendès-France resigned from the Ministry of the National Economy in April 1945, Faure followed him. He played a commendable if minor role as a French representative at the German war crimes trial in Nuremberg. A year later, after his election as Radical deputy from Jura, Faure began his parliamentary career.

In his rapid rise to power, Faure distinguished himself by utilizing a veritable arsenal of political methods. His service under Mendès-France in 1944 and 1945 later was to enable him to remark, not always ironically, that he was the first *mendèsiste*. Like Mendès-France he was an able technician; and although they were to diverge greatly in their choice of means, the

[9] *Ibid.*, p. 71. His partner on the same mission, who did catch the train and who was deported to Germany, was Jean Dumaine, brother of Jacques Dumaine, *op. cit.*
[10] *Ibid.*, pp. 65–6.

objectives of the two rivals were to coincide on more than one important question.

It was Queuille, however, who gave Faure his first cabinet post. After this happy beginning, their relationship remained cordial and mutually advantageous. In 1949, as a token of his esteem, Faure's kindly chief presented him with a photograph inscribed 'To Edgar Faure, one of my protégés'.[11] In 1952, when he became premier, Faure was in an ideal position to return the compliment. In addition to paying verbal tribute to '*le Président* Queuille, who was my patron and who will always remain so',[12] Faure provided Queuille with a more tangible expression of his respect by making him his vice-premier.

Faure's first premiership, however, contrasted strongly with Queuille's period in office in 1948 and 1949. Like Queuille, he became premier after a long governmental crisis, but far from avoiding fundamental issues, the young premier tried to meet them head-on. His government's main problems were financial ones, and Faure was still influenced by the severe financial realism that Mendès-France had long advocated. More ambitious than cautious, he made a determined effort to win the support of the Socialists who had brought down his predecessor, René Pleven. Along with making concessions in European, Tunisian, and budgetary policy, Faure agreed to support the Socialists' cherished sliding wage scale bill.

In a vote of confidence on 7 February 1952, two weeks after becoming premier, Faure succeeded in winning approval for the controversial wage scale bill, but his margin of victory was small, and, more significantly, forty deputies had abstained. Only thirty-five Radicals had voted in his favour—twenty-eight were among those who abstained.

It was not long before Radical abstainers became Radical opponents. At a meeting of the party's executive committee, held a few days after the vote on the sliding wage scale, many of those present reproached Faure for having accepted the premiership under conditions unfavourable to the advancement of Radical objectives. Repeating charges that had often been made against Queuille, they argued that by his actions Faure was serving the interests of those whom Radicals had long opposed.

In an official report on the general political situation, one

[11] *Le Canard enchaîné*, 15 September 1954.   [12] *I.R.S.*, February 1952.

speaker went so far as to refer bluntly to Faure's government as a 'transitional government'.[13] Firmly defending his actions, Faure replied that 'governmental continuity' was indispensable and argued that the strict application of the party's programme would only add to the government's difficulties. 'In order to govern with four parties, it is necessary that they all make concessions.' With the strong assistance of Herriot, Faure managed to carry the day, but only on a temporary basis. It was decided to convoke a special congress at which the debate could be continued and a final decision reached.

The latter congress met in May 1952. It was anticlimactical, however, as Faure's government had fallen on 29 February, two weeks after the meeting of the executive committee. Many Radical deputies, manifestly, had not felt it necessary to wait for a party congress in order to make their opposition official. In a preliminary vote concerning the EDC on 19 February, a few hours before Faure flew to Lisbon to represent his country at a crucial NATO meeting, nine of his fellow Radicals were among the opposition. On 29 February, when Faure unsuccessfully asked for a 15 per cent. rise in taxes, only thirty-three Radicals supported him, while six abstained and twenty-six voted in opposition. The bulk of Faure's opposition was provided by Communists and Gaullists, but the decisive votes were cast by Radicals and Moderates who refused to back the new taxes that were the price of the policies that they had reluctantly approved. The role played by Faure's fellow Radicals was particularly striking: his defeat was by a margin of twenty-six votes. . . .

Three years later, when Faure succeeded Mendès-France and became premier for the second time, he had new problems and new objectives. In 1952 he had been preoccupied with winning the support of the Socialists, and the latter were unanimous in voting for him when he fell. When he returned to power in February 1955, the Socialists were unanimous in their opposition. There had been too much competition for Faure to win a strong position of leadership on the left. The route to power had been less encumbered on the right.[14]

---

[13] Raymond Valabrègue, deputy from Drôme.

[14] In commenting on the relative ease of rising to a position of leadership among right-wing politicians, Faure is reputed to have remarked: '*Ils sont tous tellement bêtes!*' *Le Canard enchaîné*, 7 December 1955.

Although primarily dependent on right-wing support (both adversaries and admirers often referred to the new government as the Faure-Pinay government, in recognition of the important role played by conservative Antoine Pinay, Faure's Minister of Foreign Affairs), Faure's first few months in power in 1955 were marked by an able continuation of the policies undertaken by Mendès-France. Although presiding over a right-wing government and although his majority originally planned to replace him with an orthodox conservative leader, he managed to carry through a number of liberal measures. Asserting himself as an empirical man of the *juste milieu*, Faure was able to prove, during the first six months of his new premiership, that he was not a prisoner of his majority.

The latter feat constituted a remarkable *tour de force*. Faure came to power on 23 February 1955. Two weeks later, on 8 March, he risked his government's existence in order to support a financial measure designed to augment the pay of state employees. On 10 March, he won a second clear victory when he successfully repulsed an interpellation that called for the revocation of a controversial tax regulation. The major opposition to the regulation in question—it provided for jail sentences for those who opposed fiscal controls—came from the newly constituted Poujadist movement, and Faure was firm in warning France's representatives of the dangerous character of the new movement. 'Neither parliament nor the government must give in to street manifestations.' During the evening of 18 March, when Poujade himself was present in the gallery of the National Assembly, Faure again attacked those who demanded that the unpopular tax regulation be revoked, and in a new victory succeeded in having further debate on financial issues postponed for ten days. Finally, on the evening of 29 March, Faure's financial programme was approved by a vote of 302 to 269.

Faure was also active on other fronts. During the period that he was forced to devote most of his time to financial questions, he brought to a successful conclusion an onerous task undertaken by Mendès-France. After the Assembly's rejection of the EDC, Mendès-France had answered demands for German rearmament by producing a new set of proposals: the Paris Agreements. With great difficulty, he had successfully steered them through the *Conseil de la République*. In a brilliant and impromptu speech on 24 March before France's second chamber (he mounted to the tribune after a virulent attack by one of the project's many bitter opponents), Faure stressed the need for France to respect her past commitments. 'We will not be able to go on for ever telling our allies that France, after having signed, has changed her mind.' After reminding his listeners that he had been at the side of Mendès-France when the EDC treaty was rejected, he said that his predecessor had considered it essential that France should not be isolated from her allies. 'He asked with insistence, he sought with obstinacy, he obtained with difficulty the signature of an agreement.' The agreement was 'perhaps less good than people sometimes say, it is perhaps less bad than you may think it', but it did exist. It had been accepted, with difficulty, by a majority in the National Assembly; an adverse vote by the *Conseil de la République* would mean a resurgence of old quarrels. By his able speech and aided by the influential Antoine Pinay, Faure succeeded in preventing its rejection.

During the months that followed, Faure continued to carry through a programme of vigorous action. A general strike of government workers was avoided by timely wage increases, and an explosive labour situation at St. Nazaire was solved by government action. Production was increased and France's economic position improved: six months after he came to power, France was within measurable distance of an overseas trade balance.

Faure's major preoccupation, however, was with North African problems. In skilfully guiding the Franco-Tunisian Agreement through the Assembly and the *Conseil de la République*, Faure was continuing a programme inaugurated by his predecessor. 'Very fortunately,' Faure declared at his party's congress later that year, '*le Président* Mendès-France, when he arrived in 1954, took the initiative of the great and noble Declaration of Carthage.' In a statement made during a meeting of the Néo-Destour, held after relations between the two old friends had become strained, Tunisia's new leader, Habib Bourguiba, did not hesitate to link their names in expressing his country's appreciation for their respective roles. 'I wish, on this occasion, to render homage to the courageous action of M. Pierre Mendès-France who, the first, was able to promote a conception of Franco-Tunisian relations, as well as to the realism of M. Edgar Faure, who brought the negotiations to a conclusion.'[15]

[15] *L'Express*, 17 November 1955.

In formulating his Moroccan and Algerian policies, however, Faure could not follow paths traced by his predecessor; he was obliged to contend with new and quickly evolving situations. Much of Faure's time in office was devoted to Morocco. At the party's congress in November, a month before his fall from power, he described himself as 'a man who took this problem in his arms, who devoted himself to it without a halt for over two months'. Faure had started by formulating a plan which he hoped would solve the crisis caused by France's deposal of Morocco's popular Sultan Mohammed V. The new Sultan, Ben Arafa, would abdicate voluntarily and transfer his sovereignty to a Regency Council, and Mohammed V would be returned to France from his exile in Madagascar on condition that he would henceforth withdraw from Moroccan politics. On 20 June, Faure appointed the liberal Gilbert Grandval, French High Commissioner in the Saar, as Resident General in Morocco with the mission of carrying out this plan.

Six weeks later Grandval resigned. Faced with strong opposition in his cabinet and in Parliament, Faure had refused to give in to his emissary's entreaties for a prompt implementation of the plan. In Grandval's eyes, a major result of the government's lack of initiative had been the bloody riots and massacres of 20 August, on the anniversary of Mohammed V's deposition— the village of Oued-Zem was destroyed and forty French settlers, including many women and children, had been brutally killed. After his resignation on 30 August, Grandval was to reveal himself as one of Faure's severest critics. In a controversial account of his experiences in Morocco, published a few months later, he accused his former chief of having failed to give him sufficient support.[16] In Grandval's opinion, Faure had been overly concerned with remaining at the head of whatever tide of parliamentary opinion he calculated to be the strongest.

In a dramatic turn of events, however, Faure proved himself able to carry out, without Grandval, policies that the latter had advocated. A day after Grandval resigned, Ben Arafa finally left Rabat and retired to Tangier. Before a crucial debate on his Moroccan policies in the Assembly, on 6 October, Faure dismissed four of his Gaullist ministers who had strongly opposed Grandval's projects. In opening the debate in the Assembly,

[16] Gilbert Grandval, *Ma mission au Maroc*, Paris, 1956.

Faure made it clear that he favoured a liberal policy in Morocco. 'It is necessary to follow a policy of evolution and reforms. This means a Moroccan government.' Impressed by his stand, many deputies who had previously opposed him flocked to his support: he won by an unprecedented majority of 462. His only opposition came from those who had previously been most faithful in voting for him: 136 deputies of the centre-right. By the end of October, the Sultan, who had been ejected from his country by a French government largely because of the insistence of El Glaoui, the powerful Pasha of Marrakesh, had received the humble apologies of the latter and was in Paris as an honoured guest. A new era in Franco-Moroccan relations had begun, and as had been the case with Tunisia, Faure had played a central role. Although his role was the subject of much criticism, many of those who were strongest in their criticism were willing to approve the final results. In his actions, the empirical Faure had remained faithful to a passage from Montesquieu which he had cited to his fellow deputies on 17 January 1952, before becoming premier for the first time. 'It is not the means which must be brilliant, but the end. The true task of politics is to reach the latter by obscure paths.'

After the result of the Moroccan vote was announced in the Assembly, Faure expressed his regret that his government had not been able to rally all the votes of the majority which had habitually supported it. At this point, several voices on the extreme right and right interrupted him: 'It found another one!' In the Algerian debates that immediately followed, however, Faure reverted to his earlier majority. Having got the Left to vote for him over Morocco, he got the Right to vote for him over Algeria.

The situation in Algeria, Faure argued, was entirely different from those in Tunisia and Morocco. 'An Algerian state does not exist, an Algerian national entity does not exist.' Speaking before the Assembly on 13 October, he went on to voice his opinion that France was not a dominating power in Algeria—'There is a French nation that includes Algeria.' Aided by his rhetoric and by a diplomatic timetable that included a crucial Saar referendum, Faure succeeded in winning back most of his old majority and, on 18 October, by a less impressive vote of 308 to 254, won the Assembly's approval of his Algerian policy.

During the final months of Faure's premiership, his governmental record constituted a brilliant display of political gymnastics more than an impressive *tour de force*. Only too aware of his lack of a stable majority and increasingly discouraged by his government's difficulties, Faure proposed a drastic solution: a premature end to the legislature's existence.

Faure was not alone in making this suggestion. The project of holding early elections was announced to the public of 21 October, after a cabinet meeting at which a majority of his ministers had declared that they were in favour. On 23 October, speaking before a group of his constituents, Faure explained the reasons that had motivated their decision.[17] Insisting that it was not a political manœuvre, he pointed out that important tasks were awaiting the government and a stable majority was essential. During the first part of 1956 it would be necessary to establish a definite political relationship with Tunisia; a new structure for the French Union would have to be studied; and the Algerian question would have to be settled. Such problems, he argued, could not be treated during a long pre-electoral period. If the Assembly wanted to modify the electoral law, it could do so; a brief, but sufficient, time was still available. In any case, the decision was an irrevocable one. The existence of his government, he concluded, was henceforth dependent on the adoption of the new project.

Thus, the last great battle of Faure's second premiership began. It was to have widespread repercussions, particularly within the Radical party. Many of Faure's fellow Radicals were not willing to accept the reasons he advanced for holding early elections. In a speech before the Radical Federation of Drôme, Daladier declared that 'the goal of the precipitated elections is only to conceal more thoroughly a balance sheet of bankruptcy'.[18] Faure's most outspoken Radical opponent, however, was Mendès-France. The latter had been embittered when Faure succeeded him as premier. Faure's desire for early elections was in direct conflict with Mendès-France's hopes to make the Radical party the disciplined centre of a broad political movement. The rupture between the two men was now complete. Faure viewed France's problems as a premier hoping for a stable majority; Mendès-France wanted time to renovate the Radical party and to make it an instrument for the renovation and reform of France.

[17] *L'Année politique*, 1955, p. 78.　　[18] *Ibid.*, p. 79.

Mendès-France won a major victory by consolidating his control of the Radical party at the party's congress held during the first week of November. The evolution of events on the parliamentary scene was much less clear. On 28 October, Faure won a general vote of confidence by 271 to 259, with eighty-one abstentions. Forty-four Radicals supported him, ten voted in opposition, seven abstained, and four were absent. It was clear that the Radical tide had begun to turn against Faure. On 2 November, a preliminary project concerning the early end of the legislature was passed by 330 to 211, with eighty-one abstentions. Only twenty-one Radicals supported Faure, while thirty-seven voted in opposition, seven abstained and two were absent. When the project reached the *Conseil de la République*, Radical senators took the lead in adding an amendment requiring a return to the single-member constituency voting system. The latter measure was defeated in the Assembly, and on 12 November, Faure won another confidence vote by 285 to 267 with seventy-eight abstentions; his opponents were forceful in pointing out that he would have lost if he had not had the support of the Communist group. Thirty-seven Radicals had opposed him, twenty-one voted in favour, and seven abstained. After the second chamber had again voted for a return to the Radicals' favourite electoral system, Faure was forced to call for still another confidence vote. This time he met defeat. On 29 November, by a vote of 318 to 218, with fifty-three abstentions and twelve absentees, Faure was voted out of office. In this final vote, thirty-four Radicals had opposed him, twenty-seven voted in his favour, two abstained, and two were absent.

Faure's next step—his controversial dissolution of the National Assembly—aroused even stronger action on the part of his Radical colleagues. The first dissolution in French parliamentary history since MacMahon won the eternal ire of the French Left by dissolving Parliament on 16 May 1877, Faure's act had been made possible by the margin of his defeat: his had been the second government to be overthrown by a 'constitutional majority'—314 votes—within an eighteen-month period.[19] His critics, however, were quick to point out that, rather than letting the country be the judge in a major conflict between the Assembly and the government, Faure's dissolution was concerned only with

[19] Mendès-France had been opposed by 319 deputies.

the timing of the elections—and had as a major result the imposition on the country of an electoral system that was the source of widespread opposition.

In the furor that ensued, Faure's most resolute opponents were from his own party. At the cabinet level, five Radical ministers refused to associate themselves with the dissolution measures —a technicality prevented them from resigning. On the parliamentary level, Herriot, Queuille, and Mendès-France, joined by the presidents of the Socialist, Radical, UDSR, and *Républicains sociaux* groups in the National Assembly, published a manifesto in which they declared that 'such an act, although technically in conformity with the Constitution, betrays the spirit of it'.[20] It was on the party level, however, that the most direct action was taken. On 1 December 1955, after two meetings in Herriot's apartment in Paris, the party's *bureau* voted to expel the defeated premier from the ranks of the party.

'I have been overthrown, dissolved, and expelled,' Faure later informed his constituents. In discussing his unprecedented plight and in defending his controversial actions, he was forceful in insisting that he had always remained faithful to the traditional values of radicalism. Like all Radicals, Faure was convinced that *his* was the true form of radicalism.

Although Faure's period of active membership in the party had only spanned ten years, he had long since joined the ranks of prominent Radical spokesmen. After his decision in 1945 to attempt to become a Radical deputy, he had acclimated himself to his new party with remarkable rapidity. As early as the party's congress in 1946, he was able to speak like an old Radical veteran. 'During the long months while I was at Nuremberg,' he told his listeners, 'I remembered that I was a Radical and engaged in the reflections of a Radical on international justice.' Faure's reflections were of an eminently orthodox nature. When he saw the eight judges seated below the French, English, American, and Soviet flags, he said, he often found himself thinking of 'our president Edouard Herriot'. 'Why? Because, excuse me for saying it to him, but after all it was *le Président* Herriot who, in 1924, tightened our *entente cordiale* with England, who discovered Russia and established relations with this great power. It was he who in 1932 gave up power in order to maintain *l'amitié américaine.*'

[20] *L'Année politique*, 1955, p. 92.

Faure was willing to pay ritual tribute to standard Radical themes, but he also was explicit in enunciating the more specialized arguments of the *radicaux de gestion*. In March 1954, while he was serving as Minister of Finance under Laniel, he told his listeners at a special Radical congress that there were two *politiques radicales*: one was doctrinal, abstract, and idealistic; the other was *de fait*, realistic, 'a *politique* that is carried out by Radical ministers'. Faure made it clear that he was primarily interested in the latter. It was, he noted, less exalting and less impressive; it was modest, hesitant, and occasionally contradictory; but it expressed itself in everyday affairs, in statistics, and in the life of the French people. Radicals, he argued, would have to decide whether this *'politique de fait*, insufficient on many points, affected by all the ambiguities of a coalition government, but which breathes, and which occasionally advances', was truly their policy, or whether it was 'an error and an imposture'.

The following year, at the crucial special congress of 4 May 1955, when the *radicaux mendésistes* succeeded in winning control of the party's administrative machinery, Faure again discussed his concept of the role of the Radical party. Defending his actions as premier, he declared that the Radical party was a governmental party, the only party that had participated in all the governments of the current legislature. In an eloquent appeal for unity, he pointed out that there were already too many parties in France and asked his listeners not to cut their party in two. Would it not be possible, he asked, for those present to find 'what Goethe called a moment of acquiescence, one moment only?' After his speech the delegates gave him a standing ovation and sang the *Marseillaise*—but did not follow his advice.

By his eloquence, skill, and position as premier, Faure became the major spokesman for the traditional position of the *radicaux de gestion* during the crucial Radical year of 1955. A few days after the special congress of 4 May, he told a meeting of Radical deputies and senators that the party must modernize itself and affirm its doctrine. He added, however, that it did not have the right to have doubts about itself when it was managing the affairs of the country. 'What more can it propose to public opinion than to direct as it is doing the government of the Republic?'[21]

During the final months of his premiership, Faure was

[21] *Le Monde*, 13 May 1955.

presented with an abnormally large number of opportunities to defend his record both as a political leader and as a Radical. Probably his most dramatic speech was made in a debate with Mendès-France on 5 November, during the party's annual congress. Facing a hostile audience that greeted him with calls for his resignation, Faure succeeded in presenting a documented defence of his actions. He was not successful, however, in an attempt to have Herriot decide whether he should remain at his post as premier. Once again the object of Radical solicitation, the veteran leader declined in noting that 'a matter of conscience must be solved personally'.

In answering his Radical opponents, Faure utilized many of the arguments that had been used by other *radicaux de gestion*. Like Queuille, Faure often argued that a Radical premier must consider himself as 'on leave from the party'. When he used this argument, however, during the meeting at which his exclusion was voted, one of his listeners retorted: 'You may be on leave from the Radical party, but one has the impression that you have moved in with the MRP.'[22] In a statement after his exclusion, Faure noted the need to distinguish between that which belonged to the party and that which belonged to the national interest.[23] The duties of a political leader, he argued, were of a special nature. 'In my opinion, the premier cannot be a party man when there are arbitrations to undertake or decisions to make.'

In keeping with the traditional arguments of the *radicaux de gestion*, Faure prided himself before his electors on having been a member of a succession of contrasting governments. In a speech in his constituency during the electoral campaign he had done so much to provoke and to enliven, he declared that 'when one has power, one does not have the right to abandon it'.[24] 'Political life,' he told his listeners, 'consists of a series of compromises'—'In life it is necessary to compromise.'

During the ten years that had followed his entrance into the Radical party, Faure had established himself as one of the most spectacular *radicaux de gestion* in the party's history. An able technician and an excellent speaker, he was gifted with a persuasive personality and, in Herriot's words, an 'almost diabolical intel-

---

[22] *L'Express*, 2 December 1955. Auguste Pinton, senator from Rhône.
[23] *Le Monde*, 3 December 1955. Interview by *Radiodiffusion française*.
[24] *L'Express*, 5 December 1955.

ligence'.[25] A frequenter of the *salons* of the Faubourg St. Germain, he had become a well-known figure in Paris's intellectual life— his wife is editor of the progressive review, *La Nef*.[26] A versatile leader, he was able to utilize his reputation of being all things to all men to its fullest advantage. Refusing to be labelled as a man of the right or of the left, he considered himself as a man of government—ready to govern on all occasions. He was proud of his dexterity. In a debate in the National Assembly on 18 March 1955, the Socialist leader Daniel Mayer noted that one of the morning newspapers had stated that of all the governments of the 1951–6 legislature Faure's was the furthest to the right and went on to comment on Faure's versatility. 'I must admit that I personally believe that you are very capable in forming a government on the right, and also very capable in forming a government on the left.' Faure interrupted to add a third alternative. 'In that case, let's form a government of National Union!'

Of particular significance in Faure's career was his long relationship with Mendès-France. After having been youthful friends and governmental colleagues, they came to personify opposite poles of radicalism. At the same time, they continued to share many basic objectives: Faure's continuation in 1955 of many of the programmes begun by Mendès-France in 1954 provides the most striking evidence for this point.

Their differences were primarily on the level of means. Both wanted to modernize France, but Mendès-France favoured strong words and actions, while Faure preferred the more 'obscure paths' of parliamentary manœuvre and compromise. Differences in their personalities and in their choice of friends aggravated their conflicts. The intransigent young men who surrounded Mendès-France consistently served as Faure's most outspoken opponents. In January 1955 this opposition reached unprecedented heights when Jean-Jacques Servan-Schreiber, the young editor of the *mendésiste* newspaper *l'Express*, accused Faure of having lifted a tax—while Mendès-France's Minister of Finance—on imported race-horses in order to please Marcel Boussac, the French textile

[25] *Le Monde*, 21 October 1952.

[26] Mme. Faure is noted for holding independent opinions. In commenting on Faure's skill in parliamentary manœuvre, Alexander Werth, in *The New Statesman and Nation*, 17 December 1955, reported: 'A friend recently asked Madame Faure whether her husband had shown similar skill as a suitor. She replied, with some frankness: "*Oui, mais à cette époque au moins, il avait un but . . .*" '

manufacturer and race-horse owner.[27] The aroused Faure immediately challenged Servan-Schreiber to a duel, and it took all
Mendès-France's angry tact to straighten matters out.

Faure was moderate and compromising on nearly all occasions,
but he was forced to make an exception in the case of his more
vitriolic enemies among the younger *radicaux mendésistes*. The
latter continued to denounce Faure in violent terms during 1955,
their denunciations reaching a climax during the electoral campaign at the end of the year. Certain of their methods were re-
miniscent of previous political polemics. In 1949 a prominent
radical gaulliste was berated for writing in a Gaullist newspaper
that took delight in linking Herriot and Laval's names and pictures; in December 1955 *l'Express* carried on a dubious tradition
in referring to 'Faure-Laval' and in publishing a cartoon with
Laval's head superimposed on Faure's shoulders.[28]

Except when confronted by the more extreme statements of
certain of the *radicaux mendésistes*, Faure did not vary from his
faith in conciliation and moderation. At a meeting of the Radical
group in the National Assembly shortly before Mendès-France's
fall (and a few days after the cancelled duel), Faure told the
assembled deputies: 'I have two friends, Mendès-France and
René Mayer; I would like them to have a reconciliation.'[29] The
succession of events that followed may have lessened Faure's
optimism in promoting reconciliations among Radicals, but he
was always careful to avoid personal recrimination. In a speech
in Jura in December 1955, he told his constituents that 'people
will never find, in my words or in my writings, anything angry,
anything bitter, anything spiteful, even concerning my worst
adversaries'.[30] Later in the same month, while visiting cafés in
his constituency during an electoral campaign trip, Faure even
found it possible to praise his chief rival. When one constituent
asked him what he thought of Mendès-France, he began by replying, 'He's Robespierre, he was made intoxicated with power',
but immediately corrected himself. 'He is a very intelligent man.
I have great esteem for him.'[31]

[27] The incident was provoked by an article, 'Gouvernement: correction et
moralité', published in *L'Express*, 29 January 1955. For an account of the events
that followed, see *Le Monde*, 1 February 1955.
[28] *L'Express*, 3–4 December 1955. See above, p. 149.
[29] *Le Monde*, 6–7 February 1955.   [30] *Combat*, 5 December 1955.
[31] *Le Monde*, 20 December 1955.

The general elections of 2 January 1956 were a defeat for Faure's governmental majority, but he won a solid personal victory in his home constituency—in the commune of Port-Lesnay, where Faure was elected mayor in 1947, he received 255 of the 366 votes cast. As president of the small RGR, Faure henceforth lacked the support of a broad parliamentary base, and during most of the last legislature of the Fourth Republic, he remained primarily on the side lines. His exclusion from the Radical party was confirmed at a meeting of the party's executive committee in January 1956 and made official, by a vote of 924 to 333, at the party's congress at Lyons in October of the same year. Faure protested the decision, but carefully refrained from associating himself with those who were devoting themselves to bringing about a new split in the party.

Although he was expelled from its ranks, the Radical party continued to occupy a prominent place in Faure's thoughts. A year after the new legislature began, he commented with sadness on the 'break-up' of the Radical party: 'The French political system has lost its centre of gravity.'[32] The party's plight, he explained, was due to the fact that Mendès-France had wanted to 'instill it with an authoritarian style and a frenetic rhythm that was incompatible with the very spirit of radicalism'. It was time, he concluded, to rebuild the Radical party and to form a large *rassemblement centriste*.

History was to move too fast, however, for France's negotiating and temporizing parliamentary leaders. By the time that Faure was to make his long-delayed governmental *rentrée*, the Fourth Republic was in its death throes. His return to office, as Minister of Finance and Economic Affairs in the cabinet formed by Pierre Pflimlin during the night of 13 May 1958, was to coincide with the end of an era—an era that had found a characteristic leader in the person of Edgar Faure.

*
* *

Queuille had been the most noteworthy *radical de gestion* of the 1946–51 legislature; Faure succeeded Queuille in this position during the following legislature. In the meantime the rise of the *radicaux mendésistes* had taken place. After the latter won control

[32] *Le Monde*, 10 January 1957.

of the party's machinery, a showdown battle with the *radicaux de gestion* was inevitable.

Faure was the first major casualty of this struggle—his defeat coincided with that of the *néo-radicaux*. During the new legislature that opened in 1956, other *radicaux de gestion* rose to meet the challenge of the *radicaux mendésistes*. Some, following Queuille, quit a Radical party controlled by their enemies and founded another party more to their liking. Others, working from within the party, made the National Assembly their major field of action. Both groups continued to proclaim the eternal values of a conciliatory, moderate radicalism. The measure of their success was directly related to the evolution of the *radicaux mendésistes*. It is in the latter context, therefore, that the subsequent activities of the *radicaux de gestion* will be considered.

It may be assumed, in any case, that the principles outlined by Queuille and Faure will never fail to find supporters. Political power will always be a potent attraction to those who enter political life, and, for some, the exercise of power will always serve as an end in itself. The Radical party traditionally provided a political grouping for men who wanted a club, a *rassemblement*, more than a party in the strict sense of the term. A conflict was inevitable between such men and those who sought to transform the Radical party into a disciplined weapon of reform. The party could remain faithful to the easy-going traditions of its past, or it could follow the new routes outlined by Mendès-France. It could not continue, indefinitely, to remain at the crossroads.

VIII

The Radicaux Mendésistes, 1953-7

'*Nous proclamons que le radical-socialisme de la IVe République, sans doctrines, sans méthodes, sans enthousiasme, est à bout de souffle.*'
CHARLES HERNU, at Aix-le-Bains Congress, 17–20 September 1953.

'*Empruntant à Shakespeare le mot qu'il prête à César regardant les conjurés, je dis à mon tour: "Ces gens sont dangereux. Ils pensent trop. . . ."* '
LÉON MARTINAUD-DÉPLAT, at Special Congress of 4 May 1955.

Of all the political leaders who rose to eminence in post-war France, none had as great an impact on the French and international scenes as Pierre Mendès-France. His seven months and seventeen days as premier of France in 1954–5 were unprecedented in French history. With an uncompromising belief in himself and in his ideas, Mendès-France dramatically undertook a series of forceful actions. He brought an end to the seven-and-a-half-year-old war in Indo-China. He inaugurated a progressive policy in Tunisia. He brought the four-year-old EDC proposals to a vote in the National Assembly and after their rejection devised and successfully sponsored a substitute plan for German rearmament. He attacked the alcohol interests, closed the bars in the early hours of the morning, and appointed a prefect of police who stopped Parisians from sounding their horns. Above all, he aroused great enthusiasm on the part of many of his compatriots. By his dynamic and vigorous methods, he provided a contrast to many of the manœuvring and temporizing politicians who had preceded him.

Mendès-France brought new hope to many of his compatriots, but he also made many enemies. On 5 February 1955, he was voted out of office. The dramatic 'Mendès-France experiment' had come to a premature end. A new 'experiment', however, was soon to begin. Unable to continue with his plans for renovating France, Mendès-France was to devote himself to the task of renovating the Radical party.

In his new endeavour, Mendès-France was assisted by a wide variety of supporters. From 4 May 1955 to 23 May 1957, he and his followers controlled the party's administrative machinery. They enjoyed widespread support among much of the party's rank and file. After two years of diligent efforts, however, they had still not made it possible for observers to employ an unmodified form of the term 'Radical' to describe a coherent segment of political opinion. Radicalism, like the Republic itself, was still refusing to be renovated. It had only made room in its collection of political titles for one more term: the *radicaux mendésistes*.

*
* *

More than any other group of Radicals, the *radicaux mendésistes* owed their existence to the forceful personality of one man. The only possible comparison would be to the relationship between the *radicaux gaullistes* and de Gaulle. The *radicaux gaullistes*, however, were of much less significance in the evolution of radicalism than the *radicaux mendésistes* were to be—on the periphery of both Radicalism and Gaullism, they never attained more than a marginal importance in either of their allegiances. Certain of their number may have attempted to equate their two allegiances, but this was a doctrinal endeavour that never aroused the interest of the man whom they followed. Mendès-France, on the other hand, was more than a distant hero to the *radicaux mendésistes*: he was the heart and soul of their movement. A basic prerequisite for the study of the *radicaux mendésistes*, therefore, is a consideration of the career and the development of the man who brought them into their collective existence, gave them his name, and led them into battle.

Born in Paris in 1907, Mendès-France was the son of a manufacturer of women's clothing from Limoges who had established himself as a wholesaler in Paris. His family was of Portuguese–Jewish descent and settled in France long before the Revolution, perhaps as early as 1300. The family name was originally Mendès —the 'France' was added either to commemorate the establishment of the family in France or as a result of a marriage between a Mendès and a Franco in Spain or Portugal.

The future premier's family was of modest means. He grew

up in an apartment over his father's business, which was not far
from Paris's historic *Place de la République*. His record as a student
was brilliant. After passing his *baccalauréat* at fifteen, he went on
to graduate from the *École des Sciences Politiques* and to finish his
law school course—ranking first in a class of 800—by the time
he was nineteen. At twenty-one he was a member of the Paris
Bar and the youngest lawyer in France.

Mendès-France's early political career was equally precocious
and, more significantly, was Radical from a very early date. In
later years he often was to recall his long Radical past, particularly when speaking in party gatherings. In a speech at the party's
congress at Marseilles in 1954, he told his listeners that he had
become a Radical in 1923, when he was only sixteen, after hearing 'a magnificent speech' by Herriot. 'I felt that my political
feeling was to be a Radical—and it was then, *mon cher Président*,
that I joined our party which I have never left and to which
I feel even closer today than at any time in the past.' Mendès-
France's early political activities, however, were not limited to
listening to Radical oratory. In the turbulent student life of the
period, he often had to fight in support of his political ideas.
He still has a conspicuously broken nose as a result of an attack
by a group of Royalist students of *Action Française*.

His first chance in politics came after he participated in a
Radical rally at the Norman town of Louviers. Despite his young
age, he was offered the opportunity of running as the local
Radical candidate in the next elections for the Chamber of
Deputies. In 1932, four months after his twenty-fifth birthday,
he became France's youngest deputy. Two years later he was
elected mayor of Louviers, and in 1938, when he was thirty-one
years of age, Léon Blum appointed him to his first ministerial
post—Under Secretary of State for the Treasury. He was the
youngest member of the government.

By the time war broke out, Mendès-France was solidly established in Louviers and was on his way to a brilliant political
career. In 1933 he married Liliane Circurel, the daughter of a
Cairo family of Jewish merchant-bankers; Edouard Daladier and
Georges Bonnet, both cabinet members at the time, served as
witnesses at the marriage ceremony. When war came, Mendès-
France was called up as a lieutenant in the Air Force and, after
asking for flying duty, was sent to Syria, where he subsequently

won his wings as an air observer. Back in France at the time of the German invasion, he was one of the French parliamentarians who went to North Africa on the *Massilia* in June 1940.

After reaching Morocco, Mendès-France was arrested by the Vichy government. Grotesquely charged with 'desertion', he was brought to the military prison at Clermont-Ferrand, in central France, and sentenced to six years' imprisonment. In the meantime his wife, accompanied by their two small sons, had managed to flee to the United States. In June 1941, after careful plotting, Mendès-France escaped from prison, spent eight months in the French underground, and then made his way to England. After training as a navigator in Scotland, he joined the famed Lorraine group of the Free French Air Force and flew many missions over the Continent.

In November 1943 de Gaulle summoned Mendès-France to Algiers to be Commissioner of Finances in the *Comité Français de la Libération Nationale*. As part of his new duties, Mendès-France signed a financial agreement between Britain and France in February 1944 and served as leader of the French delegation at the Bretton Woods Conference in July 1944. In September of the same year, after the liberation of Paris, de Gaulle appointed him as Minister of the National Economy in the new provisional government.

In his new post, Mendès-France advanced an austere plan for economic reconstruction and proposed a bold programme of price and wage stabilization. Calling for heavy taxation of illicit profits, tight rationing, and mobilization of all French resources to speed up recovery, he argued that it was only by carrying out a plan of deliberate austerity that France could stabilize its economy and halt the inflationary rise of wages and prices. Mendès-France's ideas met great resistance, however, both within the cabinet and from the *Banque de France*. His major opponent was René Pleven, de Gaulle's Minister of Finance, who urged caution and argued that the austere programme would lose the government the confidence of producers and industrialists. Unable to carry through his programme, Mendès-France submitted his resignation in January 1945.[1] De Gaulle prevailed upon him

---

[1] Mendès-France made his letter of resignation public after the fall of the Fourth Republic in *Gouverner c'est choisir*, vol. 3, *La Politique et la Vérité, Juin 1955–Septembre 1958*, Paris, 1958, Appendix 1, pp. 329–41.

to continue in his post for a while longer, but after it became increasingly clear that his plan had no chance of being accepted, Mendès-France resigned in April 1945.

Mendès-France was henceforth the implacable Cassandra of the French political scene. During nine years in the political wilderness, he persistently warned France's successive governments of the problems darkening the nation's future. For nine long years he did not join any of the many ministries that were formed. In January 1946, after de Gaulle's resignation, Mendès-France turned down an offer to lead an expanded Ministry of Finance in the cabinet that was formed by de Gaulle's successor, Félix Gouin. He submitted a programme of drastic economic reforms to the leaders of the three parties—Socialist, Communist, and MRP—which controlled the government, but soon concluded that it was useless to try to play 'a fourth tune in an orchestra whose members were already playing three different tunes'.[2]

Refusing to accept ministerial office except on his own terms, Mendès-France combined his role of Cassandra with that of an industrious economic specialist. He served as head of the French delegation to the Savannah monetary conference in 1946, was the French representative on the International Monetary Fund later in the same year, was the permanent French representative on the United Nations Economic and Social Council from 1947 to 1950, and in 1952 again represented France on the International Monetary Fund.

Until 1953, Mendès-France's impact on the national scene was of a relatively limited nature. His precise analysis of France's political and economic problems and above all his pronouncements on the tragic war in Indo-China gradually won him an audience throughout the country, but it was not until he was nearly elected premier in June 1953 that he became the centre of many of his compatriots' hopes. By one speech, on 3 June 1953, Mendès-France became a symbol of many Frenchmen's desires for change and renovation. On the following day he was defeated by a surprisingly narrow margin (receiving 301 of the 314 votes that were necessary for election; 119 deputies voted against him and 202 abstained), but by capturing the imagination and winning the admiration of a wide variety of Frenchmen,

[2] *Le Monde*, 31 May–1 June 1953.

he was henceforth to be a central figure on the French political scene.

By its impact on public opinion, the speech made by Mendès-France on 3 June 1953 was to constitute a turning point in the post-war evolution of the Radical party. It was not until a year later that Mendès-France made his dramatic entry on the governmental scene, but in 1953 it was evident that a new and growing political force was present in the land. Mendès-France was no longer the lone wolf of French politics. The rise of the *mendésistes*—and, ultimately, the *radicaux mendésistes*—had begun.

*
* *

An important role in Mendès-France's rise to power was played by the weekly newspaper *l'Express*. Founded in May 1953, less than three weeks before Mendès-France's dramatic attempt to become premier, it not only provided him with a platform for expressing his ideas but also constituted a rallying point for some of his most enthusiastic and articulate supporters.

The most zealous of these supporters was the newspaper's able and personable young editor, Jean-Jacques Servan-Schreiber. The son of a rich French publishing family, Servan-Schreiber rapidly rose to a position of eminence in French post-war journalism. Only twenty-seven years old when he founded *l'Express*, he was well qualified to serve as a spokesman for a new generation that was coming to the fore in France. His previous years had been active ones. In 1943, after completing two years at the *Ecole Polytechnique* in Paris, he escaped to North Africa and joined the French Army. After being sent to the United States to be trained as a fighter pilot, he returned to France and was assigned to the French Army of Occupation in Germany. Married in 1947, he spent a year in Brazil and then returned to France and joined the staff of *Le Monde* as a specialist in foreign affairs. It was after leaving *Le Monde* that the young journalist decided to found his own newspaper.

L'Express was an immediate success. In its early period it was greatly aided by the support and resources of *Les Echos*, the financial daily newspaper owned by the Servan-Schreiber family —the original title of *l'Express* was *l'Express, Les Echos du Samedi*. The first issue featured a one-page interview of Mendès-France.

Many prominent French intellectuals—including François Mauriac, Albert Camus, and André Malraux—were among its early contributors. The offices of *l'Express*, on the Avenue des Champs-Elysées, became a meeting place for Mendès-France and his younger colleagues.

L'Express's star rose with that of Mendès-France. After he became premier, the newspaper's offices were sometimes referred to as 'the *Express* ministry'. During the period that he was premier, Mendès-France ceased writing in its columns, and Servan-Schreiber took a leave of absence from his newspaper and moved into the *Quai d'Orsay* as one of Mendès-France's personal advisors, but *l'Express*, more than ever, was a centre of political attention and activity.

For Servan-Schreiber and his colleagues, Mendès-France was the only Frenchman who seemed to be capable of reviving a divided French Left. They were ardent supporters of his plan to end the war in Indo-China. They were enthusiastic believers in his projects for modernizing France's economic system. They made it their mission to spread his ideas and to stimulate the younger generation to take an active interest in politics.

It was only after Mendès-France's defeat in February 1955 that many of his *mendésiste* supporters from *l'Express* considered becoming *radicaux mendésistes*. In this evolution, the special congress of 4 May 1955 was the great turning point. Hitherto many of those who supported Mendès-France did so in spite of his Radical allegiance; henceforth, however, many of them demonstrated their enthusiasm and their optimism by joining him in the second 'Mendès-France experiment'. A typical *mendésiste* reaction to the new state of affairs was expressed in a July 1955 issue of the party's newspaper. 'It is certainly the first time, for a long time, that one can dare to say one is a Radical.'

There is no doubt that *l'Express* was instrumental in encouraging many of the younger generation to participate in the difficult task of renovating the oldest party in the Republic. Servan-Schreiber himself led the way by entering the party's ranks. His rise was noteworthy. Less than a year after the 4 May congress, he spoke at a meeting of the party's executive committee as a representative of the Radical Federation of French Guinea—thereby arousing varied comments on the party's structural flexibility and wry queries as to the precise doctrinal content of '*le radicalisme guinéen*'. Several months later, transferring his interest to a more familiar Radical area of endeavour, he narrowly missed being chosen as the party's candidate in the partial elections that were called in Paris in January 1957 to find a successor for the veteran Radical deputy, Vincent de Moro-Giafferri. Despite the strong support of Mendès-France, the young editor missed being selected by a very small margin.[3] This defeat, together with the sound defeat subsequently inflicted on the Radical candidate who was chosen, was to mark a significant step in the later decline of the *radicaux mendésistes*.

Most of the activities of the *Express* 'team', however, were in the sphere of public opinion. In October 1955 the extent of this activity was greatly increased when *l'Express* was turned into a daily. After getting off to a very shaky start, the daily won a wide audience during the hectic electoral period that followed, but it did not last long after the end of the campaign, and *l'Express* returned to a weekly status in March 1956.

Whether a daily or a weekly, *l'Express* never ceased to provide Mendès-France with enthusiastic support and a platform for his ideas. In some cases, *l'Express* took stronger—or at least more violent—stands than Mendès-France himself. The vitriolic tenor of its campaign against Faure, for example, aroused the misgivings of many readers. On basic issues, however, *l'Express*'s positions continued to coincide with those of Mendès-France.

Along with *l'Express*, a second newspaper provided a centre for *mendésiste* activities: *Le Jacobin*. Unlike *l'Express* with its informal 'team', *Le Jacobin* was primarily significant as the organ of an organized club: *Le Club des Jacobins*. Founded in 1951 by a group of friends who belonged to a spectrum of political parties, the club included Radicals, Socialists, *progressistes*, members of the UDSR, and former members of the RPF. Like the members of the 'team' associated with *l'Express*, the Jacobins were young, forceful, and had as a major objective the unification of the divided French Left.

The club was founded in a mixed spirit of bitterness and

---

[3] On the first ballot, Servan-Schreiber received 115 votes; Dominique Stefanaggi, 110; and a third candidate, Amblard, 17. As no candidate had an absolute majority, a second vote followed: Stefanaggi received 122 votes, and Servan-Schreiber, 111. *Le Monde*, 8 December 1956. In the subsequent elections (first ballot), Stefanaggi received 6.5 per cent. of the votes. The Radical list had won 17.5 per cent. in the 2 January 1956 general elections.

optimism. 'A year after Korea', one member recalled in describing the club's origin, 'when France was being swallowed up in the war in Indo-China, was undertaking the EDC gamble, when the régime was definitively betraying the hopes of the Liberation, fifteen fellows, who had met by accident at meetings and in discussions, found themselves with a common feeling of revolt and of hope.'[4] They were not long in finding both precursors and a means of expressing their beliefs. The *idée jacobine* was proclaimed as their ideal, and 'the club and the newspaper were born'.

The *Jacobins* took great pride in their youth and vigour. In 1955, the average age of the fourteen members of their *comité directeur* was 31.5 years, ranging from a twenty-three-year-old student to 'a very young grandfather of fifty-two years, Charles Briandet', the newspaper's secretary-general.[5] During the first four years of the club's existence, members of the *comité directeur* participated in 272 public meetings held throughout France. In addition, they met weekly in the club's Paris headquarters in order to discuss 'great issues, doctrinal problems, and also at times less serious questions'. Sharing ideas, they also shared working habits and personal characteristics. 'How does the team of *Le Jacobin* work? In shirtsleeves, in the smell of old pipes and cheap cigarettes, in a great agitation of bow ties, and above all in friendship and in seriousness.'[6]

The best-known *Jacobin* was Charles Hernu, the club's president. Born in 1923, Hernu played an active role in the resistance. A press attaché at the *Centre National du Commerce Extérieur* and a former vice-president of the *Jeunesses radicales* of Rhône, he played a central role in the club's creation in 1951. In the general elections of 2 January 1956, he won a spectacular victory in Paris's sixth sector: his list was second only to that of Jacques Duclos. In and out of the National Assembly, he showed himself to be a staunch *radical mendésiste*—a perhaps more exact title would be that of *ultra-mendésiste*. . . .

Along with finding precursors and supporters, the *Jacobins* were also not long in finding enemies. Many Radical leaders— and in particular *néo-radicaux*—feared that the new 'jacobinism' was a camouflaged form of communism, or that at least the club had been infiltrated by Communists. In December 1953 the party's *commission exécutive* formally forbade joint membership in

[4] *Le Jacobin*, 28 October 1955.   [5] *Ibid.*   [6] *Ibid.*

the club and in the party. The *Jacobins*, however, were undaunted by the new measure. On the day after the Radicals announced their ruling, Hernu commented that they had done so only because the club's success 'risked menacing certain acquired positions or bothering certain parliamentary manœuvres'.[7]

It is undeniable, indeed, that the *Jacobins* had ideas concerning communism that contrasted with those of many Radicals. In their hopes of 'regrouping' the French Left, they did not hesitate to point out their willingness to work, sooner or later, with the party that controlled much of the left. Their attitude towards communism, certainly, was marked by conciliation more than by hostility. After declaring that the *Jacobins* wanted evolution, and not revolution, one *Jacobin* spokesman once wrote that 'the problem is not to combat communism but to compete with it'.[8] This state of affairs, he continued, was the result of France's past record. 'We were not vigilant enough to outrun it by having social progress keep up with technical progress.' In the eyes of the young *Jacobins*, their Jacobinism—and for them, *mendésisme* and Jacobinism tended to be synonymous—provided a hope for the future. 'Jacobinism is perhaps no more than an *état d'esprit* and a method. But there will be no French renaissance without this *esprit*.'[9]

Many *Jacobins* and many followers of *l'Express* were willing to join a Radical party led by Mendès-France. In order to follow the same path, members of another group of *mendésistes* had to make a much greater sacrifice. These were the most paradoxical of all *radicaux mendésistes*: the *mendésistes chrétiens*. This group, admittedly small in number, provided a graphic illustration of the widespread appeal of Mendès-France and his ideas.

The most illustrious Catholic to give Mendès-France unstinting support was the famous writer, François Mauriac. After leaving *Le Figaro* and *La Table Ronde* in 1953, Mauriac became one of the *mendésiste* group that wrote in *l'Express*. After 10 April 1954, his contributions became one of the newspaper's regular features, his '*bloc-notes*' being published on the back page of each issue.

Probably no other writer has written as many eulogies of Mendès-France and his 1954–5 premiership. 'Thanks to him we

[7] *L'Année politique*, 1953, p. 90.   [8] Charles Briandet, *Le Jacobin*, 6 May 1954.
[9] Charles Hernu, *Le Jacobin*, 6 May 1954.

are again walking, we are again under way.'[10] In praising Mendès-France, Mauriac often linked him to his other hero, de Gaulle. 'Since the departure of de Gaulle,' he wrote in August 1955, 'one statesman in France has analysed the political situation of his country with a faultless lucidity; and when a hostile majority was forced to turn to him, he was able to take, in seven months, all the initiatives that this accumulation of catastrophes imposed.'[11]

A *mendésiste*, Mauriac never carried his enthusiasm for Mendès-France to the point of joining the Radical party. There is no doubt, however, that his support for Mendès-France encouraged many Catholics, particularly younger ones, to join the ranks of Radical voters. In his *bloc-notes* published in *l'Express* on 19 October 1956, after a Radical party congress which had seen a split in the party and the departure of many right-wing Radicals, Mauriac discussed the problems inherent in asking Catholics to become Radicals. Noting that logic should have required him to join the Radical party at the time of the general elections and to have had as many of his friends as possible also join, he declared that it was 'not enough just to say that many Catholics found such an idea repugnant. And myself first of all. It would be like proposing a former stockyard to an old horse as a stable'. To persuade the faithful to vote Radical, he added, was no small affair, but to join the party of M. Martinaud-Déplat and M. Borgeaud 'went beyond what could be required of us'. By October 1956, however, times had changed. 'I no longer see,' he declared, 'why so many of the young men who have chosen Mendès-France as their political guide should not henceforth be active in a Radical party that has been liberated, by one blow, of that which made it loathsome to them.'

For Mauriac, the paradoxical union of the *Jacobins* and the *gauche chrétienne* henceforth entered into the logic of things. He was not the only influential Catholic to state such unprecedented views during this period. In an article published in the same issue of *l'Express*, Georges Suffert, the young editor of the Catholic newspaper *Témoignage Chrétien*, noted that if certain Catholics 'were entering the Radical party and if they did so with cool heads, their action could only make healthier not only the French political system, by furnishing it with a reserve of

[10] *L'Express*, 13 August 1955.   [11] *Ibid.*

generous and active men, but also the Church, which people could no longer definitively accuse of being the religious expression of a political party'.

Despite the encouragement of Mauriac and other members of the *gauche chrétienne*, young Catholics who became *radicaux mendésistes* remained a rare phenomenon. Few observers, certainly, would ever have been willing to accept the term *radicaux catholiques* as more logical than paradoxical. Other young Frenchmen, however, did not have to overcome such deep-seated sentiments in order to play an active role as Radicals. During the eight months that followed the 4 May 1955 congress, the membership of the Radical party rose from 65,000 to 100,000. The Federation of the Seine became the party's largest federation, and most of its new members made no secret of their staunch *mendésiste* loyalties. A jubilant *Association parisienne des étudiants radicaux*, opposed by certain elements of the more right-wing *Jeunesses radicales-socialistes*, held a tumultuous *Assemblée générale* in Paris on 10 May. By October they were able to claim 'about 100 new members' in Paris.[12] *L'Express*, and to a lesser degree *Le Jacobin*, continued as the most widely read organs of *mendésisme*, but in 1956 they were joined by the more academic periodical *Les Cahiers de la République*. Edited in the party's headquarters at the Place de Valois and directed by a committee of which Mendès-France was president, the new publication provided a new medium for the discussion of doctrinal and political questions.

Many *radicaux mendésistes* penetrated even further into the Radical party. After 4 May 1955, the most appealing new habitat open to many of them was the party's administrative machinery. Some of those who moved into key positions had already seen service in the party. Paul Anxionnaz, who was officially appointed secretary-general of the party in November 1955, had occupied the same position shortly after the war. Most of the remaining posts, however, went to new personnel. Georges Scali was appointed administrative secretary to assist Anxionnaz—after the latter was elected to the National Assembly and entered Guy Mollet's cabinet. Harris Puisais, who like Scali had been associated with the *Jacobins*, was appointed head of the party's propaganda section. Pierre Avril, formerly secretary of the *Association parisienne des étudiants radicaux*, was given control of the secretariat

[12] *I.R.S.*, 29 October 1955.

responsible for the administration of the party's many committees. In mid-1956 Paul-André Falcoz was given charge of an
École des Cadres in which groups of young Radicals studied contemporary problems and were instructed in the art of being
effective members of the Radical party.

On the parliamentary scene, the applicability of the term *radical mendésiste* was to become more and more subject to change.
Certain deputies, however, must be counted among the most
faithful *radicaux mendésistes*. In his bitter battles in the new legislature that was elected on 2 January 1956, Mendès-France nearly
always could depend on the support of the group of young
Radicals who had swept to victory under his banner in Paris
and in the Paris region. These included Charles Hernu, Léon
Hovnanian, Pierre Naudet, Claude Panier, Claude Leclercq, and
Pierre Clostermann. The records of the parliamentary *radicaux
mendésistes*, however, are of most direct concern in studying the
later evolution of Mendès-France's efforts to renovate the Radical
party, and it is in the latter context that their role will be treated.

*
* *

The strongest bond between most *radicaux mendésistes* was not,
manifestly, the Radical party. *Mendésistes* always outnumbered
radicaux mendésistes. Frenchmen who were willing to express their
admiration for Mendès-France were clearly much more numerous
than those who were willing to join the Radical party. It was on
the Radical party, however, that Mendès-France was to base
much of his hope for future action. What factors may be said to
have motivated him in this decision? What prompted his attempt
to mix radicalism with renovation?

It can be argued that, from a personal point of view, it was
a natural decision. Mendès-France was more 'Radical' than many
people imagined. While many of his followers hesitated to join
his party, he often expressed pride in his many years as a Radical.
He was, probably, the most Radical of all the *radicaux mendésistes*.
At certain times, indeed, he was even able to rival the more
eloquent of the *radicaux classiques* as a spokesman for the traditional themes of radicalism. In a speech at the party's congress
in 1953, he told his listeners that the Radical party was the party
of the *juste milieu* and of Reason. In October 1954, four months

after his election as premier, he discussed doctrinal questions at the party's congress at Marseilles. 'Many people ask us what profound doctrine animates our action. *Eh bien!* I reply to you that it is *la doctrine radicale* (applause).' The acclaimed premier continued: 'People have often said that radicalism is less a party than a state of mind. It is, perhaps, this suppleness which permits it today to carry to the new requirements of technology the solicitude for individual liberty that it has always maintained in the foreground during a half-century of the history of both the Third and the Fourth Republics (strong applause; cries of Bravo!)'

Closely linked to the Radical party by his past and by his personal sentiments, Mendès-France also was guided by more direct considerations. What, indeed, were his alternatives?

Many of his followers had repeatedly encouraged him to found a new party or to form a new *rassemblement*. As early as 16 September 1954, Charles Hernu, in an article in *Le Jacobin*, spoke of the possible creation of a *Ligue démocratique et républicaine*. Members of the UDSR, and in particular François Mitterrand, long wanted their group to become the centre of a new political formation led by Mendès-France. After Mendès-France's fall in February 1955, many *mendésistes* joined in making similar suggestions. The previous ten years of French political history, however, had illustrated the difficulties of forming new *rassemblements* outside the traditional party system. The prime example, of course, was that of the RPF. Created around a name with high prestige, it had nevertheless proved to be ephemeral—while older political parties had gone on to prosper.

At the same time, it was evident that it would not be profitable for Mendès-France to return to his earlier position of isolation. He had succeeded in winning widespread support in the country, but to achieve his objectives, it was necessary that his supporters be organized. In retrospect, it was clear that thirty or forty more faithful supporters in the National Assembly in 1954 would have made a great difference to his premiership. The only way to ensure such support would be to become the leader of a disciplined political party. Rather than base his hopes on a hypothetical new party or *rassemblement*, Mendès-France concluded that his best strategy was to attempt to gain control of the Radical party.

The first major consequence of this decision was the victory of the *radicaux mendésistes* at the special congress of 4 May 1955.

The *néo-radicaux* were ousted from positions of command; the *radicaux mendésistes* were henceforth in control of the party's administrative machinery—a control that they were to consolidate at the party's congress in November 1955.

Mendès-France had chosen to work through the Radical party, but he made it abundantly clear that this choice was based on a determination to have the old party change many of its traditional ways and habits. In speaking before the delegates at the 4 May congress, he was explicit both in presenting a diagnosis and in suggesting remedial action. Above all, the party lacked cohesion. After making electoral speeches, he complained, he had often had to face embarrassing questions on this subject. 'But all that you say is very fine,' his listeners would say, 'it's very interesting, but in whose name are you speaking? Your party is divided, it is contradictory. Where is its will? You have just expounded ideas which are perhaps interesting, but they are the ideas of an isolated person. But what, then, is the true doctrine of your party?'

In order to speak with a relatively united voice, the party had to have a programme. 'This great reunited party,' he told his listeners, 'no longer wants to offer—to a public which finishes by no longer believing in them—these vague billboards, these long-winded posters in which everything is promised to everybody, in terms, incidentally, that no longer fool anyone.' To express more clearly what he had in mind and to emphasize his desire to have the party break with past practices, Mendès-France added a new term to the French political vocabulary: '*plateforme*'. 'Platform,' he explained, was a word that 'people use in certain truly democratic countries'; it stood for a list of five or six clear ideas; it involved very concrete promises. The Radical party, he argued, must have a *plateforme*.

There was also a great need to reform the party's structure. In discussing this problem, he declared that there was too great a gap between 'the troops, the militants, those who are in combat in so many *départements*, on so many battlefields', and the '*bureaux*, the headquarters and the chiefs', who, 'indifferent, without control, pursue personal ends'. It was necessary to reform the party's internal organization, to revise its statutes, and to guarantee the party's 'independence from all personal, economic, or financial interests, whatever they might be'. In addition, it was necessary to provide the party with a strong propaganda machine.

Mendès-France was asking for profound changes in the party's traditional habits, but he was also insistent in arguing that by making these changes the party would be *returning* to its true vocation. Even more than most other Radicals, the *radicaux mendésistes* were forceful in arguing that they represented the true traditions of radicalism. Like the *radicaux de gauche*, they felt that the great days of radicalism were those of the early part of the Third Republic. In his speech at the 4 May congress, Mendès-France declared that the party had lost its historical mission; and because of this, 'its deep traditions were decaying and wasting away, and it was no longer able to play in the nation that dynamic role, that propelling role, which we had wanted for it'.

Thus, looking forward to a new Radical future, the *radicaux mendésistes* found much to admire in a distant Radical past. Alain continued to be a prime source of ideas and citations. Pelletan, Combes, Bourgeois, Caillaux, and Herriot were described as having represented valuable aspects of radicalism. Mendès-France, in turn, the *radicaux mendésistes* argued, was to be the leader of *le radicalisme moderne*. Renovation, certainly, did not mean denying the past. In July 1955, in an article written after the death of an old Radical veteran, Albert Milhaud, Mendès-France noted that many people spoke ironically about the generation of the 'old Radical greybeards'.[13] He added, however, that 'we who have known them, we salute these men who made the Republic and who defended it valiantly against perils'. It was the duty of contemporary Radicals to be faithful to their heritage. 'The rejuvenation of the Radical party is, for us, the return to the wellsprings of our doctrine, to the lessons of the founders and of those who succeeded them.'

While gaining inspiration from the past, the *radicaux mendésistes* continued to play an increasingly active role in the present. After the 4 May congress, a seven-member *Commission d'action*, which had been voted into existence to replace the administrative presidency, installed itself in the Place de Valois. Its first act was to call a meeting of the executive committee for 29 June. A project

---

[13] *La Concorde, organe de la démocratie poitevine*, Lezay (Deux-Sèvres), 30 July 1955. Milhaud, the author of *Histoire du radicalisme*, had a very impressive beard.

for the revision of the party's statutes was approved at this meeting. In the meantime, Mendès-France had made a series of speeches in eastern France and had paid a quick visit to Casablanca. By the time of the party's congress in November, the position of the *radicaux mendésistes* was well prepared. Mendès-France was elected *premier vice-président*, and faced by an imminent electoral campaign, he had compiled and was forcefully presenting a well-documented electoral *plateforme*.

*
* *

The new *plateforme* was a reiteration of the basic themes that Mendès-France had long advocated. Once again Mendès-France presented his compatriots with a stern diagnosis of France's problems, and once again he advanced precise plans for their treatment. The fact that the remedies were similar to those that he had advanced in 1945 and during subsequent years served to heighten the gravity of the diagnosis.

Mendès-France's diagnosis was primarily that of an economist. For years he had been arguing that without a healthy, expanding economy, France could not hope to play an important role in the world. Economic vigour was the necessary prerequisite for any coherent programme of action, whether on the international or domestic scene.

In order to modernize France's economic system, he argued, strong measures were necessary. Like many of his generation in France, Mendès-France had been strongly impressed and influenced by the methods used by Roosevelt in combating the American depression during the 1930's.[14] In a speech at the party's congress in 1953, after telling his listeners that France's level of production had not increased since 1929, Mendès-France declared that it was the first time in the history of a great people that a generation did not have more riches at its disposal than did the preceding generation. In no other great country, he added, was there such an unfavourable balance between productive and non-productive expenditures. It was necessary, therefore, that the

---

[14] A prominent role in this French 'discovery of America' was played by a book written by Georges Boris, a long-standing friend of Mendès-France. In *La Révolution Roosevelt* (Paris, 1934), Boris wrote of his newly-found admiration of the economic pragmatism that characterized '*l'Amérique Rooseveltienne*'.

State play an active role in orienting and encouraging investments in key productive industries. Cheap credit was vital for
housing and agriculture—the two activities that had the greatest
need of modernization. Marginal enterprises had to be recon-
verted; the 'dead branches' of the country's economic system
had to be eliminated. Scientific research should be encouraged,
laboratories built, educational facilities enlarged, and agricultural
training expanded. France had to adapt to the new conditions of
life in the twentieth century.

Other political leaders shared many of these objectives—the
néo-radicaux, for example, were as eloquent as Mendès-France in
calling for increased productivity. Mendès-France, however, distinguished himself by the remorselessness of his logic and the
severity of the conclusions that he drew. In order to increase
productivity, France had to be ruthless in lessening non-productive
expenditure. For Mendès-France, to govern was to choose. France
could not simultaneously carry on a multitude of expensive tasks.
It was more important to modernize France than to continue
a fruitless war in Indo-China. It was also more important to increase productive investments than to promise unrealistic wage
increases. The cure for social injustice, the amelioration of the
standard of living, and the improvement of France's international
position were all dependent on economic expansion. More than
any other French leader, Mendès-France was insistent in stressing the importance of economic expansion, and almost alone
among French politicians he was willing to pay what he considered to be the price.

One part of the price to be paid was the bitter enmity of many
of those who would be directly affected by the measures that
Mendès-France proposed. The elimination of marginal enterprises, for example, did not appeal to many of those whose personal futures were dedicated to such enterprises. The reduction
of non-productive expenditures was unattractive to those who
derived their living from such expenditures. In undertaking to
transform France's economic system, Mendès-France inevitably
aroused the opposition of the most determined supporters of
status quo France.

Mendès-France and the *radicaux mendésistes* devoted great efforts
to carefully expounding the reasons for the measures that they
advocated. It was the government's duty, they argued, to protect

P

the general interest of the people as a whole. Personal interests had an abundance of protectors in France, but the country had reached an 'absurd situation in which each group extracted advantages of protections from the national collectivity, and all Frenchmen had to pay for them by mediocrity and economic stagnation'.[15]

Of all the economic groups that Mendès-France opposed, none was more powerful or vocal than the alcohol interests, and none exacted a greater toll from the nation's finances—or the nation's health. Mendès-France's attempt to apply his logic to the alcohol question began in September 1954, when he announced his government's decision 'to attack one of the most obvious pieces of nonsense of the economic policy followed until now'.[16] In the opening speech of this campaign, he granted that it could possibly be agreed that France should produce enough alcohol for its day-to-day consumption, 'even if the alcohol that we make in France costs five or six times as much as that which we could obtain in foreign markets'. France, however, not only was systematically paying 100 francs for a product that was worth fifteen, but was stocking huge surpluses. For at least six years, the excess production had amounted to nearly 36,660,000 gallons each year. Such a policy, he said, was economic madness.

In a direct challenge to the alcohol interests, Mendès-France announced that two-thirds of the sugar-beet currently turned into alcohol would, in the future, be made into sugar. Part of the sugar would be exported under subsidies, part would be sent to the French Union, and part would be used to give sugared milk to all French school children. 'It will provide a happy modification of our country's habits,' said the premier. 'Rich and energy-making foods, like milk and sugar, have not been consumed as much as the health and the vigour of our race requires.'

Mendès-France had not gone so far as to try to abolish the system of subsidized alcohol production. In this first measure, he had only tried to reform it and to introduce some social benefits. The powerful sugar-beet lobby, however, rose up in fury

[15] Speech at Evreux (Eure), 30 January 1955. Reprinted in Pierre Mendès-France, *Gouverner c'est choisir*, vol. 2, *Sept mois et dix-sept jours, Juin 1954–Février 1955*, Paris, 1955, pp. 213–6.

[16] Speech at Annecy, 26 September 1954. Reprinted in *Sept mois*, pp. 237–47.

against him, for it was more profitable to grow beets for alcohol than for sugar. Other anti-alcoholic measures that he introduced earned additional hostility. The liquor interests and café owners opposed a sweeping new series of restrictions that included an increase in the price of drinks, the closing of bars between 5 a.m. and 10 a.m., and a limitation of the number of *bistros*. His most aggrieved opponents, however, were the *bouilleurs de cru*—France's three million private distillers. The latter had reason to fear that he was planning to limit their number and set up a system of close control over their stills.

By making himself the champion of anti-alcoholism, and in particular by making it clear that it was his objective to restrain the privileges of the *bouilleurs de cru*, Mendès-France had aroused the furious animosity of many of his compatriots. For many Frenchmen, the man who brought an end to the unpopular war in Indo-China was also the man who wanted to limit their simple pleasures. Some of his most vociferous opponents were found in his apple-growing and calvados-producing Norman constituency. In a noisy electoral meeting in December 1955, one of his listeners proclaimed: 'Yes, you are our enemy! You do not defend our interests. Allow me to tell you this: you drink milk but, as for me, milk gives me colic, and calvados is good for me!'[17] At the same meeting, another Norman interlocutor nearly choked in vituperating against Mendès-France. 'He said that American cows were better than ours! You can see it clearly: this man is against us!'[18]

It was difficult to speak of the general interest in such gatherings. Other parts of Mendès-France's economic and social projects aroused similar reactions. Few criticized his precise plans for an expanded programme of housing construction—for Mendès-France, housing and alcoholism constituted France's most pressing social problems. Many, however, opposed his plans for gradually eliminating and reconverting marginal enterprises. In presenting the latter plan, Mendès-France was careful to explain that reconversions would not be carried out in a brutal fashion. The state would provide financial assistance and technical advice; workers would be assisted in finding more

[17] 'P. Mendès-France face aux bouilleurs de cru', at Saint-Georges-du-Vienne (Eure), *l'Express*, 20 December 1955.

[18] *Paris-Presse et l'Intransigeant*, 20 December 1955.

productive employment. No steps, he asserted, would be taken without careful preparatory study.

Most of those directly affected, however, remained unconvinced. Although it was clear that, economically, marginal industries should disappear, it became equally obvious that, politically, such a move would swell the forces of movements of which the Poujadists constituted the most extreme example. Mendès-France put much faith in his persuasive abilities, but the emotions, interests and arguments of his detractors constituted a formidable barrier to understanding. His opponents preferred their own variety of logic. In a manifestation at Chartres in February 1955, shortly after Mendès-France's fall from power, farmers carried banners proclaiming 'milk=misery' and 'productivity=ruin'.[19] It was beyond the skill of even a Faure or a Mendès-France to convince such intransigent opponents that their fears were unfounded—and Faure, in any case, would not have encumbered his projects with Mendès-France's controversial milk campaign.

It was Poujade himself who provided some of the most extreme examples of the attitudes and arguments that Mendès-France and his followers—along with all other Frenchmen who wanted to 'modernize' their country—had to face. In his bombastic book, *J'ai choisi le combat*, Poujade chose Mendès-France as the target for many of what he considered as his most telling remarks. 'Is it not true, M. Mendès, that you had planned to build an experimental supermarket in Corsica in the month of November 1954?'[20] After advancing this charge, the irate Poujade proudly went on to draw what he felt was an obvious moral. 'If we had not been there, once more, friends of France devoted to our liberty, who would have denounced and prevented an infamous government from making such an attempt?'

Despite the manifest difficulties involved, Mendès-France and the *radicaux mendésistes* remained in the forefront of those fighting for far-reaching economic and social reforms in France. No other group in France was more insistent in arguing that social and economic progress are interdependent. Again and again they stressed the theme that social justice could be promoted only in the general expansion of France's economy. More than any other

[19] *L'Express*, 19 February 1955.
[20] Pierre Poujade, *J'ai choisi le combat*, Saint-Céré (Lot), 1955, p. 115.

political group, they presented precise plans for the implementation of the objectives that they proclaimed. In doing so, they made themselves the centre of many of their compatriots' hopes —particularly those of a younger generation desirous of change and new opportunities.

The solutions that Mendès-France and his supporters offered inevitably aroused the ire of well-established and powerful segments of the population. They also aroused the fears and animosity of those who were expected to adapt to new conditions of life. The widespread desire of many Frenchmen to maintain a personally pleasant *status quo* constituted a formidable barrier to any programme, or *plateforme*, calling for drastic changes. In the face of such opposition, most French leaders preferred to temporize. Mendès-France, however, never faltered in expounding what he saw as the hard facts of France's economic and social problems.

The gravity of the problems that the *radicaux mendésistes* relentlessly diagnosed may be said to have been equalled only by the difficulties that they faced in trying to win acceptance for their remedies. Jean-Jacques Servan-Schreiber, in an article published before he became an active *mendésiste*, once summarized his future hero's domestic programme by saying that 'the goal of Mendès-France may be described as that of grafting on France the liberal dynamism cultivated in the United States'.[21] He went on to add that Mendès-France believed in this goal, 'and thus shows himself to be the most optimistic of our political leaders'.

*

* *

Many of those who admired Mendès-France for his vigorous and imaginative approach to France's economic and social problems found it difficult to understand his attitudes towards the various post-war plans for European unification. His role in the defeat of the European Defence Community, as well as his subsequent sponsorship of the Paris Agreements, was a source of violent controversy among both his friends and his enemies. His later stands on Euratom and on the Common Market— where economic and not military issues were involved—were even more disappointing to those who envisaged the economic

[21] *Paris-Presse et l'Intransigeant*, 23 October 1952.

unification of Europe as a basic corollary of French economic reform and expansion.

In his actions concerning the EDC and the Paris Agreements, Mendès-France was guided both by what he considered to be parliamentary realism and by the need to maintain Western solidarity. There was no possibility of finding a majority in the National Assembly to support the EDC project, but France's allies considered German rearmament as vital for the defence of the West. The issue had embittered the French political scene for years; it was necessary to force a decision. After a fruitless attempt to find a compromise that would be acceptable to France's prospective partners and to the National Assembly, Mendès-France declined to give the project his support—he abstained from voting and did not make it a vote of confidence—and after years of delay and recrimination the EDC was finally pronounced dead.

In a statement after the final vote, Mendès-France declared that the refusal to ratify the EDC was unfortunate, but that it was not a tragedy. Stressing that the French government remained attached, without reserve or weakness, to the Atlantic Alliance, he said that it was within that alliance that new solutions must be sought and added that 'we shall not waste three years'.[22] Exactly four months later, on 30 December 1954, the Paris Agreements were reluctantly ratified by a vote of 287 to 260, with seventy-four abstentions. A British guarantee to keep troops on the Continent had been won, supranational clauses had been eliminated, and Mendès-France had given the treaty his unstinting support. To the end, however, his chief argument was the need to maintain Western solidarity. He argued as a responsible and realistic head of state, and not as an impassioned supporter of the treaty's objectives.

By his advocacy of the new treaty, Mendès-France lost much of his left-wing support. Commenting on this shift in opinion, an editorialist in *l'Express* wrote that 'the *sentimentaux de gauche*, those who have always lost the causes that they defend, cry crocodile tears on the phantom of the Mendès-France whom they liked and who was not the one who presented the Paris Agreements to Parliament'.[23] After making this preliminary ob-

---

[22] Donald McCormick, *Mr. France*, London, 1955, p. 182.

[23] *L'Express*, 25 December 1954.

servation, the writer went on to add that, 'in having had the courage to present the unpopular Paris Agreements to Parliament, PMF showed that the *gauche nouvelle* which is rising and of which he is now the chief, is no longer one of dreams, but one of responsibilities'. Drawing what may be considered an authentic *mendésiste* moral, *l'Express*'s editorialist concluded: 'We do not cherish these agreements, nor the principle of German rearmament, but we recognize that years of lies and cowardliness have made it inevitable and indispensable for France to accept paying this price for Atlantic solidarity before being able to fight with efficacy for negotiations with the East and for peace.'

Mendès-France did not kill the EDC; he presided at its burial and provided a substitute. Many of those who were willing to accept his treatment of the EDC, and who respected him for the manner in which he went on to win French acceptance for German rearmament, have found it difficult to understand his subsequent positions on projects dedicated to promoting European economic unification. In 1951 he voted in favour of the European Coal and Steel Community. In a speech in September 1954, shortly after the National Assembly's rejection of the EDC, he declared that 'the advantages of enlarging national markets no longer need to be pointed out; we will soon take constructive measures in this direction'.[24] In 1956 and 1957, however, backed by a group on loyal *radicaux mendésistes*, he voted against both Euratom and the Common Market.

In his pronouncements on European unification, Mendès-France made it clear that he favoured the construction of a united Europe, but always posed limiting questions: which Europe; and how is it to be constructed? A strong Anglophile, he always stressed his desire to see Great Britain participate in any projects that would bind France to Germany. British participation was a crucial factor in his advocacy of the Paris Agreements; the absence of Britain was a principal reason for his lack of enthusiasm for the EDC. The hasty construction of 'little Europe', he argued, of a Europe that excluded Britain, the Scandinavian countries, and Austria, would leave France isolated from her most faithful ally and subject to the dominating influence of her powerful neighbour, Germany.

Many *radicaux mendésistes* were more extreme in their criticism

[24] Speech at Nevers, 19 September 1954. Reprinted in *Sept mois*, pp. 114–7.

of the proposed 'little Europe'. Some saw it as the forerunner of a revived Carolingian Empire, administered by Catholic politicians from the banks of the Rhine. Others decried the role played by the Vatican and made wry jokes about 'the MRP International'. In a letter to the 'pro-Europe' Socialist weekly, *Demain*, one young *radical mendésiste* stressed economic and social factors. 'Yes, as for Europe and the Common Market,' he wrote, 'Mendès is right: we do not want the Europe of the Krupps and the de Wendels, but a socialist Europe, a Europe created for the well-being and security of its inhabitants.'[25]

Mendès-France's opposition to Euratom was not noteworthy for its directness. He did not participate in the five days of debates that preceded the National Assembly's adoption of the new project on 11 July 1956. When the vote took place, however, he cast a negative ballot—and was followed by twenty-six of his fellow Radicals. By the time that the Common Market project came up for discussion in the National Assembly in January 1957, however, Mendès-France was in the forefront of those who spoke against the proposed measure.

In explaining his opposition in a speech before the National Assembly on 17 January, Mendès-France declared that it was necessary to make Europe without unmaking France. Before venturing into a Common Market, France first should put her own economy in order. Before ratifying a final treaty, France's legislators should carefully consider the effects that certain of the proposed clauses could have on the future of their country. In a long and carefully documented speech, Mendès-France warned his fellow deputies of what he considered to be the dangers inherent in the proposed treaty.

Many of the treaty's clauses attracted Mendès-France's attention. He warned of the difficulties that could result from a policy of unrestrained migration of workers and argued that the treaty's provisions were not clear on this point. It was also necessary, he argued, that the treaty be more precise in providing guarantees against the risks involved in removing customs barriers. France would have to face formidable competition, a 'competition that could be beneficial in the long run if the necessary

---

[25] Jacques Frantz, Thionville (Moselle), who described himself as a '*jeune militant radical, amené à la politique par Mendès-France, comme beaucoup de mes camarades*'. *Demain*, 7–13 February 1957.

arrangements were provided'. This competition, however, could have grave long-term effects if the appropriate precautions were not taken.

Mendès-France also pointed out that prices were based on costs of production and that France was handicapped by burdens that other participating states did not have, at least in the same degree. Military expenses would not be greatly diminished by a solution to the Algerian conflict, but would be followed by larger economic investments. Other areas of the French Union would continue to be a financial burden. France's social legislation was much more advanced than that of the other countries.

The latter factor was of particular concern to Mendès-France. He noted that the only standardization that was envisaged in the treaty concerned the 'equality of men's and women's salaries within a period of four, five or six years'. No other spread of social advantage was mentioned. France's family allowances amounted to 12 per cent. of her workers' wages, but family allowances were not even mentioned in the treaty. Young people's and miners' wages were much higher in France than in Germany, Italy, and Belgium. France, in general, had social advantages that were 'much superior to those in countries with which we are going to associate ourselves'. France should insist on the rapid generalization of social advantages in all the countries of the Common Market. The only other logical conclusion, he warned, would be to abolish family allowances and to lower wages in France.

In discussing the position of France's potential associates, Mendès-France was blunt. 'Our partners', he charged, 'want to conserve the commercial advantages they have over us as a result of their backwardness in social matters.' France's policy, however, should not be to build Europe at the detriment of the working class, 'and therefore at the detriment of the other social classes who live from the workers' buying power'. It was necessary to build Europe in expansion and social progress, and not against them.

Mendès-France also noted that the size of a country's market was not the only factor that affected its living standard. Among the countries with the highest per capita incomes were Canada, Switzerland, Sweden, New Zealand, Australia, Denmark, Belgium, Holland, and Norway. Once again, he was insistent in regretting the absence of England. England, like France, had practised 'a more advanced social policy than the countries with which France was to be associated'. Most Englishmen, even the Conservatives, agreed with the need for full employment—and this opinion was not dominant in Germany.

Again and again, Mendès-France stressed the obscurity in which the treaty left many important questions and, before he concluded, once more questioned the motives of France's future partners. The Common Market project, he argued, 'such as it is presented to us, or at the very least such as we are allowed to know it, is based on the classical liberalism of the nineteenth century, according to which pure and simple competition solves all problems'. The subsequent years had shown the true character of 'this classical theory of resignation'. France must co-operate in the construction of Europe, but it must not do so at the price of betraying its heritage and sacrificing the well-being of its people.

In July 1957, when the National Assembly voted in favour of ratifying the Common Market treaty, Mendès-France was still among the opposition. After the decision was taken, however, and when it became time for the new treaty to enter into effect, Mendès-France was to declare that it was henceforth the duty of all Frenchmen to do their best to make the Common Market a success, 'a success from which France would obtain the maximum possible benefits'.[26]

*

* *

In stating his positions on European unification proposals, Mendès-France spoke primarily as an economist. When confronted with any basic problem, indeed, his most characteristic reactions were those of a practical, realistic economist. This attitude, accompanied by his insistence on following the dictates of his logic, greatly influenced the positions that he took concerning the successive crises which marked the post-war history of France's overseas possessions.

As early as 1949 Mendès-France warned his compatriots that France's economic recovery was dependent on ending the war

[26] 'Méditations sur un événement de première importance', *Les Débats économiques*, December 1958.

in Indo-China. In speeches in the National Assembly in October and November 1950, he told his fellow deputies that France would have to choose between the defence of Europe and that of Indo-China. A year later, in an address at the party's 1951 congress, he argued that France would not have an effective army in Europe as long as the haemorrhage in Indo-China continued. Once again, it was a question of making a choice, and for Mendès-France, the choice had long been clear: France had to negotiate to bring an end to the war that was bleeding her economy and preventing her from fulfilling more important tasks.

By bringing the war in Indo-China to an end, Mendès-France won great popularity among his compatriots. In his pre-investiture speech on 17 June 1954, he had promised to secure peace or resign by 20 July. By dramatically setting this time-limit on his negotiations with the Vietminh and Chinese Communists at Geneva, he caught the imagination of much of the world.

During the remainder of his premiership, Mendès-France did not hesitate to take forceful action in other parts of the French Union. After his return from Geneva, he devoted himself to finding a solution to an increasingly critical situation in Tunisia. On 31 July, accompanied by Marshal Juin, he flew to Tunis and personally told the Bey that France would carry out her previous promises to grant Tunisia internal sovereignty. By acting swiftly and by having gained the co-operation of a Marshal who had a strong reputation as a foe of Arab nationalism, he had effectively bypassed the powerful *colons* who had previously been successful in preventing the implementation of Paris-sponsored liberal programmes.

Mendès-France also extended his sphere of action to 'French India'—he negotiated an agreement by which the small group of French settlements in India were transferred to the new Indian government. His actions concerning Morocco were of a much more reticent nature. Appealing to Moroccans to put an end to the violence that was delaying the modern evolution of their country, he did not take steps to bring about what many of his supporters—including Mauriac—felt to be the only solution to the worsening situation in Morocco: the return of the Moroccans' popular ex-Sultan.

The Moroccan crisis reached its climax the following year, after the end of Mendès-France's premiership. In the meantime,

Algeria became the scene of a tragedy whose magnitude was to surpass even that of Indo-China. Mendès-France's phenomenal popularity in France was largely based on his role in ending the war in Indo-China. His decline in popularity was in great measure due to the unpopularity of his attitude towards '*l'Algérie française*'.

The first three months of the Algerian war were fought during Mendès-France's premiership. When hostilities broke out in November 1954, he was forceful in announcing his government's determination to crush the rebellion. 'One does not compromise,' he told the National Assembly in a speech on 12 November, 'when it is a question of maintaining the Nation's internal peace and the integrity of the Republic.' A split between Algeria and metropolitan France, he declared, was inconceivable. 'This must be clear for always and for everybody, in Algeria, in metropolitan France and also abroad. . . . Algeria is France, and not a foreign country that we are protecting.'

As premier, therefore, Mendès-France played a central role in the early part of the Algerian war. He did not hesitate to take strong military measures. At the same time, he made clear his intention to take more than military action. When he appointed Jacques Soustelle as Governor General of Algeria in late January 1955, he gave him instructions calling for strong military action —and also the progressive application of the Algerian statute that the National Assembly had voted in 1947.

With the passing months, Mendès-France became increasingly outspoken in his diagnosis of the Algerian problem. In a speech before the Radical Federation of Calvados in October 1955, he flatly declared that 'unkept promises are at the origin of the present situation in Algeria'.[27] 'We have not respected the statute of 1947,' he said, 'and the elections were rigged.' It was necessary, he argued, 'to apply the statute—that is to say the law— and to hold real elections'. It was doubtlessly true, he added, that 'we will see names of men who are presenting violent demands come from the ballot boxes, but it is with them that we must negotiate if they truly represent the Algerian people'.

During the election campaign prior to the general elections of 2 January 1956, he contrasted the situation in Tunisia, where negotiations had replaced civil war, with that in Algeria. In a

[27] *I.R.S.*, 29 October 1955.

speech at Marseilles a few days before the elections, he outlined his general position. 'We will not maintain ourselves in North Africa and in the other countries of the French Union as long as we count on force, repression, and violence; it is necessary to seek a reciprocal agreement among the people who live there; it is necessary to create among these populations the feeling that they must live side by side; it is necessary to want conciliation, and it can be found.'[28] France had not been true to her word and had discredited the democratic procedures that she had offered. Free elections should be held, hostages should be freed, and administrative power should be returned to civilians. As a final point, Mendès-France proposed that the new premier should personally take charge of the Algerian problem and should make his headquarters in Algeria as long as possible, 'in order to subdue there all the varieties of opposition'.

In the period that followed the elections, Mendès-France's attitude towards the Algerian problem was one of increasing pessimism. The evolution of his position in the Mollet Cabinet, as well as his position as leader of the Radical party, was largely determined by his insistence that new and conciliatory methods be tried in Algeria. In this stand he was strongly supported by the small group of *radicaux mendésistes* in the National Assembly and by his friends in *l'Express*. Their struggle to have France change her methods in Algeria constituted a central feature of the evolution of the *radicaux mendésistes* during the early part of the 1956 legislature, and it is in this context that this struggle will be treated.

*

* *

In general, the ideas advanced by Mendès-France and his supporters were marked by a desire to produce a new climate of opinion and to introduce sweeping changes in France's political, social, and economic life. On a more profound level, they sought to reinvigorate a sick régime. In a memorable speech at the party's congress in 1952, Mendès-France warned his listeners of the critical stage that France had reached. 'Here we are at the end of the *Ancien Régime*: it is the time for reforms. It is now necessary to be imaginative; we must make decisions; we must

[28] *Combat*, 27 December 1955.

choose; we must take risks.' At the party's congress the following year, he again warned of the need for action. 'Things must
change! For—listen to the clamour arising—we are in 1788!'

In discussing the 'crisis of democracy' in a speech in July
1955, Mendès-France stated that true democracy was the 'close
association of the State and the Citizen'.[29] 'Today,' he said, 'the
Citizen and the State have become strangers to each other; the
Citizen is turning away from the State, and the State mistrusts
the Citizen.' Of particular concern was the indifference of French
youth towards political affairs. Any régime that did not have the
support of the younger generations, he noted, was a fragile one.
Also of great concern was the existence of so many men and
women, particularly workers, who expressed their discontent
and discouragement by voting for Communist candidates. Communist doctrine, he explained, proclaimed that the pauperization
of the workers was inevitable until the day of a final, hypothetical, and distant Revolution; but history had illustrated
the fact that ameliorations in the living standards of the
workers could be both real and substantial. Unlike many other
countries, France had not made serious enough efforts in this
domain.

For Mendès-France and his supporters, nearly all problems
were subordinate to the basic need to further France's internal
reforms. A politician, Mendès-France often paid tribute to the
venerable issue of laicism. When asked for a statement by the
Comité national d'action laïque prior to the general elections of
2 January 1956, he declared that the Radical party was in accord
with the organization's programme, and went on to add: 'Must
I also, on the personal level, remind you of the votes that I have
cast in Parliament for twenty years which have always been in
conformity to the requirements of laicism?'[30] He never distinguished himself, however, by a passionate devotion to the cause
of laicism. In their relationships with Catholics and in their attitude towards the problem of Church schools, the *radicaux mendésistes* were always on the side of moderation and conciliation.
For them, laicism should not be the crucial dividing line in a

[29] Speech at Evreux (Eure), 23 July 1955. Reprinted in Pierre Mendès-France,
Gouverner c'est choisir, vol. 3, *La Politique et la Vérité, Juin 1955–Septembre 1958*, Paris,
1958, pp. 239–64.

[30] Letter reprinted in *Le Monde*, 26 November 1955.

modern France. In an editorial in *Le Jacobin* in 1953, Charles Hernu summarized this attitude by asking a question: 'Does being a man of the Left mean only—and naïvely—to be laic, or does it not mean, rather, to be in favour of the redistribution and growth of the national revenue?'

Mendès-France's emphasis on the need to further France's internal reform occasionally led some observers to attribute neutralistic tendencies to him. He never ceased, however, to affirm his devotion to Atlantic solidarity and eloquently stressed the close links between France, Britain, and the United States. In 1954 he was willing to sacrifice much of his popularity in France on the altar of the Western alliance by his forceful support of German rearmament. In world affairs, as in domestic French affairs, he always stressed the need for realism and honesty. He did his best to prevent the Anglo-French Suez expedition in 1956, and later expressed his surprise that those responsible for the 'adventure' had not foreseen the later British hesitancies and that they had acted without the Americans' knowledge.[31] France, he concluded, had been unfaithful to the concept of the Atlantic alliance.

For Mendès-France and the *radicaux mendésistes*, however, the decisive battleground on which France's future was to be determined was France itself. Their hopes were based, above all, on a reformed and modernized France. In working for this end, they put much faith in the role that they hoped would be played by a renovated Radical party. In May 1957, however, two years after the *radicaux mendésistes* had won control of the party, Mendès-France resigned from the party's leadership and, with

---

[31] Speaking before the Radical party group in the National Assembly, cited in *Le Monde*, 22 November 1956. In an article in *L'Observateur de l'Ile de France* (extracts cited in *Le Monde*, 15 December 1956), Mendès-France explained that he had done all in his power to prevent the expedition. On hearing rumours of the projected attack, he went to see Premier Mollet on 29 October 1956: 'I questioned him; he neither confirmed nor denied the rumours that had begun to circulate and did not say a word about the ultimatum which was to be sent a few hours later. I warned him against the risks of an armed action on our part. I told him of the improbability, if not the impossibility, of localizing a conflict, the danger of the war spreading. He limited himself to replying that he did not want war and that he did not believe it would come. I continued to argue that, in case the military operation of which it was being spoken was not crowned with a decisive and immediate success, it was necessary to be prepared for reactions on the part of the Soviets, America, the Arab countries, the United Nations. He did not want to envisage these possibilities.'

his followers, was dejected and discouraged. The hopes of the *radicaux mendésistes* were still far short of attainment.

*

*   *

The end of 1955 may be said to have marked the high-water point of the *radicaux mendésistes*. They had consolidated their control of the party's administrative machinery at the party's congress in Paris in early November. They had formed an electoral alliance—the *Front Républicain*—with the Socialists and, brandishing a carefully documented *plateforme*, were waging a vigorous campaign. Their leader, Pierre Mendès-France, was given great acclamations by throngs of voters, and his sponsorship was a coveted prize sought by many candidates—Radicals and otherwise.

After their high hopes of 1955, the *radicaux mendésistes* greeted the election returns of 2 January 1956 with mixed reactions. Mendès-France had won a great personal victory in his home constituency—the number of his electoral supporters had risen from 37,271 in 1951 to 58,822 in 1956. The most *mendésiste* of the Radical federations had made spectacular gains, in votes if not in deputies—this was particularly true in eastern France. Paris had more Radical deputies than at any time since the early years of the Third Republic. Fifty-four deputies were members of the new Radical group that was formed in the National Assembly—subsequently joined by three more deputies who replaced invalidated Poujadists. The group was smaller than the preceding Radical group, which had sixty-nine members, but after an election which had seen the eruption of fifty-two Poujadists on the parliamentary scene, and the growth of the Communist group from ninety-two to 144, Radicals and Socialists were able to claim that it was their responsibility to form the new government. With ninety-four deputies, the Socialists were the second largest group in the Assembly. Although it had not lived up to the high hopes of some of its supporters, the *Front Républicain* had been more successful than the previous governmental majority in surviving the shifting electoral patterns.[32]

[32] In January 1956, the composition of the National Assembly was as follows (figures include *apparentés*): 150 Communists; 94 Socialists; 57 Radicals; 19 UDSR; 14 RGR; 10 *Indépendants d'outre-mer*; 73 MRP; 95 Moderates (four groups); 21

L'IMMOBILISME:

un attentat
contre
le pays

VOTEZ POUR L'ACTION
VOTEZ MENDÈS-FRANCE
VOTEZ Charles HERNU !

Party poster, 2 January 1956 general elections: *Votez pour l'action!*

...la plateforme du
PARTI RADICAL

- Créer des institutions efficaces, un gouvernement capable d'agir, rétablir le scrutin d'arrondissement.

- Rendre à la France son rôle de grande puissance.

- Faire la paix en Algérie.

- Garantir le progrès social.

- Donner leur chance à tous les jeunes.

- Défendre les classes moyennes.

- Moderniser l'agriculture pour la rendre prospère.

- Construire 350.000 logements par an.

Pour que ce programme de rénovation soit appliqué intégralement, pour que le mauvais coup du 2 décembre se retourne contre ses auteurs,
votez radical socialiste
car le parti radical tiendra parole

Pierre MENDÈS FRANCE

S.P.I., 27, RUE NICOLO, PARIS-XVIᵉ

Party handbill, 2 January 1956 general elections:
La plateforme du Parti Radical

Having won a comparative success at the polls, the leaders of the *Front Républicain* were to encounter new and divisive problems when confronted with the responsibility of assuming power. After the elections, Mendès-France and Guy Mollet, as leaders of the alliance's two major parties, agreed that if one of them were called to form a government the other could choose whichever ministry he preferred. After making this agreement, Mollet declared that if Mendès-France were selected he would ask to be Minister of Foreign Affairs. He then asked whether, if their situations were reversed, Mendès-France would accept the Ministry of Finance and Economic Affairs. The Radical leader replied that before 'assuming responsibility for the economic policy of the future government, he had to be assured of an agreement between the Radical party and the Socialist party on this policy: this was an indispensable first condition'.[33] After failing to reach such an agreement after a series of conversations with Socialist economic specialists, Mendès-France declared that he would prefer to be Minister of Foreign Affairs.

When the time came to form a cabinet, however, Mollet chose a fellow Socialist, Christian Pineau, as his Minister of Foreign Affairs, and Mendès-France was made a Minister of State without portfolio. In commenting on Mollet's rejection of his request, Mendès-France later declared that 'it is now known that his attitude resulted from a veto by the MRP and the Independents'.[34] Adding that the MRP would have voted for Mollet in any case, he stated that it was 'by a sort of bluff that the parties of the Right alarmed the nominated premier by threatening not to vote for him'. 'In his desire to conciliate these parties,' he continued, 'M. Guy Mollet clearly inflicted the Radical party and one of its chiefs with a painful disavowal. The solidarity of the *Front Républicain* could not help but suffer from it.'

It was not long, indeed, before the very term '*Front Républicain*'

Républicains sociaux; 52 Poujadists; and 8 non-inscribed. The figures for the previous National Assembly were: 98 Communists; 103 Socialists; 76 Radicals; 23 UDSR; 16 *Indépendants d'outre-mer*; 87 MRP; 135 Moderates and *Action républicaine et sociale* (latter formed in 1952 after most of RPF formed group of *Républicains sociaux*); 68 *Républicains sociaux*; and 16 non-inscribed.

[33] Letter sent by Mendès-France to Radical party federations, 'Pourquoi et comment nous participons'. Reprinted in *I.R.S.*, February 1956. See also *Le Monde*, 19–20 February 1956, and *l'Express*, 20 February 1956.

[34] *Ibid.*

was relegated to the limbo of extinct French political expressions. In a meeting of the party's *Comité Cadillac* on 27 January 1956, Pierre Naudet and Charles Hernu, newly elected young *radicaux mendésistes* from Paris, opposed participation in a government formed by their party's electoral allies. With Léon Hovnanian and Claude Panier, they bitterly regretted the refusal to appoint Mendès-France Minister of Foreign Affairs and objected to the composition of the proposed cabinet. The majority of the party, however, led by Mendès-France, favoured both supporting Mollet and participating in his government. In their eyes, it was 'the best way to serve the country and the Republic, with patriotism and unselfishness, and this despite the developments of a disappointing ministerial crisis'.[35]

Subsequent developments did not improve the uneasy relationship between Mendès-France and other members of the new government. From the beginning, he was a dissenter from many of the views of the cabinet majority on economic, social, and European affairs. Of greatest import, however, were his differences with the new premier's actions concerning the tragic central problem of Algeria. Mendès-France was dismayed when, during a visit to Algiers on 6 February 1956, Guy Mollet gave in to the violent pressures of an aroused mob and withdrew his nomination of the liberal-minded General Catroux as Governor-General of Algeria. The subsequent appointment of Robert Lacoste did little to allay his misgivings. In a speech at a meeting of the party's executive committee on 15 February 1956, he attacked Mollet vigorously for his failure to carry out the electoral programme that the *Front Républicain* had adopted prior to the elections. His supporters were even more outspoken. At a meeting of the executive committee on 2 March, one young *Jacobin* declared that 'this government has done more harm in three weeks than that of M. Laniel in six months'.[36] In a speech at a meeting of the executive committee on 20 April, Charles Hernu asked, in the name of the young men who were leaving to fight in Algeria, whether the Radicals who had been elected were 'imbeciles who had promised a peace in Algeria that they thought possible when such was not the case, or crooks who had promised it when they knew perfectly well that it was impossible'. At the same meeting the newly elected president of the Federation of the Seine

[35] *I.R.S.*, February, 1956. [36] *Le Monde*, 4–5 March 1956. Paul-André Falcoz

Jacques Périer, asked Mendès-France to 'define his position clearly, as much as his presence in the government allowed', and went on to voice his opinion that his situation must sometimes be like that of 'a prisoner who looks towards the outside'.

A month later, on 23 May 1956, Mendès-France resigned from the cabinet. In his letter of resignation to Premier Mollet, he stressed his conviction that the government's failure to accompany its massive military effort in Algeria with political action designed to restore Moslem confidence in France would lead to the loss of Algeria.[37] He recalled that, far from opposing the sending of massive reinforcements to Algeria, he had urged that even more men be sent more rapidly to permit France to base subsequent actions there on a position of strength. Force alone, however, could not suffice. 'Any policy,' he warned, 'which ignores the feelings and the misery of the native population leads step by step from the loss of the people of Algeria to that of Algeria itself, and then inevitably to the loss of our whole African position.' After recalling his previous demands for measures to reassure the native population, he made a final appeal to Mollet. 'I should like at least that my resignation should have the effect of a new anguished appeal for the government to take the necessary decisions, however difficult they may be.'

Mendès-France was now on the 'outside', but his position was still not sufficiently clear in the eyes of many of his followers. On leaving the Matignon Palace, the Premier's office, where the cabinet met when he submitted his resignation, Mendès-France said that he had told Mollet that he considered his cabinet to be the best formation possible at the present time. Although he was leaving the government, he had asked the twelve other Radical ministers to remain in the cabinet. He was henceforth to be the leader of a party with twelve representatives in a government whose policies he disapproved. In the meantime, his new isolation on the governmental scene had been accompanied by increasing stresses within the party that he and his followers were trying to renovate.

*

* *

As the 'second Mendès-France experiment' moved into its second year, it was becoming increasingly clear that it was one

[37] *I.R.S.*, May 1956.

thing to have won control of the Radical party's administrative machinery, but that it was quite another to win control of the party's group in the National Assembly. The group's traditional freedom of vote, its many strong personalities and their fondness for high political office, its traditions of immobilism, and the local autonomy of the federations to which its members belonged, were all factors that hindered the transformation of the Radical group into a cohesive and disciplined unit. In addition to these problems, the party's new leaders had to face the existence within their party of deep differences of opinion on basic political issues.

The joint effect of all these factors was to lead to the largest split in the long history of the Radical party—the *scission de Lyon*, which took place at the party's congress in October 1956. The first major step towards this split took place in April 1956, when thirty Radical or ex-Radical deputies and senators—led by Henri Queuille and André Morice—issued a manifesto denouncing as 'inadmissible' certain views that *radicaux mendésistes* had expressed concerning Algeria at the meeting of the party's executive committee on 20 April.[38] The manifesto said an effort was being made to 'ignore the horrors committed by the fanatical assassins of women and children in Algeria'. Condemning 'defeatism', it called for a policy of 'firmness and resolution'. The text was prepared at the headquarters of the RGR, and among the signatories were Lafay, Laffargue, and Jean-Paul David. In a statement a few days later, Queuille declared that those who signed the manifesto had wished, in particular, to make clear their lack of agreement with 'M. Jean-Jacques Servan-Schreiber and of all the people who follow him'.[39]

The opposition within the party to the *radicaux mendésistes* was henceforth to become increasingly open and vigorous. In early June, a group of Radical parliamentarians addressed a circular letter to their Radical colleagues in parliament and throughout the country in which they called for group leadership of the

[38] See *Le Monde*, 28 April 1956, and *l'Express*, 4 May 1956. The manifesto was signed by twenty deputies and fifteen senators. *L'Année politique*, 1956, p. 46.

[39] *Le Monde*, 2 May 1956. In an article in *l'Express*, 4 May 1956, Jean-Jacques Servan-Schreiber wrote that he had sent to Queuille a copy of the speech that he had given at the meeting of the *Comité Exécutif* and asked him which of his remarks were 'inadmissible'. '*Il a reconnu par écrit,*' Servan-Schreiber noted, '*qu'en fait il n'y trouvait pas les propos inadmissibles en question. Il n'avait d'ailleurs pas assisté au Comité Exécutif, et il me demande "des égards pour son âge". . . . Mais il tient à me confirmer son "désaccord politique" avec moi sur le fond, pour l'Algérie et en général.*'

party. Mendès-France's post of *premier vice-président* would be abolished, and a quadrumvirate would be formed around Herriot. By September, forty Radical parliamentarians—including Queuille, Marie, Morice, and Tony-Révillon—had announced their agreement with the new project.[40] They made no secret of their desire to eliminate Mendès-France from the party's leadership and to promote a reunification of the party.

When the time came for the party's annual congress in October, the stage was set for a dramatic confrontation between the opposing groups within the party. In a series of speeches, supporters and opponents of the proposed projects were both eloquent and vociferous in expressing their opinions. After referring to 'this unfortunate congress of May 1955', the veteran deputy Tony-Révillon complained that 'our old party, whose tendencies were diverse but whose members were united by friendship and by respect for the *grands principes*, is deeply divided'. In his opinion, group leadership was a means of establishing unity within the party. 'For a totalitarian régime in the party,' he argued, 'we want to substitute a régime of liberty.'

The chief standard-bearer for the opposition to the *radicaux mendésistes* was André Morice. A deputy from Loire-Maritime and a former minister, Morice explained at length the reasons for his disagreement with the party's leadership.[41] In the eyes of many, he complained, 'our party no longer appears as the guarantor of French grandeur (prolonged protests)'. A second reason, he said, was that 'the Radical party no longer operates like a democratic party (Cries: *Hou! Hou!*)'. It was not playing its normal role on the political scene, and in its internal operations it was using 'totalitarian methods'. Morice then criticized the role that Mendès-France had played in the Mollet government. 'We suffered from his public opposition to Lacoste, to Champeix,[42] to Guy Mollet on this essential problem of Algeria (protests).' In a critical period in French history, he declared, the Radical party was not doing its duty, 'and this at a time when the Socialist party and its chief, M. Guy Mollet, are given the magnificent

---

[40] See *Combat*, 3 September 1956, and *Le Monde*, 10 October 1956.

[41] *L'Express*, 19 October 1956.

[42] Marcel Champeix, Socialist senator from Corrèze and Under Secretary of State for the *Administration de l'Algérie* section of the Ministry of the Interior in Mollet's cabinet.

example of a patriotic duty accomplished with zeal (hooting in the hall; cries: "Morice, you have come to the wrong congress!")'.

Morice also attacked 'the activities, which we consider evil, of a newspaper called *l'Express* (loud protests; some applause)'. Noting that people would say that '*le Président* Mendès-France is not *l'Express*, *l'Express* is not the president', he declared that whether people liked it or not *l'Express* was the 'organ of what people have called *mendésisme*, and it is in it that Mendès-France makes his opinions known'. Faced by an audience that included many young *radicaux mendésistes*, he went on to observe that 'one is not a Radical at twenty or at eighteen years of age, one becomes a Radical when one has studied the history of the Republic (*brouhaha*, loud protests)'. The Radical party was not, he said, 'the small combat formation that people wanted to make', but was a 'synthesis of diverse opinions'. The leadership of the party, he concluded, should reflect this synthesis.

Unable to carry the day (a motion condemning the activities and methods of the minority group and expressing confidence in the leadership of Mendès-France was passed by a vote of 1,006 to 426), Morice and his supporters decided to form a new Radical party. Participating in this decision—made during a dinner at a restaurant in Lyons during the evening of 13 October 1956, the third day of the four-day congress—were the two ex-premiers, Henri Queuille and André Marie, and several deputies.[43] The new party, which proudly bore the title of '*parti radical-socialiste*' until a court ruling five months later granted exclusive use of the disputed title to the senior Radical party of the Place de Valois,[44] soon grouped fourteen deputies—nine of whom had voted against Mendès-France when he was overthrown on 5

[43] Besides Morice, Edouard Ramonet and Roger Morève were present. Laffargue was also present at the dinner. *Demain*, 18–24 October 1956. Lafay was in Lyons during the congress, and René Mayer had reserved an hotel room but had not come. *L'Express*, 19 October 1956. The delegates of the three Radical federations of Algeria were expected at the dinner, but did not arrive. 'Alas!' commented *l'Express*, 'the Grouchy of this Waterloo was M. Borgeaud.' *Ibid.*

[44] *Le Monde*, 8 and 28 March 1957. The dissident group based their argument both on a technicality—the *Parti républicain radical et radical-socialiste* had neglected to register its title—and on ideological grounds—'the true radicalism was carried away by those who left, and one cannot refuse to give them the title'. At the time of the split, *Le Canard enchaîné* labelled the new party '*Le Parti radi-Queuille-socialiste*'. The title usually used was '*le Parti radical "dissident"* '.

February 1955—and over twenty senators.[45] To prove that the new party did not consist only of elderly Radical parliamentarians, it was also decided to form a *Club des Montagnards* that could oppose the *Club des Jacobins*. Declaring that the *scission de Lyon* was equal in importance to the Socialist party's *scission de Tours* in 1920 that saw the formation of the French Communist party, Morice launched an appeal for a broadly based membership. By mid-December, the new party claimed to have thirty-two federations; in April 1957, at the party's first congress, Morice noted the existence of fifty-four federations and 33,000 members.[46] Among the new members was Léon Martinaud-Déplat, who called his new party 'the refuge of radicalism'. Presided over by Henri Queuille, now the 'pope of dissident radicalism', the speakers at the party's first congress devoted much of their time to denouncing Mendès-France and the *radicaux mendésistes*. 'No,' proclaimed Morice, 'they never were, and never will be, Radicals.'

*

* *

Mendès-France and his followers were insistent in expressing their lack of regret concerning the exodus of the dissident Radicals at Lyons. 'Their departure,' Mendès-France told the congress, 'will bring us new supporters now that what was called the "uneasiness" has been dispelled. The path is now open; we call to us all men of good will. There are men and women,' he continued, 'who must join us in the great task of national renovation. In this way, this fifty-second congress will truly mark the beginning of a glorious new era (applause; the Congress rises; indescribable ovation).'[47]

It soon became evident, however, that not all the 'uneasiness' in the party had been dispelled and that the anticipated new era had yet to open. Fourteen deputies had left the party, but

---

[45] The deputies were: Arrighi (Corsica), Badie (Hérault), Bégouin (Seine-et-Marne), Devinat (Saône-et-Loire), Faggianelli (Corsica), Gaborit (Charente-Maritime), Emile Hugues (Alpes-Maritimes), André Marie (Seine-Maritime), Morève (Indre), de Pierrebourg (Creuse), Queuille (Corrèze), Ramonet (Indre), and Tony-Révillon (Ain). Of this group, only Bégouin, Faggianelli, Morève, and Queuille had supported Mendès-France on 5 February 1955. Arrighi was not a deputy at the time.

[46] *Le Monde*, 7-8 April 1957.   [47] *La Dépêche du Midi*, 15 October 1956.

Mendès-France and his faithful supporters were still a minority in the Radical group in the National Assembly. The *radicaux mendésistes*, and in particular the young deputies from Paris, continued to be strongly opposed to the policies of the Mollet government, while twelve Radical ministers continued to participate in the formulation and administration of these same policies.

The dissident Radicals, clearly, were not the only Radicals who wanted their party to resume its traditional role of conciliation and arbitration, nor were they the only Radicals who differed with the *radicaux mendésistes'* opposition to the Mollet government. André Morice had spoken of 'the magnificent example' that Guy Mollet was providing. At the same Lyons congress, Maurice Bourgès-Maunoury, who was Mollet's Minister of Defence, was emphatic in stressing his solidarity with Robert Lacoste, the controversial Resident Minister in Algeria. Speaking after Bourgès-Maunoury, René Billères, who was Mollet's Minister of Education, also defended the government's actions and went on to say that if the party did not agree with the government's policies it should tell its ministers to withdraw. The latter alternative, he noted, 'would certainly have the advantage of political purity', but, he asked, 'would a ministerial crisis bring forth a majority in this Assembly where there is none?' In replying to Billères's remarks, Mendès-France used an argument that he had used at the party's congress the preceding year when Faure's government was under strong Radical attack. 'I remain, for my part, faithful to the old tradition of our party, taught to us in other times by Herriot, according to which it is not a congress's task to overthrow a government.' It was the congress's duty, on the other hand, to formulate policies, 'and these policies bind all Radicals, whether they be militants, parliamentarians, or ministers'.

This interpretation of the role of the congress, although acceptable in theory, had long been inoperative in practice. Radical parliamentarians and ministers had always been characterized by the liberty with which they could make their own decisions and the degree to which they were unhampered by party rulings. For Mendès-France, however, the renovation of the Radical party required the reversal of this attitude. The party had to reach decisions as a unit, minorities had to give in to majorities, and the party had to take action as a unit. Such a procedure, he argued, was essential for the clarification of French political life. 'When the English vote for a Labourite,' he had declared to a meeting of Radical students in Paris in May 1955, 'they are voting for the nationalization of steel; when they vote for a Conservative, they are voting for it to be denationalized.'[48] 'When the French elect a Radical,' he added, 'their vote means that they are in favour of good, and opposed to evil.'

In order to renovate the Radical party, therefore, it was not enough to have won control of the party's administrative machinery and to have gained the enthusiastic support of a majority of the party's rank-and-file. To make the renovation meaningful, it was necessary to make it possible for the will of the party's members to be translated into action by the party's representatives in the National Assembly. The parliamentary group had to vote as a unit, and Radical ministers had to advance policies which reflected the wishes of the majority of the party's members.

The political climate both in the party's group in the National Assembly and on the evolving political scene made such objectives difficult to attain. During the months that followed the party's congress at Lyons in October 1956, hostility towards Mendès-France and the *radicaux mendésistes* continued unabated. Jean-Jacques Servan-Schreiber failed in his attempt to be selected as a Radical candidate in December, and in the elections that followed a right-wing Independent who attacked Mendès-France as 'the symbol of defeatism' won a sweeping victory.[49]

Increasingly isolated in the country, Mendès-France was also becoming more and more isolated in his party. Of particular significance in this trend was the role played by the powerful Radical Federation of the south-west. Grouping twelve *départements* and twenty-three parliamentarians, this federation consti- tuted, as in the past, a powerful force within the Radical party. Among its representatives were six members of Mollet's cabinet: Bourgès-Maunoury, Billères, Maurice Faure, Henry Laforest, Jacques Bordeneuve, and André Dulin. Its most powerful leader was Jean Baylet, who by controlling the influential *La Dépêche du Midi* was able to exercise great power over his parliamentary

---

[48] *La Jeune Tribune*, Paris, May–June 1955.

[49] *Le Monde*, 12 January 1957. Julien Tardieu. See above, p. 193.

colleagues. In the past, Baylet had more than once been instrumental in helping Mendès-France. After Mendès-France's fall from power in February 1955, the Federation of Tarn-et-Garonne, under Baylet's leadership, voted an order of the day in which it protested against the conditions in which Mendès-France had been overthrown and called for a special congress. By winning the support of many of his south-western colleagues to this plan, Baylet had played an important role in helping to engineer Mendès-France's victory of 4 May 1955.

By February 1957 Baylet and his colleagues were much less enthusiastic concerning Mendès-France's projects. At a stormy meeting of the party's group in the National Assembly on 14 February, Billères declared that he and his fellow Radical ministers had not remained in the government in order to follow the advice or the orders of Mendès-France, but that it was their conscience that had dictated their decision.[50] If his lack of accord with Mendès-France continued, he added, he would quit the party. At a meeting of the party's executive committee that was held the following day, the delegates from the south-west registered their collective disapproval of their party's leadership when, seated together in the back of the *Salle Wagram*, they raised their membership cards to vote against the executive committee's final motion.

It was clear that the familiar arguments of the *radicaux de gestion* were still not without supporters in the Radical party. On 10 March 1957, the south-western federation of Lot-et-Garonne passed a motion in which it protested against 'the calumnies aimed at M. Pierre Mendès-France', but also added that the unity of the party required the 'voluntary effacement of those who are doctrinaires more than conciliators, thinkers more than the *gestionnaires* of a great party'.[51]

Despite the rising tide of adverse opinion, Mendès-France persevered in his attempt to transform an undisciplined collection of men and opinions into a cohesive and effective political party. A major step in this attempt was made during a meeting of Radical parliamentarians at a two-day conference at Chartres, 11–12 March 1957. The *'conclave de Chartres'*, unprecedented in Radical history, was primarily devoted to discussing Algeria and the problem of party discipline. Mendès-France made concessions

[50] *Le Monde*, 16 February 195   7.[51] *Le Monde*, 12 March 1957.

in a motion on Algeria, but in return was able to secure agreement to a plan for a relative degree of voting discipline in the National Assembly. The party's group, it was decided, had to vote as a unit in all important votes and had to determine its attitude 'in accordance with decisions of the party congress or the executive committee'. Deputies who disagreed would be allowed to abstain, but not to vote the opposite way.

For the first time in the history of the Radical party, its representatives were formally committed to a future of disciplined voting. Sixteen days later, however, when the time came to put the new plan into operation, the hopes of the plan's proponents were not realized. In the first important vote that took place after the Chartres conference, twenty-one Radicals, including the twelve Radical ministers, voted in support of Mollet, thirteen voted in opposition, eight abstained, and three were absent. At a meeting of the Radical group before the vote, the deputies had split twenty-one to twenty in favour of voting against Mollet. Shortly afterwards the group's *bureau* decided to include a pro-Mollet vote that had been given orally a few hours earlier.[52] The group was as divided as ever in the past.

By the time that the party met for a special congress in Paris's *Salle Wagram* on 3–4 May 1957, incidents outside parliament had added to the disunity and disarray of the party. After six months on active service as a lieutenant in Algeria, Jean-Jacques Servan-Schreiber returned to Paris and published a series of very controversial articles based on his experiences.[53] Charged with seeking to demoralize the Army, he was soon in bitter conflict with the Radical Minister of Defence, Maurice Bourgès-Maunoury. On 10 April, the Radical party announced the organization of a *Commission d'information radicale* that would visit Algeria and make a report, but renounced this project after receiving a telegram from Mollet's Resident Minister in Algeria, Robert Lacoste, in which Lacoste spoke of 'the perilous situation' that the arrival

---

[52] *Le Monde*, 30 March 1957 and 3 April 1957. When Henri Caillavet observed that the score of twenty-one to twenty was '*un peu juste*' and argued that enforcing discipline would have meant a breaking up of the group, Mendès-France drily commented: '*Il fallait donc inscrire une clause prévoyant que la discipline ne jouerait que lorsque la majorité serait de 60 voix contre 2.*' *Le Monde*, 30 March 1957.

[53] *L'Express*, 8, 15, 22, 29 March 1957. Later published in book form as *Lieutenant en Algérie*, Paris, 1957.

of the commission at Algiers 'would be certain to provoke'.[54] 'The population of Algiers,' he ominously warned, 'would not be able to control its emotion.'

When the special congress opened in Paris on 3 May 1957, Mendès-France delivered a passionate diatribe against Mollet's Algerian policy and was bitterly critical of Bourgès-Maunoury. Before the congress ended, however, he disappointed most of his supporters by asking them to approve a motion that had been written in conjunction with Radical ministers. Calling for a new policy in Algeria and changes in the government's financial and economic policies, the motion nevertheless recommended that the Radical ministers remain in the government in order to bring about these changes. At the same time, however, the motion set the stage for a final showdown. If the government did not accept the changes that it outlined, the Radical party 'would no longer be able to participate in the government and give it support'.

The motion was presented to Premier Mollet by Billères and Bourgès-Maunoury. A week later, in a formal letter to Billères, Mollet argued that the motion's conditions were not clearly stated, regretted 'certain disobliging insinuations', and added that he was divided between his desire to maintain good relations between their two parties and at the same time to prevent his government from being unjustly criticized.[55] In the eyes of the *radicaux mendésistes*, this reply was clearly unsatisfactory. A few days later, on 21 May, Mollet asked the National Assembly for a vote of confidence on his financial policies. The willingness of Radical deputies to act on the basis of decisions reached by Radical congresses, as well as the ability of the deputies to vote as a group, was to be put to a painful test.

In a tumultuous meeting of the Radical group, the assembled deputies again found it difficult to reach a decision. In a first vote, nineteen favoured supporting Mollet, eighteen favoured voting in opposition, and four favoured abstaining.[56] As neither side had a majority, a second vote followed: twenty favoured voting in favour, twenty favoured abstaining, and one favoured voting in opposition. After a refusal by Daladier, the group's president, to cast a deciding vote, a compromise was reached:

[54] *Le Monde*, 12 April 1957.   [55] *Le Monde*, 15 May 1957.
[56] *Le Monde*, 23 May 1957.

the group as a whole would abstain, but the ministers could vote in favour.

In the confidence vote that followed and which saw Mollet's fall from power, twenty-eight Radicals abstained, twelve voted for Mollet, two were absent, and one voted in opposition. Among the twelve who voted for Mollet were four non-ministers. Two of the latter appeared before the party's *bureau* and were excused for having ignored party discipline. The remaining two refused to appear, and at a meeting of the *bureau* on 23 May 1957, Mendès-France proposed that they be expelled from the party. By a vote of seventeen to fifteen, however, the *bureau* voted in favour of only censuring them.[57] Mendès-France, concluding that he was no longer able to make the will of the party's militants respected, immediately announced his resignation from the leadership of the party. Twenty-four hours later, when the party's *Comité Cadillac* decided that the motion passed at the special congress of 3–4 May would only serve as a 'basis of discussion', and not as 'the *sine qua non* conditions for Radical participation in all future governments' as the congress had specified, Mendès-France also resigned from his position as president of the *Comité Cadillac*.[58] On 28 June 1957, at the next meeting of the party's executive committee, he officially submitted his resignation as *premier vice-président* of the Radical party.

*

*   *

Thus, after two years as leader of the Radical party, Mendès-France's political career was entering a new phase. The 'second Mendès-France experiment' had proved to be as difficult of attainment as had the first. The *radicaux mendésistes* had been able to attract many new members to the party and had won the support of a majority of the party's militants. They had been able to win control of the party's administrative machinery and

[57] See *Le Monde*, 25 May 1957, and *I.R.S.*, May 1957. The two deputies who voted for Mollet and were subsequently excused were André Bonnaire (Nord) and Léon Sagnol (Haute-Loire). The two who refused to appear before the *bureau* were Lucien Degoutte (Rhône) and Edmond Desouches (Eure-et-Loir). Mme. Yvonne Pons de Poli, one of the *bureau*'s members who voted in favour of censure, later declared that she had meant to vote for exclusion. This would have resulted in a tie.

[58] *Le Monde*, 26–27 May 1957.

had modified the statutes in order to vest more power in the militants. They had not been able, however, to extend the militants' control to include the party's deputies. Unrenovated and unrepentant, the party's parliamentary group had shown its continued disinclination to abide by the decisions of the party's congresses. And, when a showdown came between the conceptions of Mendès-France and those of his adversaries in the party's parliamentary group, a majority of the party's *bureau*, hitherto a stronghold of *mendésisme*, had refused to apply the sanctions that Mendès-France considered vital.

Unable to carry out his goals in the Radical party, Mendès-France was also increasingly isolated in the country. During a period when nationalistic fervour was running high in France, many of his compatriots insisted on equating his condemnation of the government's Algerian policy with a desire to abandon *l'Algérie française*. Seldom in France's history had a man been the subject of such strong hostility. 'When he mounts to the rostrum in parliament,' wrote an editorialist in the party's official newspaper in January 1957, 'the extreme right vociferates, the right subsides into an attitude of menacing scorn, the MRP crosses itself, the Communists maintain a hostile silence, and Guy Mollet departs shrugging his shoulders.' A month earlier, Mauriac had noted that no French politician since Clemenceau had inspired as much hatred as had Mendès-France.[59] 'When nearly everyone is guilty,' Mauriac continued, 'it is the innocent person who becomes the outlaw.'

The hope of the young, the impatient, and the enthusiastic, Mendès-France used methods that irritated many of the older Radicals. Valuing comradeship more than solidarity, and handshakes and banquets more than doctrinal purity, they constituted difficult material with which to build a disciplined and vigorous party. The sociological base of the party and the traditional flexibility of the party's structure, as well as the problem of controlling deputies who had the faithful support of their constituencies, added to the obstacles that encumbered the path of the *radicaux mendésistes*.

[59] *L'Express*, 7 December 1956. The following year, in an interview with an English writer, Mauriac described Mendès-France as a victim of French anti-Semitism. 'He is a Jew, as you know, and this has done him an incalculable amount of harm. Nobody admits it, but what really broke him was racial feeling.' Philip Toynbee, *The Observer*, 27 October 1957.

In their effort to renovate their party's doctrine, the *radicaux mendésistes* had tried to return radicalism to the methods and ideal of the radicalism of the turn of the century. To have succeeded in this aim would have meant reversing habits which had developed during the subsequent decades. Such a task was, at best, an uphill battle. Like their ideological ancestors, the *radicaux mendésistes* had stressed the need for unity with the Socialists. In 1956 and 1957, however, they were confronted with a 'neo-socialism' that made erstwhile allies into bitter opponents. And, during the period when they hoped to renovate Radical doctrine, the *radicaux mendésistes* had had to devote most of their efforts to combating recalcitrant personalities.

While the *radicaux mendésistes* were discussing their projects for the future, their party continued to provide evidence of its traditional disunity. When Bourgès-Maunoury succeeded Mollet on 12 June 1957, eleven of his fellow Radicals voted against him, twenty-seven supported him, and seven abstained. André Morice became the new Minister of National Defence, and two other dissident Radical deputies were made *secrétaires d'état*. More and more Radicals were speaking of an eventual reunification of their party and expressing their desire for a return to the calmer ways of the past.

The gravity and number of France's problems, however, showed no signs of abating. In a valedictory speech at a meeting of the party's executive committee on 28 June 1957, Mendès-France warned his listeners that France's great danger was the 'progressive collapse of this régime in which so many men no longer believe', a collapse that would be due more to the 'disgust and the discouragement of the best among the French than to the real force or the constructive value of the opposition of the extreme Right or the extreme Left'.

After referring to the party's record of the preceding two months as 'a cascade of disavowals and breaches of promises which had been solemnly made by so many important men in our party', Mendès-France declared that his decision to resign as leader of the Radical party could not be withdrawn. At the same time, with the nation's strength already divided between a large number of political formations, it was doubtful if forming one more party would help to clarify the political scene. It was to be hoped, however, that the dispersion of the progressive forces in France would not continue indefinitely and that 'under new forms yet to be explored, opportunities will ripen'. During the coming winter, he told his listeners, 'the winter of the Republic's last chance', they must take up their pilgrim's staff and go throughout the country speaking to their compatriots of their true interests. For the success of this 'crusade', they had to use, wherever they were, the means at their disposal. 'The situation can evolve very quickly,' he added. 'Let us keep ourselves ready.'

IX

Conclusions

'Il ne faut pas beaucoup de mitraillettes pour disperser cent mille citoyens armés de grands principes.'

FRANÇOIS MAURIAC, *l'Express,* 12 June 1958.

The winter of 1957–8 *was* the winter of the Fourth Republic's last chance. Maurice Bourgès-Maunoury, the young Radical who had succeeded Guy Mollet as premier in June 1957, fell from power less than four months later, on 30 September, when his government's proposal for a new 'framework-law' for Algeria was voted down by the National Assembly. After a five-week period during which France was without a government, another young Radical, Félix Gaillard, was voted into office on 6 November 1957.

When Gaillard was overthrown on 15 April 1958, it was not just one more crisis in France's long series of governmental crises—it was a crisis of the régime itself, a crisis that culminated in the 'revolution of Algiers' on 13 May 1959. Between the fall of Mollet's government on 21 May 1957, and the Algiers uprising, France had been without a government for a total of eighty-six days. The inability of the Fourth Republic to end the Algerian war and the inability of the central government to control the military and popular forces of Algiers had become increasingly evident. Again and again, Paris had been forced to capitulate to Algiers. The bombing of Sakhiet, a Tunisian village near the Algerian frontier, by a squadron of the French Air Force on 8 February 1958, was 'covered' by Gaillard as the arrest of Ben Bella in October 1957 had been 'covered' by Mollet. Even Franco, Mauriac bitterly commented, had never accepted responsibility for the bombing of Guernica.[1]

During the last year of the Fourth Republic the Radical party was as divided as ever in the past. A majority of those Radicals present at a meeting of the party's executive committee on 28

[1] *L'Express,* 13 February 1958.

June 1957—a meeting boycotted by many Radicals, particularly those from the south-west—had voted against the formation of Bourgès-Maunoury's government. When Bourgès-Maunoury fell from power, twenty-six Radical deputies supported him, thirteen voted against him, and three did not vote. When Gaillard was invested as premier, twenty-eight Radicals supported him, eleven were opposed, and four were absent.

The *radicaux mendésistes* were scathing in their opposition to both Bourgès-Maunoury and Gaillard. At the party's congress at Strasbourg in November 1957, a congress marked by a long debate on Algeria between Mendès-France and Gaillard, many of them gave vent to their bitterness. Hernu caustically referred to Gaillard's governing methods as an example of *queuillisme juvénile*. Another young *radical mendésiste* was more outspoken. 'Gentlemen,' the aroused orator declared, 'our struggle is even more difficult than that which young nationalists have carried on in other countries, because our own colonialists, those who cheat and exploit us, those who paralyse our national emancipation, are Bourgès-Maunoury and Gaillard.'[2]

Mendès-France and his supporters won a partial victory at Strasbourg. A motion calling for negotiations with Tunisia and Morocco during which all of France's problems in North Africa would be discussed was voted by the congress's delegates; and Edouard Daladier, a compromise candidate long considered favourable to Mendès-France, was elected as the party's president. Eleven of the eighteen vacant places in the party's *bureau*, however, went to opponents of the *radicaux mendésistes*, and the scene was henceforth set for the eviction of Mendès-France's supporters from the party's administrative machinery. Less than two weeks later, by a vote of eighteen to sixteen, the newly constituted *bureau* replaced its *mendésiste* secretary-general, Paul Anxionnaz, by Georges Galy-Gasparrou, a veteran deputy from south-western France. In similar votes, all other *radicaux mendésistes* in the *bureau* were removed from positions of authority. The hopes that several young *radicaux mendésistes* had entertained of maintaining and expanding their

[2] Mme. Brigitte Gros, member of the party's *bureau* and sister of Jean-Jacques Servan-Schreiber. The remainder of her speech was drowned out by the audience. After leaving the Radical party, Mme. Gros wrote a controversial novel vividly describing the experiences of a young woman who joined a political party. *Véronique dans l'appareil,* Paris, 1960.

power within the party had now been conclusively thwarted.

Weakened by its divisions and wracked by its many quarrels, the Radical party, like the Fourth Republic itself, was disintegrating as a political force. Radicals were to face the crisis that burst open on 13 May 1958, primarily as individuals, and not as members of a political party. Virtually all Radicals supported Pflimlin during the night of 13 May, but during the subsequent days and weeks most Radicals were doubtful and undecided as to what course of action they should follow. Some, including Gaillard, were to rally hesitantly to de Gaulle. Others, including Mendès-France, Daladier, Baylet, and—surprising some observers—Bourgès-Maunoury, were to join the opposition. When de Gaulle was voted into power on 1 June 1958, twenty-four Radicals voted in favour and eighteen were opposed.

Not only was the party divided, but groups within the party were also split. Baylet and Bourgès-Maunoury were united in opposition, but many of the other leaders of the powerful southwestern federations—including Billères, Laforest, and Maurice Faure—had decided to support de Gaulle.[3] Even the previously faithful contingent of *radicaux mendésiste* deputies were now divided—Pierre Naudet, a young deputy from Paris, and Pierre Clostermann, who had been an ace in the Battle of Britain, were among the founders of the *Centre de la Réforme Républicaine*, an organization of left-wing Gaullists. Both were defeated in the legislative elections held in November 1958.

Most Radical deputies who remained in the party were not much more fortunate in these elections, in which less than a third of France's deputies were returned to the National Assembly. In the months following 13 May, many Radicals had emphasized the fact that their party had opposed the constitution of the Fourth Republic from the very beginning; they were not able to cite, however, a united Radical stand concerning the new Republic's constitution. At the party's congress at Lyons in September, 56·8 per cent. of the delegates favoured an affirmative vote in the constitutional referendum while 43·2 per cent. favoured a negative vote. In the legislative elections the following month, Radicals received only 2 per cent. of the votes cast and won only fourteen seats in the new National Assembly. Despite the return of the Radicals' cherished electoral system

[3] Baylet died in an automobile accident near Toulouse on 29 May 1959.

(single-member constituencies with two ballots), the Radical party had suffered the greatest defeat in its history.

Many Radicals, including Daladier, Hernu, Hovnanian, and Masson, had given up after the first ballot. Others had decided not to stand for re-election. These included Queuille, who had rejoined the ranks of the Radical party shortly after the 13 May uprising—*his* way of defending the Republic. The most spectacular downfall was that of Mendès-France, who was defeated in the Norman constituency that he had represented for the first time in 1932. Two months later, the Radical party's *bureau* (led by Félix Gaillard, who had been elected as the party's president at the congress at Lyons in September 1958) ruled that no Radical could remain in the party and, at the same time, be a member of the *Union des Forces démocratiques*—an organization in which the *radicaux mendésistes* were playing a prominent role. Mendès-France and his followers protested against the *bureau*'s ruling and declared that they would continue to work for unity between Radicals and other democratic forces. At a meeting on 11 February 1959, the party's *bureau* decreed that Mendès-France and his friends, by refusing to renounce their new allegiance, had placed themselves outside the Radical party. Seven months later, on 20 September 1959, followed by several of his ex-Radical friends, Mendès-France moved further from the Radical fold by joining the *Parti Socialiste Autonome*, a new party that had been founded in 1958 after a split in the Socialist party. In the new era that was beginning in France, it was clear that the disillusioned and defeated *mendésistes* no longer desired to do battle under the battered banners of the Radical party.

*

* *

'Party is a body of men united for promoting by their joint endeavours the national interest upon some particular principles in which they are all agreed.' It is questionable whether the Radical party, at any period of its history, may be said to have met the specifications outlined in Burke's classic definition of a political party. There is no doubt, in any case, that it did not do so during the fourteen years that followed the liberation of Paris in August 1944. During this period Radicals occupied far-flung positions on an ideological and political spectrum that extended from near-Communists on the left to avowed Conservatives on the right. In promoting their endeavours, they often had to devote more time to combating colleagues within their party than to fighting opponents on the outside. Unity and agreement may be said to have been Radical goals, but in describing the Radical party, these terms would be most appropriate in a definition by negation.

Despite such doctrinal and semantic shortcomings, however, the Radical party played an important role on the French political scene during the post-war years. In a very real sense its ideological confusions were a major source of its political strength. In the eyes of certain of its members it could qualify as more than a mere party: it was a microcosm of France itself. Non-initiates could question the validity of such an ambitious claim, but it was undeniable that the Radical party, with the aid of its varied internal divisions, was able to represent the political viewpoints and objectives of an impressively large fraction of French opinion.

Those who were not satisfied with the Radical party's credentials as a true political party and who were not willing to transfer the discussion to the sphere of national representativeness, could not dispute, however, the Radical party's existence as an effective electoral machine. It may not have been a true political party, but it shared an objective dear to all of its political competitors: to win as many seats as possible in the National Assembly.

'*Doctrine est tactique.*' If the main objective of political action is to win elections, a diversified doctrine is a valuable asset. Tactics—and doctrine—must vary according to time and place. 'Only a Democrat who rejects at least part of the Fair Deal can carry Kansas, and only a Republican who moderates the Republican platform can carry Massachusetts.'[4] Such remarks are even more applicable to France, where candidates not only have had to alter their programmes but have also been forced to negotiate electoral alliances with their competitors. Under such conditions it is helpful to have representatives in as many segments of opinion as possible. The Radical party's post-war flirtations—and less transitory relationships—with Communists and with

---

[4] Julius Turner, 'Responsible Parties: A Dissent from the Floor', *The American Political Science Review*, March 1951, p. 151.

Gaullists provided two examples of their skill in such enterprises. The Radical party also profited by having a rich vocabulary behind which diverse interests could group themselves. *Grands principes* and *petits intérêts* (as well as some not so small) are not mutually exclusive. When these doctrinal advantages are enjoyed by a political organization with a flexible structure and a relatively varied social composition, a formidable electoral machine can result.

Despite what certain of its critics have said, however, the Radical party was considerably more than an opportunistic electoral machine during the post-war years. It was also more than a loose affiliation of able personalities who had united for electoral purposes. Its leaders were remarkably proficient in presenting basic issues to the French public. They played a vital role in the functioning of the French political régime. And, in addition to the more traditionally Radical roles played by most of their colleagues, other Radicals also dedicated themselves to the difficult task of trying to make their party the instrument that would bring about the renovation of their country.

Radical spokesmen have had few peers in the art of presenting basic issues to the French public, but this task was shared by spokesmen of all political groups and organizations. Of greater significance was the role that Radicals played in the functioning of the French political system. A great *parti de gouvernement* during the Third Republic, the Radical party again became France's most active governmental party during the Fourth Republic. In order to fulfil this role, Radical leaders once again demonstrated their skill as able practitioners of the venerable art of political compromise.

In a democracy, a *parti de gouvernement* is a party of compromise. This is particularly true in a country with a multiparty system and deep political cleavages. Where no one party has a majority, compromises *must* be made. In post-war France, where such conditions were always present, conciliatory centre parties were a prerequisite for democratic governmental action. With its flexible doctrine, its loose structure, its traditional lack of voting discipline, and its many able leaders, the Radical party was ideally suited to the difficult task of conciliating diverse interests and furthering the cause of compromise. In carrying out this task, many Radicals inevitably came to consider doctrinal unity within their own party a secondary concern. They were willing to sacrifice purity of ideas to realities of politics.

The advantages of this approach to political life are undeniable. Non-doctrinaire, compromising parties have saved more than one régime. In sixteenth-century France, the moderate and realistic *politiques* did much to heal the ravages of their country's bitter religious wars. In 1939, a French political writer declared that it was probable that if it had not been for the Radicals, the liquidation of the Popular Front would not have been possible 'except at the price of a civil war with foreign intervention'.[5] It was thanks to the Radical party's action as shock absorber and conciliator, he argued, 'that the régime still endures'. 'Perhaps,' he added, 'it was a Radical party that Spain lacked in 1936.'

The *radicaux de gestion* of the post-war years carried on the Radical party's traditional mission of compromise and conciliation. Queuille and Faure, to mention only two of the more prominent examples of this prolific Radical species, played useful roles in French post-war politics. Such men had been missing in Spain. They and their ideas, however, have been prevalent in many countries that have evolved operative democratic régimes. American political parties, for example, have not been noteworthy for the unity and clarity of their doctrine. As one distinguished professor has observed, the only time that America *did* have doctrinal parties, 'North and South found themselves at war'.[6] The immediate cause of the greatest breakdown of the American political system, he continued, was the breakdown of the party system, 'the failure of party machinery and the party leaders to remember their national function, which if carried out, was the justification of the varied weaknesses and absurdities of the party organizations and policies'.

Not all Radicals, however, were willing to sacrifice their party's future to this 'national function'. In an article published in July 1956, Charles Hernu disparagingly noted the 'touching solicitude of the *docteurs ès sciences politiques*, the soothsayers who wanted to maintain usage of a so-called *parti de raison*'.[7] In the eyes of the *radicaux mendésistes*, the Radical party had a much

[5] See *Esprit*, May 1939, pp. 174 and 187.

[6] D. W. Brogan, *An Introduction to American Politics*, London, 1954, p. 54. See also p. 90.

[7] Charles Hernu, 'Le Parti radical devant le choix', *France-Observateur*, 26 July 1956.

more noble national function to perform: the renovation of France.

For the *radicaux mendésistes*, the main task in French politics was not compromise, but the need to overcome inertia and weakness. The system of governing France by compromises between parties that disagree, they argued, had led to a series of disasters. France had suffered from the effects of this policy in Indo-China, Tunisia, Morocco, Algeria, and on the domestic scene. Excessive compromise, in their eyes, was a perversion of democracy. It was impossible, they maintained, to carry out durable measures without a logical and coherent programme of action. Calls for 'broad governments of National Union', from their point of view, were only attempts to camouflage immobilism.

It was their objective, therefore, to transform the Radical party into a disciplined instrument of reform. The great party of compromise was to become the great party of French renovation. The old party of country notables was opened to new and more dynamic elements. A valiant effort was made to inculcate new spirit into France's oldest party. France was to enter a new era, and the Radical party was to lead the way.

These high hopes, however, proved to be difficult of attainment. Putting new wine in old bottles was a hazardous endeavour. The new characteristics that the *radicaux mendésistes* envisaged for their party were the antithesis of traditional radicalism. Committees elected by Radical militants had never had control over deputies. The Radical party's rural clientèle had always voted for men more than for policies. The typical Radical deputy, with his local popularity firmly based on the services he had rendered and on his skill in mixing freely with his constituents, had always been remote from party discipline. Radicals, indeed, had traditionally revelled in their undisciplined state and gloried in their tolerance. In a poll taken in 1952, 38 per cent. of those Radicals polled affirmed that they were attracted to their party because of its '*esprit de tolérance*'.[8]

These were attitudes that were difficult to eradicate. Even those Radicals who sincerely favoured the objectives of the *radicaux mendésistes* had often rebelled when it came to paying the price necessary for their implementation. They had been willing to support the exclusion of the most prominent *néo-radicaux*. They

[8] *Sondages*, 1952, No. 3, and Williams, p. 447.

had ratified the exclusion of Faure—and the exclusion of a Radical premier was, indeed, a remarkable step for a party that prided itself on being a governmental party. More and more Radicals, however, had expressed serious reservations after the *scission de Lyon* a year later. By this time, of all the Radicals who had served as premiers after the war, only Mendès-France was left. A woman delegate at a meeting of the party's executive committee in February 1957 voiced an attitude that was to become increasingly current during the following year when she remarked that 'some are departing, others want to return; it's no longer a party but a railroad station!' Although willing to have the Radical party play the role of renovating their country, many Radicals were reluctant to have their beloved party assume, at the same time, a *rôle de saucisson*, a sausage from which a slice would be cut every six months.

The elimination of recalcitrant deputies, however, was the price that the Radical party would have had to pay if it was to become the disciplined and renovated party envisaged by the *radicaux mendésistes*. A unified parliamentary group, subject to the wishes and orders of political organs elected by the party's militants, was a basic condition for subsequent coherent political action. If only ten or fifteen deputies were willing to accept this discipline, the party's parliamentary group would have had to have been reduced accordingly. In December 1955 the Radical party had felt it necessary to adopt a liberal policy in sponsoring diverse Radical candidates: investitures were subordinated only to acceptance of the party's *plateforme*, a condition that many of Mendès-France's opponents were willing to accept. This liberal policy was established when the *radicaux mendésistes* were at the peak of their power. Later, when the *radicaux mendésistes*'s position was much weaker, most Radicals were, more than ever, unwilling to exchange parliamentary seats for party discipline.

'Logic and politics seldom slip their feet between the same sheets.' Even the *radicaux mendésistes* were unable to prove an exception to this venerable French political maxim. After two years of diligent effort, their party was as divided and undisciplined as it had ever been in the past, and 'radicalism' was still a term subject to varying interpretations.

Such a fate, however, has been the destiny of more than one political party. The range of opinion within the Radical party was probably as wide as that encompassed by both the major American political parties. Even closer analogies may be drawn between the Radical party and the American political scene. One Radical deputy, after visiting the United States in 1948, published an article in which he went so far as to argue that 'the average American is a Radical'.[9] Writing before the presidential conventions of that year, he observed that, as it was certain that Wallace would be defeated and probable that MacArthur and Taft would not be chosen as candidates by the Republican party, it could be safely assumed that the country's administration would remain in the hands of 'Radicals'. The country of William James, he remarked, had caught up with the country of the *juste milieu*.

Sharing the Radical approach to life and politics, the two major American parties have also shared Radical problems. In May 1957, Sherman Adams, a former Republican governor and the principal aide of a Republican president, declared that the Democratic party was suffering from 'a chronic and incurable schizophrenia' and was so deeply split that the party 'simply cannot put itself together again'.[10] In discussing his own party, the Republican leader was not much more optimistic. 'Today,' he said, 'we have the stalwarts, the irreconciled, and the irreconcilables. We have the liberals, the liberal progressives, the conservative progressives, the plain and simple conservatives, and the reactionaries. We have the moderns and the "un" or antimoderns, the old-fashioned and the traditionalists—each resoundingly the oracle of the true meaning of Republicanism.' After five years of 'new Republicanism', it was clear that the Republican party could still present a catalogue of internal divisions comparable in scope to any similar list that could be devised for their French counterparts. When compared to the leaders of the Republican party, the *radicaux mendésistes* had not done too badly. They had spent only two years trying to renovate *their* party.

Although few Radicals have attempted to argue that *l'Amérique est radicale*, many Radicals have echoed Maurice Barrès's similar comment concerning France. During the post-war years, however,

---

[9] Paul Devinat, deputy from Saône-et-Loire, *I.R.S.*, May 1948.

[10] Address before a regional conference sponsored by the Republican National Committee in Trenton, N.J., 24 May 1957. Reprinted in *U.S. News and World Report*, 7 June 1957.

this proud claim was not made as often as it had been in the past. 'Radicals' may have been in a majority in America after the war, but in France they were surrounded by hostile elements. In quoting Barrès in 1950, one Radical spokesman was careful to specify that it was *la France intelligente* which was Radical.[11] France, however, has never been completely Radical; it has always been Radical in a relative and comparative sense. During the years that followed the war, the Radical party continued to be at least as successful as any other French political party in representing widespread, if divided, French attitudes.

When the Fifth Republic opened, few Radicals would have thought of identifying their party with their country's new régime. It is possible, however, that the old party of the Third and Fourth Republics came closer to representing France than did many of the groups and factions which were active in setting up France's latest experiment in government.

[11] Antonin Douzet, *I.R.S.*, March 1950.

APPENDIX I

PARTY ORGANIZATION: A GLOSSARY

Comité. Basic unit of party, usually based on the canton. The *comités* existed before the party, as autonomous constituency organizations, and the party was formed by their combination.

Fédération. Exist both on a departmental and regional scale. Hold congresses, usually at irregular intervals. Some federations exist only on paper (*I.R.S.*, 23 June 1955).

Comité exécutif. After the *Congrès*, the supreme organ of the party. Makes interim decisions between congresses, arranges agendas, elects committees, and names *rapporteurs*. Under pre-1959 statutes each federation was entitled to send a delegate for every 200 members or fraction thereof, but the executive committee has always been dominated by its *ex officio* members (including both party officials and those who hold public office). Membership has varied between 1,200 and 2,000 since the war. Only 150 members needed for a quorum. According to pre-1955 statutes, was supposed to meet four times yearly. Met twice in 1947; twice in 1948; twice in 1949; three times in 1950; once in 1951; once in 1952; once in 1953; did not meet in 1954; and met once in 1955. According to the 1955 statutes, the executive committee was henceforth to meet at least six times a year. It met four times during 1956; twice in 1957; and once in 1958.

Congrès. Meets once a year, usually in September, October, or November. Each federation is entitled to send one delegate for every 100 members or fraction thereof. Elects the president of the party; elects members of the executive committee and (until 1955) the *Commission exécutive*. Elects members of *bureau* (since 1955). Establishes party's programme. A *petit congrès* was held in Paris, 19–21 December 1944. During subsequent years, congresses were held as follows: 20–23 August 1945, Paris; 5–8 September 1946, Paris; 18–21 September 1947, Nice; 2–5 December 1948, Paris; 16–19 November 1949, Toulouse; 15–17 September 1950, Deauville; 25–28 October 1951, Lyons; 16–19 October 1952, Bordeaux; 17–20 September 1953, Aix-les-Bains; 14–17 October 1954, Marseilles; 3–6 November 1955, Paris; 12–15 October 1956, Lyons; 21–24 November 1957, Strasbourg; 11–14 September 1958, Lyons; and 11–14 June 1959, Pau.

Congrès extraordinaire. Special congress. Can be called by vote of executive committee or at the request of thirty federations. Six special congresses were called during the 1944–58 period: 4–7 April 1946, Lyons; 17–18 May 1951, Paris; 23–24 May 1952, Paris; 11–13 March 1954, Paris; 4 May 1955, Paris; 3–4 May 1957, Paris.

Commission exécutive. Organ established in 1946 to replace the *bureau.* Abolished at special congress of 4 May 1955. Consisted of forty non-parliamentary members of executive committee; twenty-five parliamentarians; and eleven party officials. Met monthly and controlled the normal working of the party. Directed party between meetings of the executive committee. Many provisional delegates rarely attended. Usually about twenty members at its meetings (*Le Monde,* 7 May 1955).

Président administratif. Administrative president. Office set up to relieve Herriot of administrative duties. Held by Léon Martinaud-Déplat, 1948–55. Office abolished at special congress of 4 May 1955. Elected by congress.

Comité Cadillac. Joint sitting of the members of Parliament and the *Commission exécutive* (until 1955 when latter replaced by *bureau*). Charged with deciding policy of party in times of ministerial crisis. Set up shortly before World War I in order to allow rank-and-file members of party to participate in making crucial decisions; abolished in 1959. Name came from the town (in Gironde) whose delegate proposed its establishment. Traditionally dominated by parliamentarians.

Bureau. Replaced *commisson exécutive* in 1955. Previously elected by *commission exécutive*; after 1955 elected by executive committee. Under pre-1959 statutes had thirty-three members, including six deputies, six senators, and three members of the Assembly of the French Union. Meets weekly. Names secretary-general and treasurer.

Conférence des Présidents et Secrétaires généraux des Fédérations. Meets prior to all congresses and meetings of executive committee. May submit propositions and requests to *bureau,* congresses, or to the executive committee. Must be consulted concerning agendas of congresses and meetings of executive committee.

Commission d'Action. Group of seven Radicals who were assigned task of revising the party's statutes by the special congress of 4 May 1955. Included three parliamentarians (Mendès-France, René Billères, and André Maroselli) and four *militants* (Henri Pad; Claude Panier, elected deputy on 2 January 1956; Mme Pons de Poli; and Charles Humbert, the *rapporteur*).

Premier vice-président. Post held by Pierre Mendès-France from November 1955 to May 1957.

FRENCH GOVERNMENTS FROM THE LIBERATION TO THE END OF THE FOURTH REPUBLIC:

RADICAL PREMIERS AND MINISTERS.[1]

Date	Premier	Interior	Finance	Economy	Justice	Education
10.9.44	DE GAULLE	Tixier	Lepercq	Mendès-France	De Menthon	Capitan
			Pleven	Pleven	Teitgen	

		General Election, 21 October 1945				
21.11.45	DE GAULLE	Tixier	Pleven	Billoux	Teitgen	*Giacobbi*
26.1.46	GOUIN	Le Troquer	Philip	Philip	Teitgen	Naegelen

		General Election, 2 June 1946				
23.6.46	BIDAULT	Depreux	Schuman	De Menthon	Teitgen	Naegelen

		General Election, 10 November 1946				
16.12.46	BLUM	Depreux	Philip	Philip	Ramadier	Naegelen
22.1.47	RAMADIER	Depreux	Schuman	Philip	*Marie*	Naegelen
22.11.47	SCHUMAN	Moch	*R. Mayer*	*R. Mayer*	*Marie*	Naegelen Depreux
26.7.48	*MARIE*	Moch	Reynaud	Reynaud	Lecourt	*Delbos*
5.9.48	SCHUMAN	Moch	Pineau	Pineau	Lecourt	*Tony-Révillon*
11.9.48	*QUEUILLE*	Moch	*Queuille*	*Queuille*	*Marie*	*Delbos*
29.10.49	BIDAULT	Moch	Petsche	Petsche	*R. Mayer*	*Delbos*
2.7.50	*QUEUILLE*	*Queuille*	Petsche	*Faure* (budget)	*R. Mayer*	Morice
12.7.50	PLEVEN	*Queuille*	Petsche	Petsche	*R. Mayer*	Lapie
10.3.51	*QUEUILLE*	*Queuille*	Petsche	*Faure* (budget)	*R. Mayer*	Lapie

[1] This list includes only those ministries in which Radicals were most active. It does not include, for example, the Ministries of Foreign Affairs, Defence, Industry, Agriculture, Colonies, or Labour. The names of Radicals are in italics.

General Election, 17 June 1951

Date	Premier	Interior	Finance	Economy	Justice	Education
10.8.51	PLEVEN	*Brune*	R. Mayer	R. Mayer	*Faure*	*Marie*
20.1.52	*FAURE*	*Brune*	*Faure*	Buron	*Martinaud-Déplat*	*Marie*
8.3.52	PINAY	*Brune*	Pinay	—	*Martinaud-Déplat*	*Marie*
8.1.53	R. MAYER	*Brune*	*Bourgès-Maunoury*	Buron	*Martinaud-Déplat*	*Marie*
28.6.53	LANIEL	*Martinaud-Déplat*	*Faure*	*Faure*	Ribeyre	*Marie*
19.6.54	*MENDÈS-FRANCE*	Mitterrand	*Faure*	*Faure*	E. Hugues	Berthoin
23.2.55	*FAURE*	*Bourgès-Maunoury*	Pflimlin	Pflimlin	Schuman	Berthoin

General Election, 2 January 1956

Date	Premier	Interior	Finance	Economy	Justice	Education
31.1.56	MOLLET	*Gilbert-Jules*	Lacoste Ramadier	Lacoste Ramadier	Mitterrand	*Billères*
12.6.57	*BOURGÈS-MAUNOURY*	*Gilbert-Jules*	*Gaillard*	*Gaillard*	Corniglion-Molinier	*Billères*
6.11.57	*GAILLARD*	*Bourgès-Maunoury*	Pflimlin	Pflimlin	Lecourt	*Billères*
13.5.58	PFLIMLIN	*Maurice Faure* Moch	*Faure*	*Faure*	Lecourt	*Bordeneuve*

BIBLIOGRAPHY

A. Primary Sources

As mentioned in the introduction, the most important sources of information used in this study were the verbatim records of speeches and remarks made at the party's various meetings and congresses. These records are on file, in stenographic form, at the party's headquarters, Place de Valois, Paris. The unpublished stenographic records were of particular importance for the 1944-6 period, and for the more private meetings held during the entire period studied. The party's official newspaper, *L'Information Radicale-Socialiste*, which began publication on 8 July 1946, provides verbatim records of many of the speeches and reports made at party congresses and executive committee meetings during subsequent years. Another basic source, both for the speeches and for the voting records of Radical deputies and senators, was the *Journal Officiel*, particularly the series devoted to parliamentary debates.

In addition to *L'Information Radicale-Socialiste*, many other newspapers were of great assistance. *La Dépêche de Paris*, another official party newspaper, was founded on 28 February 1945. A daily, it continued publication until 10 December 1945; it resumed publication on 17 April 1946, but finally expired on 9 May 1947, after having published a total of 553 issues. *La Voix de Paris*, a non-party daily in which left-wing Radicals played a prominent role, was published from 30 June 1945 to 1 July 1946; it published 312 issues. *La Dépêche du Midi*, the post-war successor of *La Dépêche de Toulouse*, has continued to supply a complete coverage of the Radical party's activities. For the activities of RGR, *L'Unité Française*, which appeared irregularly after 1947, was useful. *L'Express*, published weekly since May 1953 (except from October 1955 to March 1956, when it appeared daily), was a basic source for information concerning the *radicaux mendésistes* as was *Le Jacobin*, published irregularly since 1952. *Les Cahiers de la République*, a periodical published every other month since early 1956, was also important in studying the ideas and activities of the *radicaux mendésistes*. Other newspaper and periodical references are indicated in footnotes throughout the text. Among newspapers, a special place must be accorded *Le Monde*, published daily since 19 December 1944. And, as in any study of French post-war politics, the annual editions of *L'Année Politique* (Paris: Presses Universitaires, published annually since 1945) were of great assistance.

Most of the brochures issued by the Radical party after the war were reprints of speeches previously published in *L'Information Radicale-Socialiste* or in the *Journal Officiel*. The party's statutes were published, in booklet form, in 1947 (revised in 1953), in 1955, and in 1959.

Information concerning other sources, both written and oral, has been included in footnotes. In addition to published sources and the stenographic records, these included interviews, personal observations, and information obtained from the party's archives and correspondence files.

B. Historical and General Studies of Radicalism and the Radical Party

Alain (Emile Chartier), *Eléments d'une doctrine radicale* (Paris: Gallimard, 1925).

Archimbaud, Léon, *L'Avenir du radicalisme* (Paris: Fasquelle, 1937).

Bayet, Albert, *Notre morale (Préface de Ferdinand Buisson)* (Paris: Imprimerie-éditions du Progrès civique, 1926).

—— *Le Radicalisme* (Paris: Librairie Valois, 1932).

Buisson, Ferdinand, *La Politique radicale, étude sur les doctrines du parti radical-socialiste (précédée d'une lettre de M. Léon Bourgeois)* (Paris: V. Giard and E. Brière, 1908).

Cartier, Raymond, *Histoire du radicalisme* (Paris: Imprimerie G. Lang, 1939). (Issued by the *Centre de propagande des Républicains nationaux*).

Charpentier, Armand, *Le Parti radical et radical-socialiste à travers ses congrès, 1901–11 (Lettre-préface de M. Ferdinand Buisson)* (Paris: M. Giard and E. Brière, 1913).

Halévy, Daniel, *La République des comités, essai d'histoire contemporaine de 1895 à 1934* (Paris: Grasset, 1934).

Jammy-Schmidt, *Les Grandes thèses radicales, de Condorcet à Edouard Herriot (Préface d'Edouard Herriot)* (Paris: Editions des Portiques, 1932).

—— *Idées et Images radicales (Préface d'Edouard Herriot)* (Paris: Editions Excelsior, 1934).

Jouvenel, Robert de, *La République des Camarades* (Paris: Grasset, 1914).

Krikowski, Serge, and Reynier, Raoul, *Les Radicaux de gauche au service de la République* (Marseilles: R. Reynier, 1946).

Maurice, Gaston, *Le Parti radical (Préface de Jacques Kayser)* (Paris: M. Rivière, 1929),

Milhaud, Albert, *Histoire du radicalisme* (Paris: Société d'éditions françaises et internationale, 1951).

Nicolet, Claude, *Le Radicalisme* (Paris: Presses Universitaires de France, 1957). (*Que sais-je* series.)

Semler, Rudolf, *Frankreichs Radikalsozialisten und ihre Presse*(Würzburg-Aumühle: Konrad Triltsch Verlag, 1940).

Simon, Jules, *La Politique radicale* (Paris: Librairie Internationale, 1869).

Thibaudet, Albert, *La République des professeurs* (Paris: Grasset, 1927)
—— *Les Idées politiques de la France* (Paris: Stock, 1932).

C. Biographies; Memoirs and Political Works by Contemporary Radicals

Hernu, Charles, *La Colère usurpée* (Paris: Editions C.H., 1959).

Herriot, Edouard, *Pourquoi je suis radical-socialiste* (Paris: Editions de France, 1928).
—— *The Wellsprings of Liberty* (New York: Funk and Wagnalls, 1939).
—— *Message aux pays libres* (New York: Didier, 1942).
—— *Jadis. Avant la première guerre mondiale* (Paris: Flammarion, 1948).
—— *Episodes, 1940–1944* (Paris: Flammarion, 1950).
—— *Jadis. D'une guerre a l'autre, 1914–1936* (Paris: Flammarion, 1952).

Lapaquellerie, Yvon, *Edouard Daladier* (Paris: Flammarion, 1940).

McCormick, Donald, *Mr. France* (London: Jarrolds, 1955).

Mendès-France, Pierre, *Liberté, liberté cherie . . . choses vécues* (New York: Didier, 1943).
—— *Gouverner c'est choisir. Discours d'investiture et réponses aux interpellateurs (Assemblée Nationale, 3 et 4 juin, 1953)* (Paris: Julliard, 1953).
—— and Ardant, Gabriel, *Economics and Action* (Paris: UNESCO, 1955).
—— *Gouverner c'est choisir. Sept mois et dix-sept jours. Juin 1954–Février 1955* (Paris: Juilliard, 1955).
—— *Gouverner c'est choisir. La Politique et la Vérité. Juin 1955–Septembre 1958* (Paris: Julliard, 1958).

Nicolet, Claude, *Pierre Mendès-France ou le métier de Cassandre* (Paris: Julliard, 1959).

Ray, Oscar, *The Life of Edouard Daladier* (London: Pilot Press, Ltd., 1940).

Sarrus, Jean, *Edgar Faure* (Paris: Les Editions du Parlement, 1956).

Werth, Alexander, *The Strange History of Pierre Mendès-France and the Great Conflict over French North Africa* (London: Barrie, 1957).

INDEX

Printed in Great Britain by
The Camelot Press Ltd., London and Southampton